Special Economic Zones in Asian Market Economies

Special Economic Zones (SEZs) have proliferated rapidly during the past decade and are set to multiply in the next – embracing not only Asia and Europe but also Africa and the Americas. This book is the first to examine the Asian experience of SEZs in China, India, Malaysia, and the Philippines. SEZs are usually clearly defined geographic areas in which governments use policy tools (such as tax holidays; improved infrastructure; less onerous or differentiated regulations and incentives other than those generally available in the rest of the country) to attract and promote private – usually foreign – investment from enterprises which commit to create employment and to export their products or services, and generate foreign currency for the host country. SEZs have been especially successful in bringing about economic development in Asia, especially in China.

This book examines the origins, nature and status of special economic zones in Asia, together with the current trends connected with them, and the challenges they currently face. Although the World Trade Organization cast doubts in 1995 on the future of special economic zones as a viable policy tool in the development agenda, special economic zones continue to be used, and favoured, as a way of encouraging foreign investment and economic development, with, for example, India trying to emulate China, reincorporating special economic zones into its development policy. This book provides case studies of SEZs in Asian market economies to analyse the extent to which these zones serve the changing needs of Asian development.

Connie Carter is Professor of Law at Royal Roads University; Adjunct Professor in the Faculty of Law at the University of Victoria, both in Victoria, BC, Canada; and also a Barrister of Lincolns Inn, London. Her recent publications include *Law and Economic Development in Singapore* and *Fighting Fakes in China: Legal Protection of Trademarks and Brands in the PRC.*

Andrew Harding is currently a member of the Faculty of Law, University of Victoria, BC, Canada, where he holds the Chair in Asia-Pacific Legal Relations and is Director of the Centre for Asia-Pacific Initiatives (CAPI). He is co-editor of *New Courts in Asia*, and *Constitutional Courts: A Comparative Study.*

Routledge studies in the growth economies of Asia

1 **The Changing Capital Markets of East Asia**
Edited by Ky Cao

2 **Financial Reform in China**
Edited by On Kit Tam

3 **Women and Industrialization in Asia**
Edited by Susan Horton

4 **Japan's Trade Policy**
Action or reaction?
Yumiko Mikanagi

5 **The Japanese Election System**
Three analytical perspectives
Junichiro Wada

6 **The Economics of the Latecomers**
Catching-up, technology transfer and institutions in Germany, Japan and South Korea
Jang-Sup Shin

7 **Industrialization in Malaysia**
Import substitution and infant industry performance
Rokiah Alavi

8 **Economic Development in Twentieth Century East Asia**
The international context
Edited by Aiko Ikeo

9 **The Politics of Economic Development in Indonesia**
Contending perspectives
Edited by Ian Chalmers and Vedi R. Hadiz

10 **Studies in the Economic History of the Pacific Rim**
Edited by Sally M. Miller, A.J.H. Latham and Dennis O. Flynn

11 **Workers and the State in New Order Indonesia**
Vedi R. Hadiz

12 **The Japanese Foreign Exchange Market**
Beate Reszat

13 **Exchange Rate Policies in Emerging Asian Countries**
Edited by Stefan Collignon, Jean Pisani-Ferry and Yung Chul Park

14 **Chinese Firms and Technology in the Reform Era**
Yizheng Shi

15 **Japanese Views on Economic Development**
Diverse paths to the market
Kenichi Ohno and Izumi Ohno

16 **Technological Capabilities and Export Success in Asia**
Edited by Dieter Ernst, Tom Ganiatsos and Lynn Mytelka

17 **Trade and Investment in China**
The European experience
Edited by Roger Strange, Jim Slater and Limin Wang

18 **Technology and Innovation in Japan**
Policy and management for the twenty-first century
Edited by Martin Hemmert and Christian Oberländer

19 **Trade Policy Issues in Asian Development**
Prema-chandra Athukorala

20 **Economic Integration in the Asia Pacific Region**
Ippei Yamazawa

21 **Japan's War Economy**
Edited by Erich Pauer

22 **Industrial Technology Development in Malaysia**
Industry and firm studies
Edited by Jomo K.S., Greg Felker and Rajah Rasiah

23 **Technology, Competitiveness and the State**
Malaysia's industrial technology policies
Edited by Jomo K. S. and Greg Felker

24 **Corporatism and Korean Capitalism**
Edited by Dennis L. McNamara

25 **Japanese Science**
Samuel Coleman

26 **Capital and Labour in Japan**
The functions of two factor markets
Toshiaki Tachibanaki and Atsuhiro Taki

27 **Asia Pacific Dynamism 1550–2000**
Edited by A. J. H. Latham and Heita Kawakatsu

28 **The Political Economy of Development and Environment in Korea**
Jae-Yong Chung and Richard J. Kirkby

29 **Japanese Economics and Economists since 1945**
Edited by Aiko Ikeo

30 **China's Entry into the World Trade Organisation**
Edited by Peter Drysdale and Ligang Song

31 **Hong Kong as an International Financial Centre**
Emergence and Development 1945–65
Catherine R. Schenk

32 **Impediments to Trade in Services: Measurement and Policy Implication**
Edited by Christoper Findlay and Tony Warren

33 **The Japanese Industrial Economy**
Late development and cultural causation
Ian Inkster

34 **China and the Long March to Global Trade**
The accession of China to the World Trade Organization
Edited by Alan S. Alexandroff, Sylvia Ostry and Rafael Gomez

35 **Capitalist Development and Economism in East Asia**
The rise of Hong Kong, Singapore, Taiwan, and South Korea
Kui-Wai Li

36 **Women and Work in Globalizing Asia**
Edited by Dong-Sook S. Gills and Nicola Piper

37 **Financial Markets and Policies in East Asia**
Gordon de Brouwer

38 **Developmentalism and Dependency in Southeast Asia**
The case of the automotive industry
Jason P. Abbott

39 **Law and Labour Market Regulation in East Asia**
Edited by Sean Cooney, Tim Lindsey, Richard Mitchell and Ying Zhu

40 **The Economy of the Philippines**
Elites, inequalities and economic restructuring
Peter Krinks

41 **China's Third Economic Transformation**
The rise of the private economy
Edited by Ross Garnaut and Ligang Song

42 **The Vietnamese Economy**
Awakening the dormant dragon
Edited by Binh Tran-Nam and Chi Do Pham

43 **Restructuring Korea Inc.**
Jang-Sup Shin and Ha-Joon Chang

44 **Development and Structural Change in the Asia-Pacific**
Globalising miracles or end of a model?
Edited by Martin Andersson and Christer Gunnarsson

45 **State Collaboration and Development Strategies in China**
The case of the China–Singapore Suzhou Industrial Park (1992–2002)
Alexius Pereira

46 **Capital and Knowledge in Asia**
Changing power relations
Edited by Heidi Dahles and Otto van den Muijzenberg

47 **Southeast Asian Paper Tigers?**
From miracle to debacle and beyond
Edited by Jomo K. S.

48 **Manufacturing Competitiveness in Asia**
How internationally competitive national firms and industries developed in East Asia
Edited by Jomo K. S.

49 **The Korean Economy at the Crossroads**
Edited by Moon Joong Tcha and Chung-Sok Suh

50 **Ethnic Business**
Chinese capitalism in Southeast Asia
Edited by Jomo K. S. and Brian C. Folk

51 **Exchange Rate Regimes in East Asia**
Edited by Gordon de Brouwer and Masahiro Kawai

52 **Financial Governance in East Asia**
Policy dialogue, surveillance and cooperation
Edited by Gordon de Brouwer and Yunjong Wang

53 **Designing Financial Systems in East Asia and Japan**
Edited by Joseph P. H. Fan, Masaharu Hanazaki and Juro Teranishi

54 **State Competence and Economic Growth in Japan**
Yoshiro Miwa

55 **Understanding Japanese Saving**
Does population aging matter?
Robert Dekle

56 **The Rise and Fall of the East Asian Growth System, 1951–2000**
International competitiveness and rapid economic growth
Xiaoming Huang

57 **Service Industries and Asia-Pacific Cities**
New development trajectories
Edited by P. W. Daniels, K. C. Ho and T. A. Hutton

58 **Unemployment in Asia**
Edited by John Benson and Ying Zhu

59 **Risk Management and Innovation in Japan, Britain and the USA**
Edited by Ruth Taplin

60 **Japan's Development Aid to China**
The long-running foreign policy of engagement
Tsukasa Takamine

61 **Chinese Capitalism and the Modernist Vision**
Satyananda J. Gabriel

62 **Japanese Telecommunications**
Edited by Ruth Taplin and Masako Wakui

63 **East Asia, Globalization and the New Economy**
F. Gerard Adams

64 **China as a World Factory**
Edited by Kevin Honglin Zhang

65 **China's State Owned Enterprise Reforms**
An industrial and CEO approach
Juan Antonio Fernandez and Leila Fernandez-Stembridge

66 **China and India**
A tale of two economies
Dilip K. Das

67 **Innovation and Business Partnering in Japan, Europe and the United States**
Edited by Ruth Taplin

68 **Asian Informal Workers**
Global risks local protection
Santosh Mehrotra and Mario Biggeri

69 **The Rise of the Corporate Economy in Southeast Asia**
Rajeswary Ampalavanar Brown

70 **The Singapore Economy**
An econometric perspective
Tilak Abeyshinge and Keen Meng Choy

71 **A Basket Currency for Asia**
Edited by Takatoshi Ito

72 **Private Enterprises and China's Economic Development**
Edited by Shuanglin Lin and Xiaodong Zhu

73 **The Korean Developmental State**
From dirigisme to neo-liberalism
Iain Pirie

74 **Accelerating Japan's Economic Growth**
Resolving Japan's growth controversy
Edited by F. Gerard Adams, Lawrence R. Klein, Yuzo Kumasaka and Akihiko Shinozaki

75 **China's Emergent Political Economy**
Capitalism in the dragon's lair
Edited by Christopher A. McNally

76 **The Political Economy of the SARS Epidemic**
The impact on human resources in East Asia
Grace O.M. Lee and Malcolm Warner

77 **India's Emerging Financial Market**
A flow of funds model
Tomoe Moore

78 **Outsourcing and Human Resource Management**
An international survey
Edited by Ruth Taplin

79 **Globalization, Labor Markets and Inequality in India**
Dipak Mazumdar and Sandip Sarkar

80 **Globalization and the Indian Economy**
Roadmap to a convertible rupee
Satyendra S. Nayak

81 **Economic Cooperation between Singapore and India**
An alliance in the making
Faizal Yahya

82 **The United States and the Malaysian Economy**
Shakila Yacob

83 **Banking Reform in Southeast Asia**
The region's decisive decade
Malcolm Cook

84 **Trade Unions in Asia**
An economic and sociological analysis
Edited by John Benson and Ying Zhu

85 **Trade Liberalisation and Regional Disparity in Pakistan**
Muhammad Shoaib Butt and Jayatilleke S. Bandara

86 **Financial Development and Economic Growth in Malaysia**
James Ang

87 **Intellectual Property and the New Japanese Global Economy**
Ruth Taplin

88 **Laggards and Leaders in Labour Market Reform**
Comparing Japan and Australia
Edited by Jenny Corbett, Anne Daly, Hisakazu Matsushige and Dehne Taylor

89 **Institutions for Economic Reform in Asia**
Edited by Philippa Dee

90 **Southeast Asia's Credit Revolution**
From moneylenders to microfinance
Aditya Goenka and David Henley

91 **Economic Reform and Employment Relations in Vietnam**
Ngan Thuy Collins

92 **The Future of Asian Trade and Growth**
Economic development with the emergence of China
Linda Yueh

93 **Business Practices in Southeast Asia**
An interdisciplinary analysis of Theravada Buddhist countries
Scott A. Hipsher

94 **Responsible Development**
Vulnerable democracies, hunger and inequality
Omar Noman

95 **The Everyday Impact of Economic Reform in China**
Management change, enterprise performance and daily life
Ying Zhu, Michael Webber and John Benson

96 **The Rise of Asia**
Trade and investment in global perspective
Prema-chandra Athukorala

97 Intellectual Property, Innovation and Management in Emerging Economies
Edited by Ruth Taplin and Alojzy Z. Nowak

98 Special Economic Zones in Asian Market Economies
Edited by Connie Carter and Andrew Harding

Special Economic Zones in Asian Market Economies

Edited by
Connie Carter and Andrew Harding

Routledge
Taylor & Francis Group
LONDON AND NEW YORK

First published 2011
by Routledge
2 Park Square, Milton Park, Abingdon, Oxon, OX14 4RN

Simultaneously published in the USA and Canada
by Routledge
270 Madison Avenue, New York, NY 10016

Routledge is an imprint of the Taylor & Francis Group, an informa business

Typeset in Times New Roman by Taylor & Francis Books
Printed and bound by MPG Books Group in the UK

British Library Cataloguing in Publication Data
A catalogue record for this book is available from the British Library

Library of Congress Cataloging in Publication Data
Special economic zones in Asian market economies /
edited by Connie Carter & Andrew Harding. – 1st ed.
p. cm. – (Routledge studies in the growth economies of Asia)
Includes bibliographical references and index.
1. Economic zoning–Asia. 2. Enterprise zones–Asia. 3. Asia–Economic policy–21st century. I. Carter, Connie. II. Harding, Andrew, 1950–
HC412.S64 2010
338.8'7–dc22   2010028877

ISBN: 978-0-415-59180-5 (hbk)
ISBN: 978-0-203-84186-0 (ebk)

Contents

Preface and acknowledgements

Special economic zones (SEZs) are all about FDI (foreign direct investment), economic development, poverty alleviation and policy incubators. Or so proponents would have us believe, while opponents can see only isolated free market enclaves that embrace sweat shops, low wages, gender imbalance and social and environmental degradation. Whoever is right, the fact is that following the formalization of the new global trade regime under the World Trade Organization (WTO) in January 1995, SEZs as we have known them during the past three decades should no longer exist. For under the provisions of the Agreement on Subsidies and Countervailing Measures (SCM Agreement), covered by the WTO treaty, certain export-oriented subsidies and tax preferences are prohibited. However, instead of diminishing in numbers, SEZs have proliferated rapidly during the past decade and are set to multiply in the next – embracing not only Asia and Europe but also Africa and the Americas. That is the first reason for our curiosity. The second reason involves the Asian experience of SEZs.

Today, most fully operating SEZs and those that are considered most successful exist in Asia. The majority of them still specialize in manufacturing for export. The claim is still that FDI and trade liberalization through SEZs result in economic development and poverty alleviation. It seems clear that the SEZ concept has survived its own apparent demise and instead has flourished, again in Asia. It is tempting to ask why. The purpose of this book is to provide a manageable set of regional case studies about SEZs in Asian market economies in order to capture the nature of the instrument being wielded and to discover the extent to which it is serving the changing needs of Asian development.

This book has grown from the proceedings of a conference organized by the editors by way of cooperation between the Centre for Asia-Pacific Initiatives at the University of Victoria, BC Canada; the Faculty of Management of Royal Roads University, also in Victoria, BC Canada; and Kyushu University in Fukuoka, Japan. The conference took place 15–16 February 2010 at Kyushu University and involved scholars from Asia, Canada and other parts of the world, as well as students from the LLD and LLM programmes in International Business and Economic Law, and faculty of Kyushu University

Law Faculty. The purpose was to explore the nature of the evolving concept of the SEZ across Asia from China through the Philippines, Korea and Malaysia to India, in an attempt to understand the reasons for its continuing vigour and potential challenges. In this sense the studies presented here are to various degrees critical or supportive of the Asian SEZ; but all had in common the idea that SEZs, properly conceived, organized and regulated, are at least capable of being used for beneficial purposes. The reader will find here a fascinating set of studies which raise a wide range of questions about SEZs in the context of the socio-economic, environmental, political, and governance aspects of Asian development.

The editors would like to thank Kyushu University Faculty of Law, in particular Professors Toshiyuki Kono, Caslav Pejovic, and Shinichi Ago, for their excellent and warm cooperation and financial and other assistance; Kyushu University's Antonio Formacion for his organizational flair and IT expertise; Kyushu doctoral student Sean McGinty for his assiduous help in preparing the manuscript for publication; University of Victoria law student Tricia Dayton for her research assistance in the early stages; all the conference presenters and contributors to this book; the conference participants including the LLD and LLM students and in particular Victoria and Kyushu graduate Dr Dan Puchniak of the National University of Singapore, and University of Victoria LLM student Qian Jing; Peter Sowden our Routledge editor for his assistance; and not least colleagues at our own institutions, the Centre for Asia-Pacific Initiatives and the Faculty of Law, University of Victoria, and the Faculty of Management, Royal Roads University.

Altogether seven people with Victoria BC connections were at Kyushu for the conference, and this emphasizes the extent to which the event itself and this book have been the fruit of long-standing Fukuoka-Victoria connections. There is also a profound irony in the fact that in Nagasaki, not far from Fukuoka on Kyushu Island, what was probably the first SEZ in Asia, Dejima, was established in the early seventeenth century as Japan closed its doors to the outside world, leaving this tiny artificial island-enclave in Nagasaki harbour as an oasis for international trade. The SEZ concept has thus come full circle from Kyushu to the whole of Asia and back again to Kyushu.

Connie Carter and Andrew Harding
Victoria, March 2010

Contributors

Connie Carter is Professor of Law at Royal Roads University and Adjunct Professor at the University of Victoria, both in Victoria, BC, Canada. She is a Barrister of Lincolns Inn, London. She earned her LLB and PhD in Law at the School of Oriental and African Studies (SOAS), University of London. Connie teaches business law courses in Canada and has taught International Trade Law, Competition Law, Chinese Commercial Law and Intellectual Property Law at universities in Europe, Asia and North America. She works comfortably in both the business and academic worlds, operating a training and business consultancy, often employed full time in senior positions in global companies or teaching in faculties of law or management. Before joining Royal Roads, she spent five years in China, partly as Professor of Law at Xiamen University, partly as Director of Human Resources at a China-based German multinational. Her research interests include foreign investment, WTO, Special Economic Zones, governance, law and development in Asia. Her publications include *Law and Economic Development in Singapore* (2002); and *Fighting Fakes in China: Legal Protection of Trademarks and Brands in the PRC* (1999).

Arnel Paciano D. Casanova is General Counsel and Corporate Secretary of the Bases Conversion Development Authority (BCDA), Manila, Philippines. He earned a Master's degree in Public Administration from Harvard University (2007) and an LLB from the University of the Philippines (1998). An awardee of the Philippine Legion of Honour Medal, the highest military merit medal (non-combat) in the Philippines, he divides his time between work at the BCDA and as a visiting lecturer at the Ateneo de Manila School of Government. He is the founding Director and Philippines Country Manager of Avantchange Ltd.

Shankar Gopalakrishnan is National Secretary in India of the Campaign for Survival and Dignity, a federation of tribal and forest dwellers' organizations from eleven states working on issues of forest rights – particularly the Forest Rights Act. His responsibilities include actively working with parliamentarians, government officials, media persons and other civil society groups on the forest rights issue, co-ordinating national mass mobilizations on the forest rights issue, co-ordinating various legal teams to prepare for the court defence of the Forest Rights Act, writing and participating in media debates, and preparing and producing documentation on forest rights issues. He has a BA (double major in Mathematics and Community, Regional, Environmental Studies) from Bard College, New York (2000) and an MSc in Development Studies, from the School of Oriental and African Studies (SOAS), University of London (2004).

Andrew Harding graduated with an MA from Oxford University in 1974, and was awarded an LLM (Singapore) in 1984, and a PhD in law (Monash) in 1987. He is a former Head of Department and Professor of Law in the Law Department at the School of Oriental and African Studies (SOAS), University of London, having previously taught at the Faculty of Law, National University of Singapore and as a Visiting Professor at Harvard Law School. He is currently a member of the Faculty of Law, University of Victoria, BC, Canada, where he holds the Chair in Asia-Pacific Legal Relations and is Director of the Centre for Asia-Pacific Initiatives (CAPI). He has published widely in the field of Asian and comparative public law, and is co-General Editor of Hart Publishing's Series 'Constitutional Systems of the World'. He is co-editor of *New Courts in Asia* (2010), and of *Constitutional Courts: A Comparative Study* (2009).

Charles Krusekopf is Head of the Master's program in Environment and Management at the School of Environment and Sustainability at Royal Roads University in Victoria, BC, Canada, where he has been a core faculty member since 2005. Prior to joining Royal Roads he was Assistant Professor of economics at Austin College in Sherman, Texas. In 2004, Charles taught international trade at the Mongolian National University on a Fulbright Fellowship. He has done fieldwork on institutions of land tenure and agriculture in China. He has worked for *Fortune* magazine in New York; for the US Trade Representative's Office in Washington, DC; for the US Embassy in Mongolia; and as a consultant on economic development with organizations such as the World Bank and the Soros Foundation. He is Executive Director of the American Center for Mongolian Studies. His research interests include carbon trading markets and systems; environmental economics; economic ethics; international trade; economic development, land and agriculture; China and Mongolia.

Peter Muchlinski is Professor in International Commercial Law at the School of Oriental and African Studies (SOAS), University of London. Prior to joining SOAS he was Professor of Law and International Business at Kent Law School, University of Kent (2001–5). He has taught at the London School of Economics (1983–98), and was the Drapers' Professor of Law in the Law Department of Queen Mary and Westfield College, University of London, from 1998 to 2001. He specializes in international and European business law, international investment law, competition law,

law and development, and commercial regulation, in which fields he has authored numerous papers and articles. He is the author of *Multinational Enterprises and the Law*, second edition, 2007, and co-editor of the *Oxford Handbook of International Investment Law*, 2008. In 1990 he qualified as a barrister and is a door tenant at Brick Court Chambers, London. He is a Principal Adviser to the United Nations Conference on Trade and Development (UNCTAD) on investment issues, Co-Rapporteur to the International Law Association Committee on the International Law on Foreign Investment, and occasionally advises in international investment arbitrations.

Tey Tsun Hang joined the Faculty of Law of the National University of Singapore in 1997. Between 2000 and 2003 he served as a Justice Law Clerk to the Chief Justice of Singapore, State Counsel at the Attorney-General's Chambers and District Judge of the Republic of Singapore. He was a member of the editorial committee of the *Singapore Journal of Legal Studies, Singapore Journal of International and Comparative Law, Singapore Year Book of International Law*, and the executive committee of the Centre for Commercial Law Studies. He is editor of the *Asian Journal of Comparative Law*. He teaches Media Law, Personal Property, Equity and Trusts and also practises at a law firm. His recent publications include *Singapore's Jurisprudence of Political Defamation and its Triple-Whammy Impact on Political Speech* (2008); and *Singapore's Electoral System: Government by the People* (2008).

Feng Xu is Assistant Professor in East Asia Politics at the Department of Political Science, University of Victoria, Victoria, Canada. Her book, *Women Migrant Workers and China's Economic Reform* (2000), investigated the lives and survival strategies of women migrant workers in silk factories of southern Jiangsu province. She is currently researching a new project on unemployment, community/*shequ* building and urban governance in contemporary urban China. Recent publications include (with James Lawson) 'SARS in Canada and China: Two Approaches to Emergency Health Policy', 2007; 'New Modes of Urban Governance: Building Community/*Shequ* in Post-*Danwei* China', 2008; and 'Gated Communities, Migrant Enclaves: A New Conundrum for Urban Governance in China', 2008.

Abbreviations and acronyms

CADZ	China Association of Development Zones
CSR	Corporate social responsibility
CSSD	China-Singapore Suzhou Industrial Development Co. Ltd.
CIS	Commonwealth of Independent States
DTA	Domestic Tariff Area
ECER	East Coast Economic Region (Malaysia)
EKC	Environment Kuznet's Curves
EMS	Environment management systems
EPZ	export processing zone
FDI	foreign direct investment
FIAS	Foreign Investment Advisory Service [a World Bank division]
FTA	free trade agreement
FTZ	free trade zone
GATT	General Agreement on Tariffs and Trade
IBRD	International Bank for Reconstruction and Development
ICFTU	International Confederation of Free Trade Unions
ICT	information communications technology
IFC	International Finance Corporation
ILO	International Labour Organization
IR	integrated resorts [Singapore]
IRDA	Iskandar Regional Development Authority [Malaysia]
ISP	Initial Incentive and Support Package [Malaysia]
IT	information technology
MIGA	Multilateral Investment Guarantee Agency
MSC	Multimedia Super Corridor [Malaysia]
NCER	Northern Corridor Economic Region [Malaysia]
NDP	National Development Policy [Malaysia]
NEP	New Economic Policy [Malaysia]
NTBs	non-tariff barriers
OECD	Organisation for Economic Co-operation and Development
PPP	private-public partnership
SCM	[Agreement on] Subsidies and Countervailing Measures
SCORE	Sarawak Corridor of Renewable Energy

SDC	Sabah Development Corridor [Malaysia]
SEZ	special economic zone
SEZAME	special economic zones in Asian market economies
SOE	state owned enterprise
TNC	transnational company
UMNO	United Malays National Organization [Malaysia]
UNCTAD	United Nations Conference on Trade and Development
WCO	World Customs Organization
WEPZA	World Economic Processing Zones Association
WTO	World Trade Organization

1 SEZs

Policy incubators or catalysts for development?

Connie Carter and Andrew Harding

To set the scene and provide a context upon which this volume can be viewed, we underline three important factors.

First, during the past three decades, foreign direct investment (FDI) rather than trade has become the most important vehicle for bringing goods and services to foreign markets and for integrating national production systems (Sauvant 2008: 3).

Second, special economic zones (SEZs) have been the most potent and most successful vehicle for transporting FDI into developing countries and emerging market economies (Graham 2004; Jones et al. 2003; Lall 2000a).

Third, global FDI inflows, which were only about US$50 billion during the early 1980s, reached US$2.09 trillion by the end of 2007 (UNCTAD 2009) but have slowed significantly during the 2008–9 recession (Kedic 2009: 1). However, during the same three decades SEZs have proliferated worldwide, whether as policy incubators or providers of the ideal environment for capitalism and FDI promotion, while only showing signs of becoming somewhat 'less special' during the recent recession.

China's FDI inflow experience (Graham 2004; Ota 2003) and emerging markets such as the Philippines (UNCTAD 2003), Bangladesh and Mexico (Sadni-Jallab and Blanco de Armas 2002), serve as examples to validate the claim that SEZs greatly increase FDI inflows and may help alleviate poverty. However, although both SEZs and FDI inflows are evidenced in developed as well as developing countries, in the past three decades it is developed countries that have accounted for the lion's share of FDI inflows (UNCTAD 2009), while the proliferation of SEZs has occurred predominantly in developing countries and emerging market economies. Nevertheless, developing countries, especially those in Asia, accounted for some 30 per cent of global FDI inflows in 2006 (ibid.) and, according to the pundits, the Asian SEZs have been the most successful and most prolific (Graham 2004; Ota 2003; World Bank 2008). It is also worth remembering that most of the FDI inflows are in the services sector while agriculture and industrial manufacturing still dominate the economies of most developing countries. In light of these trends, it should be both satisfying and challenging to observe the development of

FDI and modern SEZs and their effect on economic development and poverty alleviation in the new century.

The main purpose of this volume is to deconstruct the nature of SEZs in Asia and examine the 'specialness' of their contribution to development in Asia. To this end, the task of this introductory chapter is to explore key definitions that form a backdrop to the contributions in this volume and flag the surprisingly multifaceted nature of the individual contributions.

Key definitions: foreign direct investment (FDI), development and SEZs

Three concepts require definition in the context of this book: FDI, development and SEZs. Of course, FDI is now an everyday term. And yet, given the fickleness of foreign money as displayed during the so-called Asian crisis of 1997–99, to set the scene, it is perhaps worthwhile to proffer a definition of FDI here. FDI is

> an investment involving a long-term relationship and reflecting a lasting interest and control by a resident entity in one economy (foreign direct investor or parent enterprise) in an enterprise resident in an economy other than that of the foreign direct investor (FDI enterprise or affiliate enterprise or foreign affiliate).
>
> (UNCTAD 2007: 245)

Critically, the operative words in this definition are somewhat fuzzy and imprecise: how long is a long-term relationship? And what is the meaning of a lasting interest and control? On the facts, all that can be said is that in 2006, some 80,000 parent companies controlled more than 800,000 foreign affiliates (Sauvant 2008: 4), many of which were acquired rather than founded and grown organically. However, not all controlling parent companies originate in developed countries. Increasingly, many multinational companies (MNCs) originate in emerging market economies and developing countries, and control assets outside of their home countries. They too make foreign acquisitions and become expansionist in response to the liberalization of FDI regulations around the world. They also increasingly make use of advanced information and communication technologies to forge global networks for production and distribution. And they focus on outward FDI – sometimes by establishing themselves in SEZs – in order to exploit ownership, location and internalization advantages proffered by host countries.

Development is another of those words that everyone seems to know and bandy about comfortably, until it is time to say what it means – especially in relation to developing countries and emerging market economies. It is often said that China used its SEZs to kick-start its economic development in 1980 and that SEZ status specifically increased the annual growth rate in cities and provinces that were awarded preferential treatment through the establishment of SEZs (Demurger et al. 2002; Jones et al. 2003; Wang and Hu 1999; Wang and Meng 2001). However, is development merely a matter of economic growth rates, of GDP and GNP? A proper discussion of this issue is beyond the scope of this volume, although it is considered briefly in Connie Carter's Chapter 4 on China. However, for a full discussion, readers are encouraged to consult the excellent contributions in Trubek and Santos (2006); the book's focus is the law and development paradigm; however, the crux is a deconstruction of the concept of development especially in order to realize the incorporation of its social aspects and its overarching objective, which Amartya Sen (1999) claims is 'freedom'.

What then of SEZs; what are they? Conventionally, an SEZ is a clearly defined geographic area in which national, provincial or local governments use policy tools such as tax holidays, improved infrastructure, and less onerous or differentiated regulations and incentives other than those generally available in the rest of the country (the domestic tariff area) to attract and promote private, usually foreign, investment from enterprises which commit to create jobs and export their products or services in order to generate foreign currency for the host country.

Two decades ago, this might have been an excellent definition of the SEZ, particularly of the modern SEZ in China. But gone are the days when that definition will suffice universally. In the twenty-first century, SEZs have evolved into a different animal. For a start, nowadays, SEZs are not necessarily clearly defined geographic areas – in some countries (for instance in Togo, Senegal, Cameroon and Nigeria) single enterprises may obtain the privileges and benefits that once were bestowed only upon SEZs in their guise as geographically defined areas. In other countries, SEZs are configured specifically to meet the needs of clearly defined industries and even specially designated activities. Thus, one can find special zones designed only for high technology and science-based industries (Malaysia, Korea, India); for financial services (Singapore, Malaysia, Korea); petrochemicals (Singapore, Thailand); software and information communications technology (China, Vietnam, India, Dubai); zones to support aviation and airline-based activities (China, Malaysia); tourism zones (Baru Island in Colombia); mining and extraction-based enclaves (Philippines, Indonesia); logistics parks, cargo villages and distribution centres (Czech Republic); zones that provide supply chain management, call centres and other trade supporting services. This list is not exhaustive and is set to grow as countries invent new ways of circumventing strictures laid down by the World Trade Organization (WTO).[1]

Second, SEZs are no longer just government-initiated or government-operated affairs; many are established and managed under public-private partnerships or purely private partnerships as allowed, for example, under the Indian SEZ Act 2005 (see Harding, Chapter 9 in this volume).

Third, not all SEZs crave the coveted foreign currency; some provide competitive advantage havens for companies which seek to trade in a lucrative domestic market, by manufacturing the products or services inside that market at substantial cost savings in labour and transportation. In such cases even domestic companies may import duty-free components and assembly kits, manufacture the goods domestically and only pay designated import duties and taxes once the finished goods are sold into the domestic market. Often the payback sought includes skills and technology transfer – so-called spillover effects through backward linkages. And often, host countries are disappointed as no such spillover effects are discernable.

The scenarios above illustrate not only the diversity of SEZs but also go a long way to explaining why it is so difficult to give a universally accepted definition of the concept, or even to agree on how many SEZs exist worldwide and what the future holds for them. In this volume, the term is used generically to denote any area or zone in Asia which operates under a special legal or regulatory framework and offers incentives to enterprises to locate or which are located within the specific area.

'Open SEZAME'

The working title of this book was SEZAME, an acronym for Special Economic Zones in Asian Market Economies. The catch phrase was 'open SEZAME', because we sought to open the doors to the mysteries of SEZs in Asia. The following section gives an overview of the next eight chapters, tying them together in light of the themes and issues raised.

Peter Muchlinski's Chapter 2 explores the conceptual issues of SEZs and locates them within the evolving regime of international economic law. He considers the nature and origins of the SEZ idea and examines the possible future impact of its implementation on economic and social development in a host country. At the economic level, he acknowledges the general trend towards trade and investment liberalization, and the increased regulatory strain which the introduction in 1995 of the WTO prohibition of export trade subsidies has placed on the use of SEZs. In such an environment, he questions the further utility value of the SEZ concept to twenty-first century players. In addition, as regards social development, he asks two crucial questions: how far can the SEZ concept be used to lower social standards? Or can it become a vehicle for the protection or enhancement of such standards (for example, of labour conditions and environmental standards)?

Three chapters on China follow. As if to suggest answers to Muchlinski's social development questions, Feng Xu's Chapter 3 focuses on the governance of China's labour market regime, arguing that SEZs as laboratories for experiments in capitalism became the first instances where laws, rather than the Chinese state, became the lead regulatory mechanism in labour allocation. She observes that nowadays the Chinese state as a whole not only exhibits an increasingly free market economy, but also uses law as the specific regulatory tool for governing the labour market. However, this optimistic stance is tempered by further observations of both new and old impediments. For instance, she argues that the newer forms of mediating agencies that have emerged, particularly temporary employment agencies, have had the effect of making regulation of the Chinese labour market less effective overall than it could be. She also asserts that the relatively limited independence of the Chinese judiciary and the historical legacy of close relations between business and local government, mean that implementation and adjudication of laws are generally less effective than the making of them in China.

Connie Carter's Chapter 4, presenting a tale of two Chinese SEZs, examines, inter alia, the minimalist legal environment under which early SEZs functioned and, using China's first Equity Joint Venture Law 1979 (EJV Law) as an example, she would dispute even the efficacy of China's early law-making skills as postulated by Xu. The EJV Law itself comprised only fifteen articles and was three pages long. However, the thrust of Carter's chapter is to compare the performance of two Chinese SEZs: one, Wenzhou in Zhejiang province, which according to some Beijing policy-makers and scholars, has succeeded mightily and outperformed the other, Suzhou in Jiangsu province, by employing a predominantly endogenous growth scenario with domestic private investment as opposed to Suzhou's exogenous growth with reliance on FDI (Hu 2008). There are limits to the clarity of the comparison itself owing to the limitations and integrity of the data collected. In particular, there is some speculation that key official data may have been manipulated or 'over-reported'.[2] However, the gist of Carter's findings suggests convergence of the development models, which leads her to conclude that, under the strain of reduced Western demand for China-made goods, China should encourage endogenous growth and allow its population to reap the benefits of its own labour. This includes paying attention not only to social welfare benefits, housing and education for the rural poor, the urban poor, the aged, unskilled migrant workers, and other disadvantaged, but also to accelerating the remediation of the environment.

It is on the latter area that Charles Krusekopf's Chapter 5 focuses. Basing his observations on the theories of Kuznets' curves, he posits that due to their relatively well educated, newly affluent populations and ties to international firms and markets, China's SEZs are well positioned to become leaders in environmental fields such as the development of pollution control technologies, green product design, environmental finance and other environmental services. Furthermore, he argues that a proper focus on environmental management will offer a double benefit for SEZs, by helping to improve the local environment while also supporting their economic development plans. Krusekopf analyzes the environmental situation not only in the SEZs themselves but also in the 'donuts' around them, and makes recommendations about how environmental management can be improved. He welcomes the newly popularized idea that China's SEZs can be transformed into special 'environmental' zones acting as incubators and laboratories for experiments in sustainable development. This analysis runs counter to the popular notion of SEZs as promoters of unsustainable development.

The situation in the Philippines is significantly different from that of China. The last decade of the twentieth century ushered in major international and domestic upheavals in the Philippines, both politically and economically. The fall of the Marcos dictatorship gave birth to a new democracy and new Philippine Constitution. It also witnessed a rise in nationalistic fervor, one result of which was the Philippine government's termination of its military bases agreement with the United States. This compelled the US military to withdraw from the Subic Naval Base, the Clark Air Base and other smaller military camps in the Philippines. Arnel Casanova's Chapter 6 charts the challenges and opportunities involved in the conversion of the former military bases into SEZs and free trade zones. Casanova tells the story from an operational and management perspective and we benefit from his personal insights as general counsel and corporate secretary to the Bases Conversion project. He relates the decisions that led to economic loss and recounts the effects of abuse of privileges and incentives, corruption and smuggling, and ambiguity in the legal framework intended to govern the economic zones; and points to other factors that curtailed the full potential of these catalysts for national development. The Philippine experience testifies to the fact that Asian SEZs are not all models of perfect performance; furthermore, that SEZs may be established for complex reasons which go far beyond giving tax and other incentives, and that regulatory and governance defects may reduce the benefits to be derived from them.

Tey's Tsung Hang Chapter 7 on Malaysia's Iskandar project shows how the SEZ concept can play an important role in a political economy which displays ethnic complexity. In its attempt to create economic growth and distribute significant wealth and opportunity to the majority *bumiputera* (Malays and natives of Sabah and Sarawak) community, extensive use has been made of the SEZ concept. Given the need for incentives for SEZ investment, this raises the difficult issue of whether affirmative action provisions, which ordinarily require 30 per cent *bumiputera* investment in a particular project, are also to apply in SEZs. Tey explains and traces this issue through a discussion of Malaysia's dualistic political economy and a study of the Iskandar project, where the 30 per cent *bumiputera* investment rule does not apply, and where, in line with our discussion above of the transformation from the original 'sweatshop' SEZ, Iskandar is designed to attract investment in creative industries, educational services, financial advisory and consulting services, healthcare services, logistics services and tourism. The SEZ can still fulfil the 'best of both worlds' principle, allowing investment incentives in a limited area without necessarily challenging the prevalence of contrary rules in the domestic trade area (DTA). But the heavy implication of Tey's study is that when the irresistible force of FDI for economic development meets the immovable object of political necessity it is the former that will ultimately prevail. If so, the SEZ in the Malaysian context will have fulfilled a useful purpose.

The final two chapters in this book concern SEZs in India: Shankar Gopalakrishnan's Chapter 8 and Andrew Harding's Chapter 9. They take contrasting approaches but reach similar conclusions. Gopalakrishnan places the Indian SEZs in the context of India's developing political economy and argues that SEZs are not merely another FDI incentive policy but are rather a political intervention in India's governance institutions. He explains why, uniquely among SEZs discussed in this book, India's SEZs have become flashpoints of protest. Harding on the other hand takes the Indian SEZ Act 2005 as a contemporary example of SEZ governance and analyzes it from a public law standpoint. He finds that the breathtakingly wide provisions of this statute are unconstitutional, in that they breach basic notions of fundamental rights and the rule of law. Harding advocates a rethinking of the governance and regulation of SEZs and addresses the constitutional dimensions and plausibility of the discrimination inherent in the SEZ concept. India's SEZ experience can be contrasted with Malaysia's Iskandar project as discussed by Tey Tsung Hang in Chapter 7, where SEZs became part of the solution in Malaysia's dualistic political economy which focuses on empowering the *bumiputera* community while growing the economy for the benefit of all. Gopalakrishnan concludes that the Indian experience 'constitutes the logical culmination of the zone concept', and that it is 'difficult to imagine a more extreme or more dangerous formulation of the concept of the SEZ than the Indian one'. That conclusion, together with Harding's public-law critique of SEZ governance, Tey's indication that the *bumiputera* policy may be in the throes of reformulation, and Casanova's reports of corruption and abuse of power, all suggest that the emerging pluralistic nature of Asian SEZs may involve grave political issues. Furthermore, that the Chinese experience, with its strong authoritarian background, is a unique, one-of-a-kind model, which might not lend itself to transplantation. In light of these conclusions, we may see a less than featherbed landing for the SEZ concept in Asia.

SEZs and the contemporary literature

A survey of up-to-date literature analyzing modern SEZs in Asia – or elsewhere – reveals a relatively sparse library. As might be expected there are many monographs from the 1980s and 1990s, especially about China's early SEZ experience. But there are fewer from the most recent decade, and again those that exist focus mainly on exploring China's development experience – especially its economic (Wang and Meng 2001), urban (Jones et al. 2003), labour (Gallagher 2005; Lee 2007), sociological (Pun 2005) and environmental issues (Richardson 2004). There are also a few studies of general interest about SEZs in selected Asian countries, for instance, Jayanthakumaran (2003) and Lall (2000b); monographs about individual countries such as Thailand: Poapongsakorn et al. (2000); studies evaluating the economic impact of zone development (Jayanthakumaran 2002; Sinclair 2001); and those exploring the relationships between SEZs and economic reform and trade liberalization in developing countries (Cling and Letilly 2001;

Madani 1999; and Schrank 2001). However, in recent years, scholars and others seem to have lost interest in SEZs or their fate.

But the tide might be turning now because SEZs have proliferated recently – from about 500 worldwide in 1995 (ILO 1998) to some 3,000 or 5,000 only a decade later. And it is not only the number of zones which have multiplied but also the number of countries that host the zones. The World Bank (2008) identifies particularly Organisation for Economic Cooperation and Development (OECD) countries – industrialized or developed countries – as key growth areas for SEZs. And with countries as diverse as India, Russia, Ukraine, Pakistan, Vietnam, Jordan, Uganda, Nigeria, Kenya, Ghana and so on showing an increased appetite for this economic development model, interest in SEZs is clearly on the rise in the twenty-first century.

Furthermore, although the World Trade Organization (WTO) in 1995 cast doubt on the future of SEZs as a viable policy tool in the development agenda, the World Bank and aid agencies such as US-AID (US Agency for International Development) have been reviving the SEZ model as a way of overcoming what they claim are obstacles which often stand in the way of foreign investment and development. Thus, in April 2008, the World Bank, through its multi-donor investment climate advisory service, FIAS, published a study entitled *Special Economic Zones: Performance, Lessons Learned, and Implications for Zone Development*, in which it lends credibility to the revival of SEZs as a viable policy tool. According to its interpretation (World Bank 2008: 54),

> SEZ regimes are consistent with the WTO so long as benefits are not contingent on export performance, use of local content, or maintenance of a foreign exchange balance; or primarily benefit a specific firm, industry, or other interest. Zone regimes that have specific incentives linked to export performance – such as minimum export requirements, subsidized rent or utilities, or a lower tax on export income – are not compatible with WTO mandates and need to be altered.

There is nothing new in this interpretation and the World Bank's publication is a very general study about the configuration, management and performance of SEZs. However, what is new is that the Bank raises the issue at all and that it presents such an overly optimistic view of future trends and the sustainability of SEZs. The Bank therefore confirms a renewed interest in SEZs worldwide and signals an increase in the number of policy-makers, professionals, and researchers who might benefit from knowledge about them. It is therefore a pity that the World Bank's publication is so adamant about recommending the private-owned and private-operated model of SEZs even while admitting that, owing to lack of data, it is difficult to conclude that private zones outperform public ones.

However, the Bank does suggest that from the host country's point of view, private zones are less expensive to develop and operate, 'mainly because private developers finance onsite infrastructure and facilities; governments are required only to provide offsite (external) infrastructure facilities, which are only a small part of the total development costs (usually a maximum of 25 per cent of onsite costs)' (World Bank 2008: 45). The crux seems to be that because private zones are run on a cost-recovery basis, they are usually more responsive to tenants' needs, and therefore provide a wider range of property management services and amenities, including specialized on-site facilities for telecommunications, healthcare, day-care centres, and business support services (ibid.). This begs the question of whether government-owned facilities can operate on a cost-recovery basis. The Suzhou SEZ established as a joint venture between the Chinese and Singapore governments is operated by a government-owned corporation and uses a cost-recovery basis (Carter 2003). However, throughout the study the Bank excludes China – or 'East Asia' as it prefers to call China. For instance, it claims that '[o]utside East Asia, government-developed and -run zones are generally less profitable than their private counterparts, and have a worse track record in terms of negative social and environmental impacts as well'. Instead of using anecdotal evidence to suggest that private zones generally cost less to establish, develop and operate than public zones and that they also yield superior economic results than public zones, our interests and insights might have been better served if the Bank had spent its money on conducting systematic research and analysis of the facts in individual zones. The Bank now runs a real risk of repeating its fiasco of the 'Asian Miracle' pronunciations of the 1990s.

This book, on the other hand, attempts a timely analysis of the genesis, status, trends and challenges concerning the implementation of SEZ policies in an array of Asian countries. It is unique in that it highlights a range of experiences from Asian countries with a variety of political and economic regimes: from communist, authoritarian China in the process of becoming a fully fledged free market economy; to the sixty-odd-year-old democracy of an independent India struggling to liberalize, modernize and deregulate its economy; to modern democratic, multi-ethnic Malaysia and the newly democratic Philippines fighting to curb corruption and abuse of privilege. By covering a range of Asian experiences, this volume offers a natural platform for those who wish to explore the transfer and adaptation of Asian SEZ policies and practice to countries outside of Asia, as well as those who want to consider prospects for the sustainability of the Asian SEZ model.

Key questions for SEZ promoters

There are at least five key questions to which policy-makers in a potential SEZ host country should seek answers: first, choice of the nature and configuration of the zone required to fulfil the country's development goals, including location and the private–public dilemma; second, an appropriate legal, regulatory or governance framework which pays due regard to designation criteria if private zones are to be allowed, and to incentives, privileges, rights and obligations of zone developers/operators vis-à-vis the government and the private companies and other stakeholders; third, the incentive package and core policy features of the zone; fourth, the regulatory framework including investment approvals, expatriate permits, on-site customs clearance procedures, automatic access to foreign exchange and so on; fifth, the institutional framework and management autonomy of the zone.

Following are some specific considerations (dos and don'ts) that policy-makers might want to take into account if they wish to maximize the success of their SEZs.

- Location, location, location. Most successful SEZs are not hidden away in inaccessible rural areas but are located near ports and have easy access to public transportation and other infrastructure.
- Establish a comprehensive policy framework in which your SEZs' objectives, markets, and preferred activities are clearly set out.
- Remember that SEZ is a generic term so specify what kind of zone you envisage will help fulfil your country's specific needs, and remember that an SEZ program is only one of the tools available in your development policy toolbox.
- In your policy framework, remember to include a long-term objective and strategies regarding how you will integrate the SEZ activities into the rest of the country's development programme in due course.
- Fiscal incentives, tax holidays and so on are not the major part of the SEZ package. As the fiscal incentives being offered in SEZs around the world become more and more similar, there is a veritable price war in this area; like discounts in detergents on a supermarket shelf. Avoid this. Spend the money on enhancing the facilities and amenities.
- Ensure that the incentive framework complies with the WTO by removing any export obligation and allowing companies within the zone full access to the domestic market on a duty-paid basis.
- Even the most generous incentive package will not compensate for or offset disadvantages such as poor location, grossly restrictive practices, abundant, time-consuming red tape, and malfunctioning or inadequate utilities.
- Simplify and streamline the procedures necessary for complying with and gaining all required approvals, permits, licenses and so on. In the best run zones, such as the Suzhou Industrial Park SEZ in China, the authorities establish a one-stop shop (Carter 2003). This will require legislation to provide the one-stop entity with single-point authority over the functions of other government agencies.
- Ensure that the powers of and regulatory structure for SEZs mesh with the country's constitutional and rule of law structure, taking account of human rights, central and local powers, proper delegation, and rights to judicial review and other forms of oversight.

Finally, the original SCM deadline agreed in the Uruguay Round (of the WTO) for the elimination of export subsidies in developing countries was extended from January 2003 to 2010. The Doha Round established procedures under which eligible developing countries can submit applications to extend the original SCM deadline. Eligible countries are those whose share of total global exports was below 0.10 per cent in 1998–2000, and whose gross national income was under US$20 billion in 2000. So far, most of the thirty eligible developing countries have filed applications for extension of the deadline for compliance. However, of the ineligible developing countries only Thailand seems to have amended its zone-related legislation so as to comply with the WTO rules. Thailand has removed mandatory export requirements and export subsidies from its legislation (World Bank 2008: 57).

With or without WTO compliance, it seems clear that SEZs or zones of one form or another will continue to exist, and even continue to multiply in the twenty-first century. But they will also evolve to meet the challenges of globalization or global integration, international trading rules, and the advent and proliferation of free trade agreements (FTAs) and bilateral international treaties (BITs). SEZs will continue to exist both in developing countries or emerging market economies as well as in highly industrialized developed countries. For instance, the USA alone is home to 266 foreign trade zones (FTZs), which is considered one of the main reasons why manufacturers were able to operate 'just-in-time' systems in that country (World Bank 2008: 57–58). It is clear that the advantages of flexibility, cost reduction in production, logistics and distribution, trying out new policies in a discrete location, and so on, which SEZs offer are available to and required by all countries, developed and developing.

However, economist Paul Romer might be treading a new path – at least in name – when he suggests the fanciful idea of 'Charter Cities'.[3] He claims that the secret of transforming a poor nation into a rich one is modelled by the British Empire, not World Bank reports. Romer's plan calls for a rich country to take over part of a poor country (establish an SEZ?) and imbue it with the rich country's laws, institutions, regulations including justice mechanisms, and so on. His example proposes that the USA close Guantanamo Bay and hand over the land to Canada, which would agree to develop it. A new city, a Charter City, would blossom, muses Romer. It would do for Cuba what Hong Kong, administered by the British, did for China; it would connect Cuba to the global economy. The scenario includes property developers and contractors, lured by rising property values, rushing in to construct turnkey factories and other commercial and residential buildings, and a massive influx of migrant workers (from inner Cuba and beyond) lured by better wages and a fair (British-style) judicial system – similar to the Singapore experience. Eventually the Cuban authorities would decide to replicate the Guantanamo SEZ all over the island, in a similar fashion to the Chinese plans for cloning the Singapore–China Suzhou Industrial Park all over China (Carter 2003), or of taking the Hong Kong model to Shenzhen and beyond.

So is the ultimate fate of SEZs a reversion to the colonial experience of treaty ports and national factories? In other words, old wine in new bottles: the colonialism of the twenty-first century? Romer would say absolutely not. Establishing a Charter City (modern SEZ) does not involve coercion and therefore there is no colonization, no colony, just a modern well-functioning city with all amenities, human rights and 'development' for everyone. Whether or not Paul Romer is correct remains to be seen. And the entire issue of neo-colonialism must await a separate book, perhaps with a focus on China's expansion into Africa and elsewhere in Asia.

Notes

1 Under the provisions of the Agreement on Subsidies and Countervailing Measures (SCM Agreement), covered by the WTO, certain export-oriented subsidies and tax preferences are prohibited. For a discussion, see Torres 2007: 217.
2 For an analysis and discussion of distortions in China during the reform process, see Young (2000).
3 The scenario described here derives from an interview with Paul Romer conducted by Anne Marie Tremonte on CBC Radio One, 8 February 2010; see www.cbc.ca/The Current.

Bibliography

Aggarwal, A (2004) 'Export Processing Zones in India: Analysis of the Economic Performance', Indian Council for Research on International Economic Relations Working Paper no. 148.

Carter, C (2003) 'The Clonability of the Singapore Model of Law and Development: The Case of Suzhou, China', in Antons, C, ed. (2003) *Law and Development in East and Southeast Asia*, London: Routledge/Curzon.

Cling, J and G Letilly (2001) *Export Processing Zones: A Threatened Instrument for Global Economy Insertion?* DIAL/Unite de Recherche CIPRE Document de Travail DT/2001/17 (November).

Demurger, S, J Sachs, W Woo, S Bao and G Chang (2002) 'The Relative Contributions of Location and Preferential Policies in China's Regional Development: Being in the Right Place and Having the Right Incentives', *China Economic Review* 13: 444–65.

Gallagher, M (2005) *Contagious Capitalism: Globalization and the Politics of Labour in China*, Princeton, NJ: Princeton University Press.

Graham, E (2004) 'Do Export Processing Zones Attract FDI and Its Benefits? The Experience from China', *International Economics and Economic Policy* 1: 87–103.

Hamada, K (1974) 'An Economic Analysis of Duty-Free Zones', *Journal of International Economics* 4: 225–241.

Healey, D and W Lutkenhorst (1989) 'Export Processing Zones: The Case of the Republic of Korea', *Industry and Development* 26: 1–56.

Hu, K (2008) 'Made in China: The Cultural Logic of OEMs and the Manufacture of Low-cost Technology', *Inter-Asia Cultural Studies* 9(1): 27–46.

International Confederation of Free Trade Unions (2003) *Export Processing Zones: Symbols of Exploitation and a Development Dead End*, International Confederation of Free Trade Unions (September).

ILO (International Labour Organization) (1998) 'Labour and Social Issues Relating to Export Processing Zones', Geneva: ILO.

Jayanthakumaran, K (2002) 'An Overview of Export Processing Zones: Selected Asian Countries', University of Wollongong Department of Economics Working Paper Series, WP 02–03.

—— (2003) 'Benefit-Cost Appraisals of Export Processing Zones: A Survey of the Literature', *Development Policy Review* 21(1): 51–65.

Jones D, Cheng Li, and A Owen (2003) 'Growth and Regional Inequality in China during the Reform Era', *China Economic Review* 14: 186–200.

Kedic, L. (2009) 'The Global Economic Crisis and FDI Flows to Emerging Markets', *Columbia FDI Perspectives* 15 (8 October).

Kusago, T and Z Tzannatos (1998) 'Export Processing Zones: A Review in Need of Update', World Bank Social Protection Discussion Paper 9802.

Lall, S (2000a) 'Export Performance and Competitiveness in the Philippines', Department of International Development Working Paper 49, Oxford: University of Oxford.

—— (2000b) 'Technological Change and Industrialization in the Asian Newly Industrializing Economies', in *Technological Learning and Economic Development: The Experience of the Asian NIEs*, Cambridge: Cambridge University Press.

Lee, C-K (2007) *Against the Law: Labor Protests in China's Rustbelt and Sunbelt*, Berkeley: University of California Press.

Madani, D (1999) 'A Review of the Role and Impact of Export Processing Zones', World Bank Development Research Group Policy Research Working Paper 2238 (November).

Miyagiwa, K and L Young (1987) 'Unemployment and the Formation of Duty-Free Zones', *Journal of Development Economics* 26: 397–405.

Ota, T (2003) *Industrial Policy in a Transitional Economy: The Role of China's Special Economic Zones in Economic Development*, Tokyo: Tokyo University.

Poapongsakorn, N, P Santanaprasit and N Srianant (2000) *Assessing Export Platforms: The Case of Thailand*, Harvard Institute for International Development, Continuing Assistance on Economic Reform II Discussion Paper no. 73.

Pun, N (2005) *Made in China: Women Factory Workers in a Global Workplace*, Durham, NC: Duke University Press.

Radelet, S (1999) *Manufactured Exports, Export Platforms, and Economic Growth*, Harvard Institute for International Development, Continuing Assistance on Economic Reform II, Discussion Paper no. 43.

Rhee, Y, K Katterbach and J White (1990) *Free Trade Zones in Export Strategies*, Industry Development Division, Industry Series Paper no. 36, World Bank.

Richardson, B (2004) 'Is East Asia Industrializing Too Quickly? Environmental Regulation in Its Special Economic Zones', *UCLA Pacific Basin Law Journal* 22(1): 150–244.

Sadni-Jallab, M. and E Blanco de Armas (2002) *A Review of the Role and Impact of Export Processing Zones in World Trade: The Case of Mexico*, Brighton: Institute of Development Studies, University of Sussex.

Sanchez-Ancochea, D (2004) *Following the East Asian Miracle? The Limitations of Manufacturing Specialization of Small Latin American Countries in the New Global Economy*, First Annual Report, Institute for the Study of the Americas, London: University of London.

Sauvant, K (2008) 'The Rise of International Investment, Investment Agreements, and Investment Disputes', in *Appeals Mechanism in International Investment Disputes*, New York: Oxford University Press.

Schrank, A (2001) 'Export Processing Zones: Free Market Islands or Bridges to Structural Transformation?' *Development Policy Review* 19(2): 223–42.

Sen, A (1999) *Development as Freedom*, Oxford: Oxford University Press.

Torres, R (2007) 'Free Zones and the World Trade Organization Agreement on Subsidies and Countervailing Measures', *Global Trade and Customs Journal* 2(5): 217.

Trubek, D and A Santos, eds, (2006) *The New Law and Economic Development: A Critical Appraisal*, Cambridge: Cambridge University Press.

UNCTAD (United Nations Conference on Trade and Development) (2003) *World Investment Report 2002: Transnational Corporations and Export Competitiveness*, New York and Geneva: United Nations.

—— (2007) *World Investment Report 2007: Transnational Corporations, Agricultural Production and Development*, Geneva: UNCTAD.

—— (2009) *World Investment Report 2009: Transnational Corporations, Agricultural Production and Development*, Geneva: UNCTAD.

United Nations Center on Transnational Corporations (UNCTC) (1991) *The Impact of Trade-Related Investment Measures on Trade and Development*, New York: UNCTC.

Wang, S and L Meng (2001) 'A Reevaluation of China's Rapid Growth', *China Economic Review* 12: 338–46.

Wang, X and A Hu (1999) *The Political Economy of Uneven Development: The Case of China*, Armonk, NY: ME Sharpe.

Wei, S-J (1995) 'The Open Door Policy and China's Rapid Growth: Evidence from City-Level Data', in Takasoshi Ito and A Krueger, eds, *Growth Theories in Light of the East Asian Experience*, Chicago: Chicago University Press, 73–97.

World Bank (1992) *Export Processing Zones*, Policy and Research series, Volume 20 (March), Washington, DC: World Bank Group.

—— (2001) 'Export Processing Zones: Has Africa Missed the Boat?', Africa Region Working Paper series 17 (May), Washington, DC: World Bank Group.

—— (2008) *Special Economic Zones: Performance, Lessons Learned, and Implications for Zone Development*, Washington, DC: World Bank Group.

Young, A (2000) 'The Razor's Edge: Distortions and Incremental Reform in the People's Republic of China', *Quarterly Journal of Economics* 115(4): 466–84.

2 SEZs

A policy tool in search of a new agenda?

Peter Muchlinski

The special economic zone (SEZ) represents a specialized form of investment incentive regime that has played a significant role in the evolution of globalized production by multinational enterprises (MNEs). The basic concept is that of a 'dual legal order' which separates a specialized policy enclave from the rest of the jurisdiction in which the zone is located (Likosky 2005a: ch. 4). It is the purpose of this chapter, first, to consider the nature and origins of the SEZ concept in the first section and, second, to examine the possible future impact of the concept on economic and social development. At the economic level the general trend towards trade and investment liberalization, and the introduction, since 1995, of WTO disciplines prohibiting export trade subsidies, has placed the use of SEZs under increased regulatory strain. In such an environment, what further use does the SEZ concept have? In addition, as regards social development, how far can the SEZ concept be used to lower social standards? Or can it be a vehicle for the protection of such standards? These questions will be addressed in the second section of the paper.

Origins, nature and development of SEZs

SEZs come in many forms and names.[1] Very commonly the zone is referred to as an export processing zone (EPZ) which has been defined as, 'a designated specialized industrial estate which produces mainly for export and which constitutes an enclave from the trade and customs regime of a country in which free trade applies' (ESCAP/UNCTC 1985: 1).[2] The EPZ has a distinct regime of customs and trade regulations which may be coupled with a package of investment incentives, designed to attract internationally mobile inward direct investment, preferably in the manufacturing sector (see Wall 1976). According to the most recent survey of EPZs undertaken by the World Bank in 2008 there are around 2,301 zones in 119 developing countries clustered mainly in the Asia-Pacific region (World Bank 2008: 23). The terms EPZ and SEZ can be used interchangeably and their adoption is often a matter of preference rather than substance. For example India has redesignated its earlier EPZs as SEZs governed by the provisions of the more recent Special Economic Zones Act 2005 (see Harding in this volume).

The EPZ phenomenon has been viewed as an evolution of the ancient free port concept (ESCAP/UNCTC 1985: 9–10). This is correct so far as both approaches involve the creation of a 'policy enclave'. Nevertheless, a crucial difference between a traditional free port (or free trade zone [FTZ]) and an EPZ is that, while both are created by a special customs regime, the former aims mainly at the encouragement of free trade in finished products and commodities, while the latter is specifically concerned with encouraging export-orientated manufacturing investment. This is not to suggest that elements of a 'free port' cannot co-exist with an EPZ. Indeed the free port concept has itself evolved beyond its traditional roots. According to the World Bank, free ports have become something more than just export drivers and investment magnets being designed as, 'liberalised platforms for diversified economic growth that not only could but should spill over into the national economy' (World Bank 2008: 16).

In this connection, special mention should be made of China's unique SEZ policy, the most prominent example of the use of this newer free port concept. It aims not only at encouraging inward direct investment by MNEs but, more importantly, at the creation of a capitalist economic enclave within the PRC, which can act as a testing ground for the creation of a new Chinese socialist market economy. Thus, in the PRC, the EPZ and FTZ concepts have been adapted into a new kind of administrative regime for the reorganization of socialist relations of production. This forms a pivotal part of China's wider open door policy, leading, eventually, to that country's integration into the international division of labour, while at the same time preserving its socialist ideological perspective.[3]

In essence, the EPZ grew out of a compromise between two conflicting strategies of economic development pursued by developing countries (Muchlinksi 2008: 227). During the late 1960s and 1970s, numerous such countries adopted policies of import-substituting industrial development, which aimed at the creation of an independent domestic industrial base by means of, inter alia, restrictions on imports and inward foreign investment. However, such policies were strongly biased against export activity. The result was that these countries failed to earn adequate returns on domestic investment. By way of response, in the 1970s, certain developing countries, not wishing to abandon import substituting policies entirely, introduced EPZs as a means of partial and limited liberalization (Kumar 1989: 4–6). The aim was to attract MNEs into the EPZ, by means of favourable customs regulations and other incentives, so that these firms would set up production facilities in the zone. From these, they would service global export markets in both finished and intermediate products. Thereby, it was believed, the host state could earn increased export earnings. Furthermore, investment in EPZs by MNEs was thought likely to bring further benefits in the form of increased employment opportunities, improved training and skills for the workforce and the transfer of modern productive technology (ESCAP/UNCTC 1985: 15–21).

The first EPZ was established in Ireland in 1956 with the creation of the Shannon Free Zone around Shannon Airport (Sklair 1988; World Bank 2008: 30). However, the principal developments in this policy have occurred in developing countries, particularly in East Asia. Thus, inter alia, India, Taiwan, Malaysia, the Philippines, and South Korea have all adopted EPZs.[4] In Africa, the first EPZ was created in Mauritius in 1970.[5] Other Sub-Saharan countries have since established EPZs.[6] In North Africa, Egypt has established similar zones as part of its *infitah* (open door) policy.[7] In Latin America, Puerto Rico was the first to adopt the EPZ concept in 1962 (ESCAP/UNCTC 1985: 10). In Mexico, a unique policy based on EPZ principles has emerged as a means of stimulating industrial development along the US-Mexican border. US firms have, for some years, been taking advantage of conditions in ss. 806.30 and 807 of the US Tariff Schedule (now 9802.0). These allow for the export of goods from the US for assembly abroad and for their re-importation at favourable rates of tariff, in that import duties are only levied on the value added abroad (Hood and Young 1979: 207). These regulations have made it profitable for US firms to export labour-intensive production activities to low labour-cost areas. The low labour costs attract low re-importation tariffs due to the low value added. Indeed, such tariff concessions may be seen as a significant home country contribution to the growth of EPZs in developing countries. In 1965, the Mexican government introduced the Border Industrialization Programme, so as to encourage US industrial investors to exploit this concession in US tariffs by locating labour intensive production in Mexico. Special customs concessions were introduced for the importation of parts and raw materials required for the processing, assembly and finishing of products destined entirely for export, within a 20-kilometre strip parallel to the international border or to the coastline (Sklair 1993: 45). Since the 1960s the in-bonded factories of the so-called *maquiladora* industry have extended hundreds of miles inland from the border, thereby straining the 'enclave' character of the original border zone (ibid.). Other countries also allow single factory EPZ schemes that provide incentives to individual enterprises regardless of location.[8]

The most important legal and administrative features of an EPZ are: the relationship between the EPZ and the rest of the host state referred to as the domestic tariff area (DTA); the applicable incentive regime and facilities offered to investors and pre- and post-entry administrative procedures.[9] As noted earlier, the essential feature of an EPZ is its status as an enclave within the host state bounded by a distinct customs regime. In effect, the EPZ is outside the territory of the host state for trade and investment purposes. Thus, a common feature of EPZs is that they are bounded by two frontiers: the political, fiscal and excise frontier between the host state and the rest of the world, and an internal fiscal and excise frontier between the zone and the rest of the host state (the DTA). This has significant effects upon the manner in which relations between the EPZ and DTA are arranged. In order to preserve the enclave status of the EPZ, certain states have specified the total or partial exclusion of local capital from investment in the EPZ, although the policies of individual states differ in this respect. More significantly, the local authorities must ensure that goods entering the zone are employed for the purposes of consumption or production within it, and are not smuggled into the DTA. Smuggling has proved to be one of the undesired, but perhaps inevitable, side-effects of EPZs.

In order to protect domestic producers from adverse competition, and to preserve the export orientation of the zone, firms operating in the EPZ may be prohibited or restricted from selling in the domestic market of the host state (Muchlinski 2008: 28–29). However, there may be schemes that permit sales into the local market. For example, in India, SEZ located firms are permitted to sell goods and services on the local market provided all necessary import licences have been obtained and duties paid.[10] Similarly, the Egyptian Foreign Investment Law of 1997 states in Article 33 that, 'import into the country from the free zones shall be in accordance with the general rules on import from abroad. Customs taxes shall be payable on goods imported from the free zone to the local market as though they were imported from abroad'. By contrast, sales by local producers to firms within the EPZ are generally encouraged. These will be treated as deemed exports from the DTA, and may attract fiscal and/or other benefits for EPZ firms as incentives to utilize local sources of supply.[11]

The major incentives offered in EPZs have traditionally related to tax exemptions and duty-free imports. These are usually supplemented by exemptions from import quotas and the freedom to import capital and to remit profits. There may also be non-fiscal financial incentives such as export allowances or subsidized interest rates (ESCAP/UNCTC 1985: 21–27; UNCTC 1988: 274–75). Many EPZ projects include the provision of facilities in the form of transport links, factory buildings, commercial services and housing and social services for the workforce. In areas of low population, it may also be necessary to bring in workers from other regions, or to use foreign migrant workers (ESCAP/UNCTC 1985: 30–32). The development of such facilities is particularly characteristic of EPZs that are aimed at the industrialization of underdeveloped regions of the host state.[12] Of especial significance to the early evolution of EPZs has been the harnessing of low-cost labour. Thus, the legal control of labour relations within the EPZs has acquired considerable importance as a means of preserving this advantage. Consequently, it is not uncommon to find that the employment rights of workers, and the right to establish trade unions or to take industrial action, are more limited within the EPZ than in the DTA (ESCAP/UNCTC 1985: 33; International Confederation of Free Trade Unions 1983: esp. paras 35–55; Kumar 1989: 112–13).

It is common for the administrative regime of an EPZ to establish eligibility criteria for investments. Most often, these include a combination of one or more of the following: the export-orientation of the investment; limited or no local equity participation; substantial foreign capital investment; significant local content in production; employment promotion effects and possibilities for technology transfer (ESCAP/UNCTC 1985: 33–34). The authorization required for entry into the EPZ will usually be within the power of a specialized agency set up to administer the EPZ on behalf of the host state government. Some countries have a central authority for this purpose.[13] Others have established separate authorities for the administration of EPZs.[14] Ideally, the relevant authority will have sufficient links with government departments to enable it to act as a 'one stop' service for the foreign investor, thereby reducing administrative inconvenience. In this way the EPZ authority can be used to bypass bureaucratic delays. Apart from administering the entry of foreign investors, the authority will usually have responsibility for the provision of infrastructure and services within the EPZ, the promotion and marketing of investment opportunities within the zone, and the recruitment of workers.

Historically, most EPZs have been established and operated by public sector bodies. However, an increasing number are privately managed and public-private partnership (PPP) arrangements have become increasingly common.[15] Indeed, according to the World Bank (2008:19):

> Perhaps the most notable trend over the past 15 years has been the growing number of privately owned, developed, and operated zones worldwide ... According to the stocktaking exercise conducted for this study, 62 percent of the 2,301 zones in developing and transition countries are private sector developed and operated. This contrasts greatly with the 1980s, when less than 25 percent of zones worldwide were in private hands. The key factor behind the rise of private zones is the perception that private zones are more successful than most public zones, as well as a general lack of funding for new government zone development.

With the entry of the private sector into zone development, most countries have either set up specialized public sector zone development and management agencies, or increasingly divested the physical project development function to the private sector, and transformed their zone authorities into purely regulatory, planning, and promotional bodies (ibid.: 20). Some zone authorities have reorganized themselves as corporate entities so as to become less bureaucratic and to ensure substantial private sector participation at the level of the board of directors (ibid.: 21).

Mapping a future role for SEZs

As devices for attracting inward investment by MNEs, EPZs have met with considerable success. Since the 1960s such zones have become locations for the more labour-intensive stages of production undertaken by MNEs. Taking advantage of the lower labour costs found in EPZs, MNEs in assembly-type industries (particularly consumer electronics, light machinery, clothing, textiles and resource processing) have established plants therein. These investments have increased jobs in the host countries and have contributed to export promotion in that most of the production in EPZs has been orientated towards supplying developed country markets.[16] According to Wall, the success of pioneering EPZs in Ireland, South Korea and Taiwan may have led many developing countries to believe that this was attributable to the zone instrument itself and not to the inherent attractions of those countries to export-orientated investment (Wall 1976: 485). This may explain why the idea has since been emulated by so many countries. However, the results have not been uniformly good in terms of the objectives behind such zones. It may be said that the traditional EPZs with their stress on low value added, light assembly production methods, have not helped to develop higher value added production of the kind needed for effective development. Equally many such zones have failed to establish lasting backward linkages into the local economy or to resolve labour surplus problems (World Bank 2008: 37). In addition there have been instances in which the costs of setting up the EPZ have not been recouped due to poor decisions on location, contradictory policies and the lack of effective marketing to potential investors.[17] As Kumar points out, a major difficulty with EPZs has been that they have been given a multiplicity of incompatible goals to achieve. It may not, in fact, be possible to do more than achieve a net increase in foreign exchange and employment through the establishment of EPZs. The wider goals of developing economically backward regions should, in his view, be dropped (Kumar 1989: 184–85). On the other hand, according to the UNCTAD *World Investment Report 2002*, EPZs can be successful if they have coherent and comprehensive policies, provide for human resource development, have good working and living conditions and aim to transform themselves into higher value added industrial parks (ibid.: 217, 219).

It is against this background that this second part of the chapter considers the future development of the SEZ concept. In particular the economic role for SEZs in a more liberalized international trade environment will be examined, as will the often made claim that SEZs are used as engines of social exploitation and environmental degradation.

The economic role

As more developing host states liberalize investment conditions within the country as a whole, the justification for retaining special economic enclaves within the economy is weakened (Muchlinski 2008: 233). As noted above, EPZs were set up as exceptions to a general policy of import substituting growth through the encouragement of domestic enterprises. Once the host country abandons such a policy and tariff reductions and trade and investment liberalization become generalized throughout the national economy, the need for an EPZ is less apparent. This may undermine the economic rationale behind the EPZ, and encourage firms to invest in the DTA. For example, a significant reason behind the failure of the Bataan EPZ in the Philippines appears to have been the extension of the bonded warehouse scheme, at first initiated exclusively within the zone, to other EPZs, coupled with the easier availability of investment incentives to investors outside the zone (ESCAP/UNCTC 1985: 240–41).

Indeed, the traditional EPZ may be a redundant concept in an open, developing, economy that is managing to attain more advanced levels of efficiency, institutional capacity and skills upgrading (UNCTAD 2002: 219). Yet such zones continue to attract the attention of countries and analysts, and countries continue to apply laws and regulations establishing and operating EPZs. In this light two issues in particular are worthy of discussion. The first concerns the impact of the multilateral disciplines prohibiting export subsidies under WTO rules, while the second concerns the regulatory consequences of the economic role played by SEZs in a more open economy.

Impact of the WTO subsidies code

Membership of the WTO entails adherence to the Agreement on Subsidies and Countervailing Measures (SCM Agreement) which, as was noted above, prohibits certain export-oriented subsidies (Torres 2007). While this will not affect services-oriented export subsidies, which fall outside the scope of the SCM Agreement, many manufacturing-oriented export subsidies will fall foul of the prohibition on 'specific' subsidies covered by that agreement.[18] By Article 1 of the SCM Agreement, a subsidy is defined as a financial contribution by a government or any public body within the territory of a WTO member that confers a benefit on the recipient. Article 2 adds that subsidies must be specific to an enterprise, an industry or a region to become 'actionable' within the required procedures under the agreement, while Article 3 prohibits two types of subsidy outright: those attaching to the export of goods or to the substitution of imports. Actionable subsidies will give rise to a right to seek remedial action, by way of countervailing duties being imposed on imports from the WTO member that initiated the subsidy, where it can be shown that the subsidies have caused, or threaten to cause, material injury to the industries or enterprises of another WTO member (ibid.: 220; Trebilcock and Howse 2005: 266–75; UNCTAD 2002).

EPZs are not prohibited as such by the SCM Agreement. Thus they may be kept in place provided that any incentives or subsidies used do not fall within the prohibited subsidy category (Torres 2007: 220; World Bank 2008: 54). According to the World Bank (2008: 54):

> SEZ regimes are consistent with the WTO so long as benefits are not contingent on export performance, use of local content, or maintenance of a foreign exchange balance; or primarily benefit a specific firm, industry, or other interest. Zone regimes that have specific incentives linked to

export performance – such as minimum export requirements, subsidized rent or utilities, or a lower tax on export income – are not compatible with WTO mandates and need to be altered. In addition, some analysts conclude that the broad exemptions of import duties and charges granted to EPZ enterprises may constitute a prohibited export subsidy since firms operating under other regimes are permitted duty-free importation of only those inputs used in the production of goods. This 'excess' may be incompatible with the WTO.

As to the requirement of specificity EPZ subsidies will come within this category where the zone is geographically delimited, or where it is industry specific, or where an enterprise is authorized to benefit from subsidies, or is required to export part of its production, as part of the authorization or licensing procedure (Torres 2007: 218).

The options open to members using EPZs are, either, to maintain EPZ subsidies but eliminate the conditionality of restricting sales on the domestic market or establishing a new system of incentives for all domestic companies that is not contingent on export performance either in law or in fact. WTO rules also permit border tax adjustments, so EPZs can continue to exempt exports by companies in these zones from indirect taxes (such as sales taxes) border taxes (such as consular fees) and import charges (UNCTAD 2002: 34; Torres 2007: 220–21).

So far there have been no disputes brought before the WTO Dispute Settlement Body concerning the use of SCM inconsistent subsidies specifically in SEZs or EPZs. A plausible explanation may be that since so many members maintain SEZs, and since they are not the most important single trade distorting instrument, no disputes have arisen.[19] It is a question for further investigation. However, the need to control and monitor the use of such policy instruments is inherent in WTO membership. Thus, upon accession to the WTO, China had to make certain undertakings as to the use of subsidies in the SEZs.[20] In addition the SCM Agreement provides only temporary respite for the least developed countries from its disciplines. By Article 27 of the agreement, developing countries were given an eight-year period of transition towards full conformity in recognition of the fact the export subsidies may play an important role in the economic development programmes of such members. That period ran out at the end of 2002. However, under Article 27(4) of the SCM Agreement, qualifying countries can apply for annual extensions of this period with a two-year transition to full conformity from the period of the last extension. This approach created much opposition from members who wished to enjoy the certainty of an extended period of transition. Accordingly, as part of the preparations for the Doha Round of trade negotiations a fast-track approval procedure for extensions was introduced.[21] Countries whose share of total world exports was below 0.10 percent in 1998–2000, and whose gross national income was below $20 billion in 2000, were eligible to apply. To date, most of the thirty eligible developing countries have submitted requests for extension of the deadline (Torres 2007: 222; World Bank 2008: 54).

Regulation for new functions

In its recent survey of SEZs the World Bank rejects the view that they are an obsolete policy tool. To the contrary, the case for zones may actually be strengthened in the context of trade liberalization (World Bank 2008: 57):

> First, even with full implementation of the Uruguay Round, tariff and non-tariff barriers will remain in most countries. Developing country exporters will still need to compete with exporters in other countries who are operating in a duty- and tax-free environment. Second, even with lowered tariffs, anti export biases will not be removed. Various policy distortions, procedural inefficiencies, and infrastructural inadequacies – many that can be directly addressed only over the long term – will deter exporters. This places great importance on the continued development of focused investment promotion and export competitiveness mechanisms such as SEZs that can provide a simplified regulatory environment.

This implies the need to reassess the economic role of EPZs. In particular the World Bank urges greater integration between zones and the wider host economy. The barriers between the zone and the DTA should be weakened with the zone becoming less of an enclave and more of a catalyst that serves to increase the integration of the domestic and international economies (ibid.: 14, 42). As noted above, this has happened in Mexico in relation to *maquiladora* factories. Similarly, in Egypt, firms have been encouraged to locate on the outskirts of EPZs by having the benefits of the zone apply to their operations, creating individual 'Private Free Zones' (Sklair 1988). Furthermore, domestic firms might be encouraged to enter the zone to take advantage of more favourable export conditions (UNCTAD 2002: 215). Apart from increased regulatory integration between the DTA and the zone further regulatory reforms may be needed. In particular the reduction of bureaucratic delays, simplified authorizations, use of a WTO-compliant incentives framework and the development of a uniform national system of tax incentives may be required (World Bank 2008: 51–57). Equally, the social and environmental impacts of zone operations will need to be dealt with. These are considered in the next section.

A further dimension to consider is the use of PPP structures in zone regulation. The World Bank advocates the use of private zone systems but it has noted that some countries have tried to develop these without an adequate legal and regulatory framework. The result may be excessive variation in the terms and conditions applicable to each zone in the host country and increased legal uncertainty. What is needed is a clear delimitation of the rights and responsibilities of the private and public partners with respect to all aspects of zone development, financing and operation, regulation and promotion (ibid.: 52). The implications of the use of PPPs need to be considered more fully. In particular the precise relation between the private and public elements needs to be clarified, the relationship between private profits and public service provision determined and the social and environmental aspects of the partnership regime need to be addressed. This is, after all, a form of business association used in specific industrial projects. How it needs to be adapted to the operation of SEZs is not a well understood issue.

Social and environmental role

This aspect of EPZ operations is difficult to map. In part this is due to the presence of much contradictory information about the social effects of EPZs. Examples exist to show how some EPZs suppress basic labour rights, condone poor working practices and low wages while others uphold ILO labour standards or offer better than average practices and conditions including wages. Further examples show that EPZs often employ and segregate young unskilled women workers and pay them lower wages while ignoring essential women's rights at work, while other examples show that EPZs offer women new working opportunities and higher wages than anything they would have had before. Finally, in relation to environmental effects there are examples of lax environmental controls aimed at attracting polluting industries and examples of better environmental controls and practices within the zones. The challenge is to see how new forms of SEZs can enhance positive social and environmental effects and minimize negative effects in these areas.

Effects on workers' rights

Evidence of disadvantageous effects on workers' rights appears to come from mainly government-controlled zones that operate in low value added industries which require low wages to remain competitive (World Bank 2008: 40). The most common complaints, according to the ILO, relate to respect for freedom of association and the right to collective bargaining.[22] Assaults on these rights may be effected by legal restrictions on unionization and union membership, blacklisting of union officials, interference in the affairs of workers' organizations, refusal to negotiate, harassment, violence and reprisals, legal restrictions on industrial action including its prohibition by classifying EPZs as essential services, as well as exemptions and ambiguity regarding the application of labour law and access to zones (Gopalakrishnan 2007).

In some countries there is virtually no worker organization in EPZs. According to a 2008 ILO survey (paras 13–14):

> [I]n Costa Rica the few unionized workers face harassment and unfair dismissal. In Indonesia, there are numerous restrictions on workers' rights and significant anti-union sentiment and repression. In China, official

> unions have had only weak negotiation capacity ... In Madagascar, only one of every 62 enterprises is party to a collective agreement. Furthermore, 28 per cent of enterprises do not have any staff representative and 54 per cent of workers do not know what a collective agreement means. There is a clear need for training and mobilization. In Sri Lanka, the creation in 1994 of employees' councils, encouraged by employers and the Board of Investment (BOI), hampered the creation of free and independent unions and the exercise of the right to collective bargaining. According to the trade unions, the councils are set up without consultation with unions, are under the control of the BOI and their members are not freely elected. To represent workers in collective bargaining, a union has to represent 40 per cent of the workforce – otherwise the employees' councils negotiate on their behalf. Trade unions have therefore started to organize within a collective called the Apparel-Industry Labour Rights Movement, which seems to have improved cooperation between trade unions and the employees' councils under certain conditions.

The ILO supervisory bodies have sought to change these situations. In response to recent pressure from the ILO (2008: paras 14–15),

> Sri Lanka has indicated that a Social Dialogue and Collective Bargaining Unit has been set up within the BOI and that measures have been taken to promote collective bargaining at the EPZ level ... Several countries have indicated that they are in the process of taking legislative measures to give effect to the recommendations of the supervisory bodies. For example, Nigeria and Pakistan have indicated that they are in the process of taking legislative measures to grant freedom of association to EPZ workers. Costa Rica has indicated that it is amending its Labour Code, so as to provide for a speedy investigation procedure into complaints of anti-union discrimination. Mauritius has indicated that legal measures to strengthen collective bargaining processes at the enterprise level will be taken.

Thus ILO intervention may help in reducing such abuses.[23] That said, even where laws and practices are ILO compliant there may be weak implementation policies and a lack of adequate supervision.[24] To counter such problems countries may establish special mechanisms for dialogue and dispute resolution. Thus zone authorities in the Philippines, Singapore, and Trinidad and Tobago have trade union representatives on their boards. Other zones have promoted labour–management committees at enterprise level (ILO 2003: para. 29). According to the ILO, 'where at the zone level, through union pressure, employer or government initiative, social dialogue has taken place, it appears that zones have benefited from lower levels of industrial unrest and labour turnover' (ibid.). Indeed initiatives to develop better social dialogue are now being undertaken by Sri Lanka, Indonesia and Madagascar, which have had histories of opposition to such policies (ibid.: paras 31–32).

As the nature of production changes in SEZs from labour-intensive low technology assembly operations to higher value added, more technologically advanced production, an improvement in labour rights and general conditions of work is likely to result (UNCTAD 2002: 217). There is, however, considerable danger that certain zones may be in a 'low value-added trap' and it may prove hard to escape this (ibid.). According to UNCTAD, the major policy response to this risk should be investment in the upskilling of the workforce and the fostering of local entrepreneurship often through increased linkages between the zone and the DTA (ibid.: 215). It is zones that cannot beat the 'low value-added trap' that will continue to concern the ILO and other bodies charged with the improvement of workers' rights. Although they may allow for higher than average wages, they will continue to compete on labour-intensive processing which depends on low labour costs. Thus there will remain an incentive to restrict labour, safety and health regulations. In legal terms the extended use of so-called 'no lowering of standards clauses' in international trade and investment agreements could ensure that labour-related incentives are not permitted. However clauses of this type are often no more than best efforts provisions that do not carry mandatory force. Future agreements should change this weakness.

From the foregoing discussion it is clear that the economic and social evolution of SEZs is intimately interconnected and this must not be forgotten when developing new approaches to this policy instrument. That said, technological development may have a significant social consequence for female employment, to which our attention now turns.

Female employment

A long-standing controversy concerning EPZs has been the fact that the majority of workers in EPZs are young, single, females (Sklair 2002: 128–32).[25] It has been suggested that this may depress overall wage rates and create a more docile workforce, less inclined to espouse trade union membership, which, traditionally, has been geared to male concerns (Madani 1999). On the other hand, women may in fact have opportunities for employment and pay within the EPZ that far surpass anything they could otherwise have expected (Sklair 2002: 129). However, there is discrimination in terms of pay equity and equal treatment between male and female EPZ workers (ILO 2008: para. 17). In addition there has been less attention paid to the specific requirements of women workers as regards working hours, pregnancy, maternity leave and childcare. For example, until the practice was outlawed, pregnancy tests were imposed by some employers in the *maquiladoras* of Mexico. Complaints were made to the ILO and under the NAFTA labour side agreement. Mexican legislation now explicitly prohibits discrimination on the basis of pregnancy (ILO 2003: para. 21).

The issue of women's rights has not been adequately addressed. Discrimination and non-recognition of the special needs of women workers continues in some zones (World Bank 2008: 40). A further risk to women workers arises out of technological change. As the ILO states (ILO 2003: para. 11):

> Export-led industrialization has been strongly female-intensive, with no developing country having increased manufacturing exports without greater recourse to women workers. Zones have created an important avenue for young women to enter the formal economy at better wages than in agriculture and domestic service. Women make up the majority of workers in the vast majority of zones, reaching up to 90 per cent in some of them. However, there is a suggestion that as the nature of employment in zones evolves, with higher technology inputs, the gender profile of the workforce changes.

Thus, as economic development goes forward, women may be disadvantaged in the access to new value-added jobs that should follow. This raises the question of whether special attention needs to be paid in the employment and training practices of SEZs to ensure equal access to new opportunities for female and well as male workers.

Environmental impacts

The environmental impact of FDI has been analyzed from two main perspectives: the 'pollution haven' and the 'pollution halo'. According to the former, multinational enterprises (MNEs) operating in 'dirty' industries are likely to invest in countries that have low regulatory standards, thereby allowing them to take advantage of a location-specific advantage for absorbing imported environmentally harmful practices (Muchlinski 2008: 543). It has been suggested that some developing countries ought to act as pollution havens, given that the cost of assimilating environmentally hazardous substances may in fact be lower in such locations, given the higher absorptive capacity of some developing countries (Low and Yeats 1992: 89; Stewart 1993). This view is contested by the pollution halo argument, which sees the systematic raising of environmental standards by developing countries as a means of attracting the most environmentally advanced technologies possessed by MNEs originating from home countries with high levels of environmental regulation. This is an aspect of the concept of 'eco-efficiency' whereby firms will raise their environmental standards and practices in response to market stimuli such as regulatory penalties for environmentally harmful activities and incentives to develop new environmentally friendly technologies and practices (Schmidheiny 1992).

Both positions can be supported by evidence from the practice and operation of EPZs. The most notable example cited by adherents of the pollution haven approach is the Mexican *maquiladora* industry. The stimulus given by this programme to rapid industrial development along the US-Mexican border failed to keep up with the available waste treatment facilities and was compounded by a weak regulatory regime and lax monitoring and enforcement. In addition there was some evidence that between 1982 and 1990, US chemical industry investment grew dynamically following a tightening of environmental regulation there (Richardson 2004: 202; World Bank 2008: 41). Some evidence of pollution haven investment can also be found in East Asia.[26] However, the economic evidence for pollution havens appears to be weak, being based in the main on unreliable data (UNCTAD 1999: 298). Indeed, even the Mexican case has been explained as the result of 'regulatory chill' rather than a deliberate pollution haven strategy (Richardson 2004: 202).[27] Equally, the large scale of US investment could be more convincingly explained by the low labour costs of the region (ibid.).

As to the pollution halo position, there are at least two factors that point to the possibility that EPZs and other SEZs can act as magnets for best environmental practice. First, the internal environmental policies of MNEs may require the use of higher home country standards or global industry standards based on best practice (ibid.: 206–7). Firms have adopted techniques such as 'life cycle analysis', whereby the design of a product is based on the capacity to salvage and reuse components or to dispose of them in an environmentally friendly manner (OECD 1997: 71–72; Schmidheiny 1992: 98), voluntary eco-labelling and eco-audits, or a commitment to the development of environmentally friendly new technologies and products. Of especial significance in relation to self-regulation has been the widespread adoption by MNEs of the International Standards Organization (ISO) 14000 series of environmental management standards (Clapp 2005; Krut and Gleckman 1998; Lally 1997–98; UNCTAD 1999: 302–4).[28] The ISO 14000 series covers six main areas, including environmental management systems, environmental auditing, environmental labelling, environmental performance, evaluation, life cycle assessment and terms and definitions. Of the already adopted ISO 14000 series it is ISO 14001, *Environmental Management Systems – Specification with Guidance for Use*, which allows for corporate certification (Muchlinski 2008: 548). Though open to criticism on numerous grounds (Clapp 2005), these standards offer a means whereby firms can create a process of self-examination which should lead to better environmental performance regardless of local regulatory conditions.

A second important factor is that a significant number of zones place environmental concerns as a high priority in the regulatory structure. For example, China has extensive environmental regulations applicable to its SEZs and requires foreign firms to comply with strict environmental standards, though there have been some notable exceptions made in practice (Richardson 2004: 207–17 and 222–23). Indeed, in China, domestic firms may be more favourably treated in this regard than foreign firms (ibid.: 223–28). In other countries the state of environmental regulation in SEZs varies considerably. Some have very lax regimes while others have strong requirements.[29] That said, the encouragement of state-of-the-art environmental standards may be easier in a SEZ than in a country-wide regulatory regime. In particular, newer SEZs will have better infrastructure and resources to tackle environmental issues. Furthermore, some zones have been set up as 'eco-parks', as in Taiwan where the Environmental Protection Administration has named a number of such zones.[30] Thus the SEZ concept may be very suitable to such an environmental policy application.

The furtherance of good environmental practices in SEZs can be enhanced by international action. Just as in the case of international labour standards, international environmental standards could encourage host countries to adapt their regulatory regimes to conform to international obligations. In particular, membership of the main Multilateral Environmental Agreements (MEAs) may entail an obligation to ensure that national laws and regulations conform to the international standards they contain. This obligation will apply as much to zone regulations as to the rest of the country. SEZs cannot be used as vehicles for the exclusion of international legal duties. In addition, Bilateral Investment Agreements (BITs) could be used as a means of ensuring improved environmental protection. Specifically, such agreements could be used to challenge attempts to lower environmental, health or labour standards as a means of attracting FDI through the inclusion of a 'no lowering of standards' clause. The most recent US BITs contain provisions asserting that it is inappropriate for host countries to seek investment through the lowering of environmental or labour standards, while the Canadian counterpart applies to health, safety and the environment.[31] However, as noted above in relation to labour rights, such clauses are often non-binding on the signatory states, and this situation should be changed.

On the other hand, where foreign investors are expected to conform to higher standards than domestic investors, this could amount to a breach of the national treatment clause, which exists in most BITs. This requires that foreign investors from the other contracting party be treated no less favourably than investors of the host country contracting party. Thus environmental or other social regulations should apply equally to both kinds of investors. However, it may be arguable that where the SEZ prohibits investment by domestic investors, and the applicable regime applies to foreign investors only, domestic and foreign investors are not in a comparable situation and so the national treatment rule cannot apply.

Conclusion

From the foregoing discussion it is clear that the SEZ concept is at a crossroads. The original purpose for which such zones were established, the creation of export-oriented enclaves in otherwise unliberalized economies, is no longer dominant. As national economies liberalize, the need for such a physically delimited dual legal order is lessened.[32] Equally, WTO disciplines will not permit certain types of export subsidies characteristic of the old style SEZs. However, it is premature to proclaim the SEZ as a piece of regulatory archaeology. SEZs retain the attraction of a specialized regulatory regime that can be adapted to new economic and technological opportunities. Thus, rather than undertaking the old role of a low labour cost, light assembly, export oriented enclave, new SEZs can act as the motors of a higher skill and higher technology model of investment and as the sites of economic integration between the domestic and international economies. In this their administrative and infrastructural advantages can serve to simplify and make more convenient the process of investment by both foreign and domestic firms. In addition, the new types of investment may allow for improved working conditions and positive environmental impacts in SEZs. Thus the future appears positive.

Nonetheless, it would be foolish to leave this as the last word on SEZs. At the economic policy level it is clear that not all SEZs can escape the 'low value-added trap'. This may be simply a fact of locational disadvantage and/or historical mismanagement coupled with limited resources. It is not clear what can be done to help overcome such structural problems. In these cases, social and environmental problems may continue and will challenge the legitimacy of the SEZ as a policy instrument. In such cases recourse to international standards as benchmarks for acceptable minimum labour, safety, health and environmental standards may be required. As stated above, SEZs cannot be used as an excuse for non-compliance with international standards. Here intergovernmental organizations, particularly the ILO and international environmental regimes, have a responsibility to continue in their monitoring and enforcement activity or to develop such activity. Equally, international trade and investment agreements could serve to control excessive declines in standards through legally binding 'no lowering of standards' clauses.

In relation to newer 'high value added' zones other regulatory problems arise and must be tackled. In particular the trend towards private sector zones and the increased use of PPPs requires a clear demarcation of the relationship between private contractual rights and public law obligations. This is normally done in the PPP agreement itself. However, there remain important problems of accountability that emerge from the private performance of public functions that contractual clauses may not always answer adequately.[33] In addition there remain questions of the relationship between the PPP and the wider community in which it operates. Where that PPP is set up as an industrial zone these wider social questions will need to be thought out so as to ensure that they are not sidelined in the process of rapid economic development. One such question was mentioned above in relation to the employment effects upon women of the move to higher value added production. Should the zone authority have a duty in this regard to retrain women or to offer quotas for women? Or does its private character mean that there is no such duty? In such a case what role does the state itself play? Such questions will no doubt emerge in relation to other social issues as well. It is not hard to see environmental questions raising similar problems of responsibility.

Thus the SEZ concept has a future, but one that is not free of new regulatory problems and issues at the levels of both economic and social regulation. What is certain is that the old style 'enclave' model offers us little guidance on these new-generation problems.

Notes

1 This section draws upon and develops Muchlinski 2008: 226–32.

2 According to the ILO, EPZs are 'industrial zones with special incentives set up to attract foreign investors, in which imported materials undergo some degree of processing before being re-exported'. With developments in information technology, 'imported material' would also include 'electronic data' today, as well as call centres located in zones. EPZs have evolved from initial assembly and simple processing activities to include high tech and science parks, finance zones, logistics centres and even tourist resorts. Their physical form now includes not only enclave-type zones but also single-industry zones (such as the jewelry [sic] zone in Thailand or the leather zone in Turkey); single-commodity zones (like tea in Zimbabwe); and single-factory (such as the Export Oriented Units in India) or single-company zones (such as in the Dominican Republic): www.ilo.org/public/english/dialogue/sector/themes/epz.htm. According to a recent World Bank survey EPZs are, 'industrial estates offering special incentives and facilities for manufacturing and related activities aimed mostly at export markets'. Typically these take two forms:

> In the traditional EPZ model, the entire area within the zone is exclusively for export-oriented enterprises licensed under an EPZ regime. Hybrid EPZs, in contrast, are typically sub-divided into a general zone open to all industries regardless of export orientation and a separate EPZ area reserved for export-oriented, EPZ-registered enterprises.
>
> (World Bank 2008: 10)

3 On the relationship between economic policy and ideology in the PRC's policy on SEZs, see: Chan et al. 1986: ch. 5; Sit 1985; Sklair 1991; see further Richardson 2004; World Bank 2008: 29.

4 See ESCAP/UNCTC 1985: Table 1.7 at 45. For a comprehensive survey of EPZs around the world, see Singa Boyenge (2007) at www.ilo.org/public/english/dialogue/sector/themes/epz/epz-db.pdf

5 See Mauritius Export Processing Zone Act (no. 51) 1970 as amended by Acts nos. 50 of 1975 and 13 of 1980. See further Alter (1990); Hein (1989); and the Enterprise Mauritius website, www.epzda.intnet.mu

6 These include Senegal, Liberia, Ghana, Zaire, Togo and Madagascar, Cameroon and Kenya. See: UNCTAD/ ECDC/225, 1992) and the *ILO Database* at Singa Boyenge (2007) note 4. See too: Nigeria Export Processing Zones Decree 1991 (Decree no. 34, 13 June 1991) repealed and replaced by Nigeria Export Processing Zones Decree (no. 63, 1992) of 19 November 1992: Federal Republic of Nigeria, *Official Gazette* no. 62 vol. 79 of 1992. This decree empowers the president of Nigeria to designate areas of the country as EPZs. It also establishes the Nigeria Export Processing Zones Authority (NEPZA) to manage, control and coordinate all activities within the zones. The first Nigerian EPZ was set up in Calabar, the capital of Cross River State, see: 'Goose with the Golden Egg', *Newswatch Magazine*, 16 March 1992, 29. See further NEPZA *Investment Procedures, Regulations and Operational Guidelines for Free Zones in Nigeria 2004* at www.nepza.org/downloads/NEPZA%20FREE%20ZONE%20REGULATIONS.pdf

7 See Law no. 8 of 11 May 1997 Promulgating the Law on Investment Guarantees and Incentives in *ICSID Investment Laws of the World* (1997) Dobbs Ferry, Oceana, vol. II. Release 97–2. See for preceding laws: Law no. 230 for 1989 of 20 July 1989: unofficial English translation in 4 *ICSID Rev-FILJ* at 376–95 (1989) comment by Marchais, ibid. at 297. For a discussion of the origins and effects of the original Free Zones established under Law 43 of 1974 see: Sklair 1988: 132. See further General Authority for Investment and Free Zones (GAFI) website at www.gafi.gov.eg/docs/freezones.htm

8 Apart from Mexico, countries relying exclusively on a single-factory scheme include Mauritius, Madagascar, Mexico and Fiji; other countries such as Costa Rica, the United States, and Sri Lanka allow both industrial estate-style zones and single factory designations: World Bank 2008: 11.

9 The following paragraphs draw on and revise Muchlinski 2008 at 229–32.

10 See Kumar 1989 at 47–48 for the old EPZ regime and see the Special Economic Zones Act 2005 (India SEZ Act 2005) s. 30 and the Special Economic Zone Rules 2006 (India SEZ Rules 2006) Rule 47 for the current regime available at http://sezindia.nic.in/

11 ESCAP/UNCTC 1985: 29–30.

12 See e.g. the Kandla Free Trade Zone in India described by Kumar 1989: 36–37; the Bataan EPZ in the Philippines described in ESCAP/UNCTC 1985 at 220–45.

13 E.g. South Korea and Thailand: ESCAP/UNCTC 1985: 34. See India's Central Board of Approval established under the India SEZ Act 2005 s.8 and explanatory note at http://sezindia.nic.in/HTMLS/about.htm

14 See ESCAP/UNCTC 1985: 35–38 for a comparative analysis. See India's Special Economic Zones Authority established for each SEZ under the India SEZ Act 2005 s. 31.

15 See UNCTAD 2002: 214 citing the example of the Philippines where forty privately run economic zones have been established since 1995 under the Philippines Economic Zone Authority. For legal basis see H. no. 14295 S. no. 1061 Republic Act no. 7916 Special Economic Zone Act of 1995 as amended by S. no. 1136 H. N. 5992 Republic Act no. 8748 An Act Amending Republic Act no. 7916 available at www.peza.gov.ph/about_peza.htm. Similarly under the Indian Special Economic Zones Act 2005 (India SEZ Act 2005) s. 3 (1) an SEZ can be set up either by governmental bodies or by 'any person'. 'Person' includes,

> an individual, whether resident in India or outside India, a Hindu undivided family, co-operative society, a company, whether incorporated in India or outside India, a firm, proprietary concern, or an association of persons or body of individuals, whether incorporated or not, local authority and any agency, office or branch owned or controlled by such individual, Hindu undivided family, co-operative, association, body, authority or company.

Available at http://sezindia.nic.in/HTMLS/SEZ%20Act,%202005.pdf. On the use of PPPs see World Bank 2008:18–19.

16 See Muchlinski 2008: 232 and World Bank 2008: 34–35, which suggests that while EPZs might be effective tools for employment generation their direct employment effects are less significant than their indirect effects, and at 35–36, where export development is seen as a major advantage of EPZs.

17 See, in particular, Kumar's analysis of the relative failure of the Kandla Free Trade Zone in comparison to the Santa Cruz Electronics Export Processing Zone in India: Kumar 1989; and the reasons given for the failure of the Bataan EPZ in the Philippines in ESCAP: World Bank 2008: 240–44; see too Warr 1989: 84.

18 Other types of incentives will also fall outside the scope of the SCM Agreement. According to Torres 2007: 218, 'less onerous labour regulations or facilities in the

creation and incorporation of companies, particularly with respect to participation of foreign capital, and access to improved general infrastructure, such as roads, phone lines or ports and trade facilitation measures' will generally fall outside the scope of the SCM Agreement, as they are not considered to be financial contributions.

19 On the other hand EPZs may have distorting effects upon Regional Trade Agreements (RTAs). According to the International Labour Office's *Report of the InFocus Initiative on Export Processing Zones (EPZs): Latest Trends and Policy Developments in EPZs* (Governing Body GB.301/ESP/5, 301st Session, Geneva, March 2008) at para. 12 at www.ilo.org/wcmsp5/groups/public/-ed_norm/-relconf/documents/meetingdocument/wcms_090223.pdf at para.11:

> Regional trade agreements (RTAs) are meant to reduce trade and investment barriers between their members. EPZs are not, however, considered to belong to national customs areas and their inclusion in RTAs may lead to trade circumvention whereby a non-RTA member producing in the EPZ of an RTA member would gain access to the favourable conditions offered by the RTA. Moreover, such practices may disadvantage local firms in an RTA member. As a result, some RTAs have adopted restrictive policies to prevent circumvention of tariffs. Duty drawback schemes have generally been limited and accompanied by transitional periods, for example under the North American Free Trade Agreement and the free trade agreements between the European Union and Chile and the European Union and Mexico. A recent study by the Organisation for Economic Co-operation and Development (OECD) indicated that the lack of provisions on the treatment of EPZs in RTAs may lead to an unintended increase in trade circumvention.

Citing M. Engman, O. Onodera and E. Pinali: 'Export Processing Zones: Past and Future Role in Trade and Development', OECD Trade Policy Working Paper no. 53, Working Party of the Trade Committee, TD/TC/WP (2006)39/FINAL, at www.olis.oecd.org/olis/2006doc.nsf/8d00615172fd2a63c125685d005300b5/4f4eb906a942a783c12572e300558929/$FILE/JT03227583.PDF

20 In the Accession Protocol (WTO Accession of the People's Republic of China, Decision of 10 November 2001 (WT/L/432 23 November 2001) available at www.docsonline.wto.org) China makes the following commitment in respect of special economic areas:

(B) Special Economic Areas

1. China shall notify to the WTO all the relevant laws, regulations and other measures relating to its special economic areas, listing these areas by name and indicating the geographic boundaries that define them. China shall notify the WTO promptly, but in any case within 60 days, of any additions or modifications to its special economic areas, including notification of the laws, regulations and other measures relating thereto.
2. China shall apply to imported products, including physically incorporated components, introduced into the other parts of China's customs territory from the special economic areas, all taxes, charges and measures affecting imports, including import restrictions and customs and tariff charges that are normally applied to imports into the other parts of China's customs territory.
3. Except as otherwise provided for in this Protocol, in providing preferential arrangements for enterprises within such special economic areas, WTO provisions on non-discrimination and national treatment shall be fully observed.

In Annex 5B to the Accession Protocol, China commits itself to phase out by 2000 the subsidies of 'the priority in obtaining loans and foreign exchange based on export performance' and 'preferential tariff rate based on localization rate of automobile production'. However, China does not commit itself to rescind the subsidies of 'preferential policies for the economic and technology development areas', 'preferential policies for the economic zone of the Pudong area of Shanghai', 'preferential policies for foreign invested enterprises', and 'preferential income tax rate for high-tech enterprises', which are contained in Annex 5A of Access Protocol and notified to WTO and its members.

21 'Procedures for extensions under Article 27.4 for certain developing country Members', adopted November 2001 WTO document G/SCM/39.
22 See ILO 2008: para. 12; another emerging issue is the treatment of migrant workers in EPZs see para.18.
23 Equally regional organizations can also help in monitoring labour standards in EPZs located within their member countries: see Gerbracht 2006–7.
24 According to the ILO,

> Chinese labour and trade union laws apply to all enterprises and economic organizations. They cover most employment issues, including contracts, wages, working conditions, occupational safety and health, the female workforce and dispute resolution. However, enforcement and labour practices vary between regions, as provincial and local labour departments have fairly wide discretion in handling local labour matters; and local governments are also concerned to attract investment.
>
> (ILO 2008: para. 29)

and see too paras 33–36 on similar issues in Sri Lanka, Indonesia and Madagascar.
25 According to the ILO report of 2008, para. 21,

> In Madagascar, more than 50 per cent of EPZ workers are young adults aged between 19 and 24 and, in Costa Rica, 40 per cent of EPZ workers are aged between 20 and 39. Women workers represent 71 per cent of EPZ workers in Madagascar, 40 per cent in Costa Rica and almost 70 per cent in Sri Lanka. It is estimated that, in 2005, the Sri Lankan garment sector provided direct employment to around 340,000 people, 87 per cent of whom were women. In China, women workers make up about 40 per cent of the workforce across the whole economy; this figure has always been 10 per cent higher in EPZs. In Batam, one of the main Indonesian EPZs, 80 per cent of workers were women in July 2007. Contrary to the situation in many countries, the share of female employment in India has always been less than 50 per cent and has tended to decrease over recent years.

26 Richardson 2004: 204–5, noting such investment in poorer East Asian countries by Japanese firms, the migration of Japanese cement producers to China and Hong Kong manufacturers of Styrofoam and electrical circuit boards produced with ozone-depleting CFCs in China's SEZs given China's longer phase-out period for the use of CFCs under the Montreal Protocol.
27 'Regulatory chill' denotes the unwillingness of a host country to raise regulatory standards for fear of losing FDI.
28 The ISO 14000 series standards are available upon payment from the ISO website, www.iso.org
29 Richardson 2004: 217–22, covering South Korea, Taiwan, Vietnam, Thailand, the Philippines and, in passing, Costa Rica, Belize, Zambia and Sri Lanka.

30 Ibid.: 218. These are known as Environmental Science and Technology Parks (ESTPs). There are four such parks: Kaohsiung, Hualian, Taoyuan, and Tainan; see the Power Point presentation of the Environmental Protection Administration at www.epa.gov.tw/en/epashow.aspx?busin=11949&path=11949&guid=86098c8c-4071-4a63-68a0b-4566024cf144&lang=en-us and see further the ESTP webpage at http://ivy3.epa.gov.tw/H/ESTP/en/index.htm

31 US-Uruguay BIT Articles 12, 13: 44 *ILM* 268 (2005) 217 also at http://ustr.gov/assets/World_Regions?Americas/South_America/asset_upload_file440_6728.pdf, Canadian Model BIT Article 11 at http://ita.law.uvic.ca/documents/Canadian2004-FIPA-model-en.pdf

32 This is not to say that dual legal orders are in themselves redundant. Host countries will continue to offer preferential treatment to foreign investors in their national laws and so continue with a dual legal order but will do so in the country as a whole rather than in an enclave. See Likosky 2005a: ch. 7.

33 See Likosky, ibid., at 44–51, and see further Likosky 2005b.

Bibliography

Alter, R (1990) *Export processing zones for growth and development: The Mauritian example*, IMF Working Paper 122, Indian Ocean Division.

Belser, W (2003) *Special economic zones of China and WTO: Will the privileges survive?* WTO Beijing Office.

Chan, T, EKY Chen and S Chin (1986) 'China's special economic zones: Ideology, policy and practice', in YC Jao and CK Leung (eds) *China's special economic zones: Policies, problems and prospects*, Oxford: Oxford University Press.

Clapp, J (2005) 'The privatization of global environmental governance: ISO 14000 and the developing world', in DL Levy and PJ Newell (eds) *The Business of global environmental governance*, Cambridge, MA: MIT Press.

Engman, M, O Onodera and E Pinali (2006) *Export processing zones: Past and future role in trade and development*, OECD Trade Policy Working Paper no. 53, TD/TC/WP (2006) 39/FINAL.

ESCAP/UNCTC (1985) *An evaluation of export processing zones in selected Asian countries*, New York: United Nations, ESCAP/UNCTC Publication Series B, no. 8.

Gerbracht, B (2006–7) 'Export processing zones and free trade agreements: Lessons from the North American Agreement on Labour Cooperation', *Transnational Law and Contemporary Problems* 16: 1029.

Gopalakrishnan, R (2007) *Freedom of association and collective bargaining in export processing zones: Role of the ILO supervisory mechanisms*, Working Paper no. 1, ILO.

Hein, P (1989) 'Structural transformation in an island country: The Mauritius export processing zone 1971 to 1988', *UNCTAD Review* 1(2): 41–57.

Hood, N and S Young (1979) *The economics of multinational enterprise*, London: Longmans.

International Confederation of Free Trade Unions (1983) 'Trade unions and the transnationals', *Information Bulletin*, Special Issue no. 3, 'Export Processing Zones', Brussels: ICFTU.

ILO (International Labour Office) 2003) *Employment and social policy in respect of export processing zones (EPZs)*, Governing Body GB.286/ESP/3 286th Session, Geneva.

—— 2008) *Report of the InFocus Initiative on export processing zones (EPZs): Latest trends and policy developments in EPZs*, Governing Body GB.301/ESP/5 301st Session, Geneva.

Jauch, H (2002) 'Export processing zones and the quest for sustainable development: A Southern African perspective', *Environment and Urbanization* 14(1): 101–9.

Krut, R and H Gleckman (1998) *ISO 14001: A missed opportunity for global sustainable industrial development*, London: Earthscan.

Kumar, R (1989) *India's export processing zones*, Delhi: Oxford University Press.

Lally, A (1997–98) 'ISO 14000 and environmental cost accounting: The gateway to the global market', *Law and Policy in International Business* 29: 501.

Likosky, M (2005a) *The silicon empire: Law, culture and commerce*, Aldershot: Ashgate.

Likosky, M (ed.) (2005b) *Privatising development: Transnational law, infrastructure and human rights*, Leiden: Martinus Nijhoff.

Low, P and A Yeats (1992) 'Do dirty industries migrate?', in P Low (ed.) *International trade and environment*, Washington, DC: World Bank Discussion Paper 159.

Madani, D (1999) 'A review of the role and impact of export processing zones', Washington, DC: World Bank Policy Research Working Paper no. 2238.

Muchlinski, P (2008) *Multinational Enterprises and the Law*, 2nd edn, Oxford: Oxford University Press.

OECD (1997) *Economic globalization and the environment*, Paris: OECD.

Richardson, B (2004) 'Is East Asia industrializing too quickly? Environmental regulation in its special economic zones', *UCLA Pacific Basin Law Journal* 22(1): 150–244.

Schmidheiny, S (1992) with the Business Council for Sustainable Development (BCSD) *Changing course: A global business perspective on development and the environment*, Cambridge, MA: MIT Press.

Singa Boyenge, J-P (2007) *Database on export processing zones*, Geneva: ILO.

Sit, V (1985) 'The special economic zones of China: A new type of export processing zone?', *The Developing Economies* 23(1): 69–88.

Sklair, L (1988) 'Foreign investment and Irish development: A study of the international division of labour in the mid-west region of Ireland', *Progress in Planning* 29 (whole issue): 149–217.

—— (1988a) 'The costs of foreign investment: The case of the Egyptian free zones', in E Kedourie and S Haim (eds) *Essays on the economic history of the Middle East*, London: Frank Cass.

—— (1991) 'Problems of socialist development: The significance of Shenzhen Special Economic Zone for China's open door development strategy', *International Journal of Urban and Regional Research* 15 (special issue): 197.

—— (1993) *Assembling for development: The Maquila industry in Mexico and the United States*, first published Unwin Hyman 1989, updated US publication by the Center for US-Mexican Studies, San Diego, CA: University of California Press.

—— (2002) *Globalization capitalism and its alternatives*, 3rd edn, Oxford: Oxford University Press.

Stewart, R (1993) 'Environmental regulation and international competitiveness', *Yale Law Journal* 102 (June): 2039–46.

Trebilcock, M and R Howse (2005) *The regulation of international trade*, 3rd edn, London: Routledge.

Torres, R (2007) 'Free zones and the World Trade Organization Agreement on Subsidies and Countervailing Measures', *Global Trade and Customs Journal* 2(5): 217.

UNCTAD (1999) *World investment report 1999*, New York and Geneva: United Nations.
—— (2002) *World investment report 2002*, New York and Geneva: United Nations.
UNCTC (1988) *Transnational corporations in world development trends and prospects*, New York: UN Doc ST/CTC/89.
Wall, D (1976) 'Export processing zones', *Journal of World Trade Law* 10(5): 476–98.
Warr, P (1989) 'Export processing zones', *World Bank Research Observer* 4(1): 65–88.
World Bank (2008) *Special economic zones: Performance, lessons learned, and implications for zone development*, Washington, DC: World Bank Group.

3 SEZs and China's attempt to govern the labour market by law

Feng Xu

The first Special Economic Zone (SEZ) in Shenzhen, set up in 1979, was hailed as a laboratory for capitalism in China. The Chinese government settled on the name 'Special Economic Zone' rather than the then commonly used term, 'Export Processing Zone' (EPZ), which was considered more clearly capitalist and narrower in focus (Lu 2008). By 2003, an estimated 100 special zones or more were recognized by the central government (Naughton 2007: 410). Debates on the meaning, the role, and the future of SEZs have continued unabated since the first one was set up in China (Crane 1994). One of the latest debates on SEZs is whether they have fulfilled their historic mission in China, now that a full-blown market economy has emerged there, confirmed by official membership in the World Trade Organization (WTO) in 2001 (He 2009).

This chapter does not engage directly with these debates. Instead, I argue that the SEZ, as a laboratory for experiments in capitalism, has had a real demonstration effect on the rest of the Chinese economy, which in 1979 was still very much oriented to central planning (Gallagher 2005). In particular, SEZs were the first instances where laws, rather than the Chinese state, became the lead regulatory mechanism in labour allocation. Now the Chinese state as a whole not only exhibits an increasingly marketized economy, but also uses law as the specific regulatory mechanism to govern the labour market (Potter 1994).

This is not to suggest that an Anglo-American labour market has taken root in China. One of the clearest signs of this has been the ongoing importance of institutionalized brokerage between employees and employers amidst the emergence of a genuine labour market. This observation of a simple difference is not offered in praise or in criticism. But beyond that observation, I do suggest that in some important respects the newer forms of mediating agencies that have emerged, particularly temporary employment agencies, have had the effect of making regulation of the Chinese labour market less effective overall than it could be.

In addition, the intensified logic of so-called 'flexible production' in SEZs to date and global capital's powerful need for flexible and cheap labour, both unskilled and skilled, has made it exceptionally difficult to regulate the labour market in SEZs. Further, effective regulation depends on rule-implementing and rule-adjudication, in addition to rule-making. Because of the relatively limited independence of the judiciary and because of the historical legacy of close relations between business and local government, implementation and adjudication of laws are generally less effective than the making of them in China (Lee 2007).

These features of SEZ regulation in China remind us that regulation in general (like law in particular) is not simply a compilation of rules and standards. If we turn to consider the implications of regulation for society, it is also noteworthy that particular forms or kinds of regulation also tend to produce particular kinds of subject – that is, particular kinds of social identity that shape individuals and groups in their characteristic actions. In the contemporary Chinese turn to law as regulation, the subject that is intended is one that is attractive to global capital. Specifically, this subject is a member of a labour force, a subject that in a very specific sense is 'disciplined' and at the same time 'self-governing' (Foucault 1991).

In turning to laws as regulatory mechanisms, and in formulating them in particular ways, the Chinese state has consulted intensively with international organizations such as the ILO and the World Bank (Bottelier 2007). This consultation covers best practices and international standards for regulating the labour market. The extent of this consultation contradicts a commonly held assumption in the West that China necessarily opposes outside influence. The dominant consideration affecting government responses to these outside influences in technical matters appears to be whether the measures are presented as imposed and mandatory. While this exchange of non-binding technical practices is crucial with respect to the state, it is not the only outside influence that has a bearing on changes in China's labour market. Alongside the reform of state law and regulation, international NGOs such as Asia Labour Watch and Human Rights Watch have been pressuring foreign capital in China to adopt international standards (both public and private) of corporate social responsibility.

So this chapter is about laws, rules, and standards as regulatory mechanisms in China's emergent labour market, with SEZs acting as a laboratory for experimentation. New forms of mediating bodies such as temporary staffing agencies play an active role in this market. The restructuring of this crucial aspect of the Chinese economy fits into the overall goals for the Chinese state over the past three decades: to retreat from the active, coercive administrative measures typical of the Maoist period, and to move towards a more stable role of regulating relatively autonomous markets. But I suggest that some important aspects of the newer forms of mediating agencies have had the effect of making regulation less technically effective.

The first part of the chapter is a brief discussion on SEZs. The second part discusses tensions among stakeholder interests in SEZs. The final section looks at the social and economic sustainability of an economic development model based on cheap labour and export-oriented industrialization, and the inherent difficulties of accountability and regulation associated with China's place in global supply chains. I use temporary staffing agencies as an example to illustrate the point.

Special economic zones (SEZs)

As the editors of this book have stated, SEZs are 'geographically defined areas set apart from the rest of the country or region and endowed with policy incentives by a national or regional government(s) to entice foreign investors (Carter and Harding, Chapter 1 in this volume). SEZs come under different names. Of particular importance, however, is the common characteristic they share: well defined/demarcated zones within the internationally recognized boundaries of a country that have a different administrative and legal structure from the rest of the country.

The initial SEZs in China, however, were truly 'special' in several key ways that set them apart from Asian EPZs:

- they acted as national laboratories for experiments with the market economy;
- they were much larger in size;
- they were governmental bodies with higher levels of autonomy;
- and they served multiple functions, 'seen as "windows" on the world, absorbing advanced experience in technology, administration, and business' (Naughton 2007: 408).

SEZs: state sovereignty and globalization

The first four SEZs in China were set up in 1979 amidst a perceived crisis in the Chinese economy. George Crane argues that Deng Xiaoping, in a power struggle with Mao's appointed successor Hua Guofeng, presented China as an economy in crisis, and used this to justify special measures to deal with the crisis. According to Crane, opening up SEZs as a laboratory for market economy was not only an economic policy. It was also an attempt to reform China's national economic identity, away from an inward-looking and self-reliant national identity and towards an outward-looking identity, opening up to the outside world (Crane 1994). The TV series *River Elegy* made a national sensation in the late 1980s that built on this transformative project. It presented the image of a blue ocean symbolizing 'transparency, openness and western civilization', over against the yellow of China's Yellow River. The latter symbolized both the cradle of Chinese civilization and static self-enclosure (Cui 1988). Against this symbolic backdrop, SEZs won legitimacy, distributed as they all were along China's eastern seaboard. However, some feared that the SEZs would simply surrender sovereignty to international capital, based on parallels with China's treaty ports under the unequal treaties with European and Japanese imperial powers. Internationally, this concern was fanned by the literature on globalization that either celebrated or mourned the erosion or outright loss of national sovereignty.

SEZs are not the end of sovereignty, even if there are some interesting parallels – they are not treaty ports. But SEZs do force us to rethink what we mean by sovereignty in a globalized world. Sovereignty remains central to our understanding of the shifting scales and relationships amongst the state, society, and market under globalization. It is misleading to see the openness of SEZs to foreign capital as a sign of eroded state sovereignty under globalization. Aihwa Ong (1999: 215–16), drawing critically on Carl Schmitt's work on sovereignty, presented the notion of 'graduated sovereignty' with specific reference to similar developments in Southeast Asia. By this term, she means that different labour populations are subject to different kinds of surveillance and enjoy different kinds of rights.

In the case of China, we can clearly see 'graduated sovereignty' in action between SEZs and the rest. Guided by two of Deng's widely publicized sayings ('let a few people get rich first,' and, 'let the coastal regions get developed first'), the Chinese national economy has been re-spatialized into zones/regions of development: the Pearl River Delta and the Yangtze River Delta development zones, for example. Decentralization of economic regulation was one of the special policy arrangements surrounding SEZs; to put the same point in more abstract terms, these zoning 'technologies' represent a political-economic re-scaling from the national to the sub-national. Zoning technology still guides development strategies today, even in cases where it is addressing regional inequalities that emerged or intensified under earlier zoning schemes. The 'Develop the West Strategy' (DWS) is a clear contemporary example.

SEZs and zoning have complicated implications for working conditions. SEZs employ unskilled or semi-skilled migrant labour in manufacturing for export and high-tech zones. This well-known feature derives from their place in a low-wage, low-cost, low-skill national competitive strategy. But the same SEZs typically employ skilled white-collar labour in their service outsourcing, and professionals who are engaged in high-wage, high-status innovation.

The segregated labour market in China divides in very broad terms between unskilled and semi-skilled internal migrants on one hand, and university graduates on the other, with the urban working classes standing somewhere in the middle. This facilitates a graduated sovereignty, with its differentiated treatment of citizens. This differentiation is further maintained by (1) the household registration (*hukou*) system of differentiated internal residential status; and (2) the discourse of 'population quality' (*suzhi*), which is widely and unselfconsciously accepted in Chinese society. China's household registration (*hukou*) system divides its citizens into urban and rural *hukou* holders. The former enjoy full citizenship rights, while the latter are treated as second-class citizens, especially in urban areas. Most internal migrants working in SEZs are rural *hukou* holders from China's inland provinces (Solinger 1999). According to the unofficial *suzhi* (population quality) discourse, individuals are assigned to sharply differentiated status groups based on perceived levels of 'civility' in education, behavioural refinement, class status, and personal hygiene. These characteristics are assumed to run together, and are widely attributed on the basis of superficial appearance. Those associated with higher 'population quality' are reliably better paid than those with low *suzhi* (Anagnost 2002). The past decades have seen the rapid elaboration and intensification of these socially accepted divides, alongside the gradual attenuation of the *hukou* system to allow large but controlled volumes of internal migrants to occupy the lower end of the coastal employed populations.

Low-wage, low-cost industrialization was the original basis for China's opening to foreign investment during the first decades of economic reform. But today, with other Asian economies providing significant wage-competition for such jobs, innovation and invention are considered essential to China's economic success in the knowledge economy. This attempt to move up the global supply chain does not mean that China will abandon its reliance on cheap labour and a 'made-in-China' model.[1] The latter is still a necessary part of its industrial strategy: first, the enormous reserve army of peasant labour must somehow be employed, at the very least for reasons of social stability; and second, development between the coastal and interior areas is still sharply uneven. Instead, China is trying to diversify industrialization strategies so that its economic growth does not solely rely on the made-in-China model. Coastal areas now compete with each other to set up high-technology zones that will contribute to a new 'invented-in-China' model, while the inland provinces are left to specialize in outsourced 'made-in-China' manufacturing.

At the same time, the made-in-China strategy now faces additional challenges in the face of the global financial crisis. As is well-known, the impacts of crisis on this strategy have important implications far beyond economic ones. Ominously, job losses have cut across different segments of the labour market. It is reported that over 20 million out of about 130 million migrant workers have recently lost their jobs (Mackinnon 2009). There is also a looming crisis of unemployed university graduates. The large numbers of unemployed in each major demographic group have huge adverse impacts on social stability.

Talk of 'new SEZs' has circulated in China since 1997. The new SEZ (NSEZ) emphasizes comprehensive reform that includes economic growth based not only on the made-in-China model, but on the invented-in-China model as well. The NSEZ model also strives to restore harmony across the rural/urban divide, develop social policies, and advance institutional reform – three areas now perceived to be essential for sustainable economic growth (Zhang 2009). The stated desired results of forming NSEZs – no longer simply GDP growth, but rather comprehensive reform – points to another rationale behind the Chinese government's initial decision to set up SEZs, namely to create models for experimenting with policy reform.

SEZs as model

When thinking of 'graduated sovereignty', it is tempting to think about SEZs as somehow operating outside or alongside the 'real' mainland China. However, this is in some ways quite misleading. Besides thinking about SEZs in terms of 'graduated sovereignty', we should therefore also consider them in terms of a distinctive feature of ordinary governance that occurs throughout China: policy innovations are typically tested first at experimental sites. These models, if judged successful, are subsequently implemented nationwide. In this way, exceptional models are intended to produce norms that ultimately are to be emulated elsewhere.

A side note on the social role of norms is important. In English, the norm is typically viewed as normative, i.e., something against which deviation is measured. But it is also viewed as a kind of presumed statistical average – simply what is normal. Norms in China, however, are more often presumed to be both exceptional and exemplary. A classical example is the Maoist role model, Lei Feng, and the way his behaviour was meant to be replicated generally. The contrast with exceptional and even exemplary figures in the West is striking. North Americans and Europeans are rarely expected to match the performance of their sports heroes, statesmen, or religious leaders, at least not to this degree. In China, model cities and SEZs of this exceptional kind have tremendous power to inspire emulation, because of the prestige and pride they bring to their people and government officials (cf Bakken 2000). The result in Western eyes is a paradox: the norm is set out as deliberately exceptional, and yet there is enormous pressure to emulate the exception that ultimately 'normalizes' it (this time in the Western sense of the word) and makes it ubiquitous.

China's first four SEZs (Shenzhen, Xiamen, Zhuhai, and Shantou) are practical examples of this pattern. They were created in 1979 as an experiment in capitalism, while the rest of the economy was still organized around central planning. As Deng Xiaoping said in 1979, explaining the rationale behind the Shenzhen SEZ, a space can be demarcated and called a 'special zone'. He said Shanganning (the three inland provinces of Shanxi, Gansu and Ningxia), the communist revolutionary base during the rule of the Guomindang or Nationalist Party, had also been a 'special zone' that experimented with communism in China. But what was initially an experiment in the special zone became national policy with the establishment of the People's Republic in 1949. So in Deng's mind, there was a clear parallel in setting up the Shenzhen SEZ to experiment with 'socialism with Chinese characteristics' (Yu and Li 1992: 318). He was reported to have said to the Guangdong officials of the time that the central government had no money, so they had to 'shachu yitiao xuelu'. This phrase can mean open up a bloody path or cut an escape route. By using this war-time analogy, Deng normalized the pattern of experimentation and minimized the exceptional nature the SEZ, in that the Communist Party had experimented before in this way during their fight against the Nationalists. In this sense, the SEZ is not 'special' at all.

The war analogy also meant that Deng and his reform-minded colleagues were fighting with equally strong opponents, perhaps the persistent poverty of China, or perhaps those 'conservatives' within the Party who opposed to the idea of SEZs for fear of encroaching capitalism. The use of words with such a powerful resonance indicates that the success or failure of SEZs was no small matter to Deng and his reform-minded colleagues. It was not until mid-1980s that SEZs were embraced as national models for economic development, culminating in then-premier Zhao Zhiyang's Coastal Development Strategy. Shenzhen was not only the place where migrants from the inland provinces would go in search of jobs and a better life. It was also seen nationally as a 'sacred place' for people to visit, just like Yan'an used to be during the Mao era. The 'pilgrimage' to Shenzhen contributes to a strong desire to emulate Shenzhen in the rest of the country: they've seen their future there!

Unsurprisingly, given this pressure to emulate, coastal cities have not been alone in competing to open up SEZs since the 1990s. China's hinterland also aspires to them: indeed, the new hot spots for SEZs are Chengdu and Xi'an. Many local government officials succumb to 'zone fever' because SEZs brought them both material and status rewards. For example, in Shanghai, there are at least six national zones and fourteen municipal zones. The 'zone fever' evident since early 1990s has created problems: regulations in flux, weak quality control of zone regulation, not to mention enormous agricultural land loss.

In its use of model zones, the Chinese governance style exemplifies the point that the 'difference' granted to SEZs cannot be considered in isolation from the rest of China. For example, at the initial stages of the SEZs, companies within the zones were given special treatment in terms of being able to implement capitalist labour practices (flexible labour practices), while most of the state-owned enterprises (SOEs) outside the zones continued the Maoist 'iron rice bowl' labour practices. Contract labour was first introduced in SEZs. However, in the 1990s, as SOEs in the regular Chinese economy were asked to turn themselves into 'modern' profit-making companies, they also demanded, and eventually got, permission to adopt capitalist labour practices similar to those implemented in the SEZs (Deng 2005: 245–47).

Because capitalist labour practices were allowed to exist first in the SEZs, the Labour Law of 1994 was first meant to be applicable to companies in the SEZs. The flexibility of capitalist labour practices were deemed unconducive to social stability, but the Chinese state could not influence foreign capital in the zones through the active administrative measures it exercised over SOEs. This made the Labour Law the only viable policy instrument by which it could intervene. As Piquet argues, the Labour Law legitimizes these labour practices, but counterbalances them with new developments protecting workers' rights (Piquet 2008: 51).

However, as the so-called 'iron rice bowl' was later broken in the rest of China, more and more workers have joined the ranks of the flexible labour force. Workers in SOEs protest against forced lay-offs and other wage-related matters, almost on a daily basis. Perceiving this to be a real threat to social stability, the central government drafted and passed the Labour Contract Law (LCL) of 2007. Unlike the preceding Labour Law, this law applies to the entire Chinese workforce, both inside SEZs and beyond.

Now I would like to turn to what might be called the patterns of politics (writ small) that are characteristic of SEZs in order to understand some of the difficulties in implementing labour-related laws and regulations. Policy actors influencing developments in SEZs clearly include the following: foreign capital, local government officials, the central government, international organizations such as the World Bank and ILO; and (at least in terms of their growing attempts to influence SEZ policy) international civil society organizations such as Human Rights Watch and Asia Labour Watch. While migrant workers themselves do not have a voice in SEZs in any direct sense, they can be considered stakeholders in an indirect sense. On the one hand, international civil society organizations purport to monitor and recommend changes in the name of these workers. On the other hand, the Chinese state continues to claim that as the Communist Party, it represents working-class interests. Perhaps especially in the face of international civil societal attention, but also internally, the state is drawn to policy questions, based on its claim to represent the interests of the working class.

Tensions of interests among stakeholders

The rationale for foreign capital to move to China's SEZs is to avoid more stringent and costly labour, environment, and other regulations at their home base. The widespread shift from Fordist to post-Fordist production methods intensifies capital's desire for flexible labour. However, foreign companies, especially the multinational corporations (MNCs) that are more visible to consumers, are also subject to international campaigns for corporate social responsibility. Therefore, MNCs often care more about their international corporate images, and hence are often more willing to abide by costly or cumbersome laws, regulations, and even non-state codes of conduct. The politics surrounding the international societal pressures directed at corporate brand images has been a matter of considerable international scholarly reflection, including the work of Keck and Sikkink (1998). However, as Sum and Pun argue based on their ethnographic studies of a textile subsidiary of an MNC in the Pearl River Delta, China is at the low end of global supply chains and subject to the pressures of global just-in-time production. The pressure to deliver goods faster, cheaper, and better has often meant that corporate social responsibility is sacrificed to the fiscal bottom line. Consequently, the two authors argue, the global pressure to demonstrate corporate responsibility has led to 'a commodification of the codes of conduct' in China. These codes become mere marketing strategies to garner 'reputational capital', and as a result, the original intent of labour codes, (namely, to develop and institutionalize 'ethics for the market') is not realized (Sum and Pun 2005: 197).

Further, international pressure on MNCs in the global supply chain to be accountable for labour rights, environment protection, and so on already assumes that a prior power relationship exists between capital and labour that third parties cannot verify directly. As James Lawson (2008) argues,

> acts of accountability occur as acts of mediation and representation because the acts or events for which actors are being held accountable for the exercise of power cannot be experienced directly by those holding the actors to account. Accounts are in this sense always both asymmetric (they do not cover their objects of inquiry comprehensively) and 'biased' … (they are mediated communications, and all media bias the reception of their content in particular ways).

Under economic decentralization since the 1980s, local government officials at SEZ locations have been motivated to attract as much foreign capital as possible. This is a consequence of China's reliance on performance-based techniques for managing lower-level government officials. The amount (and increasingly the kind) of foreign capital attracted to an official's area of jurisdiction is linked closely to the official's personal promotion and welfare. SEZs are currently administered by committee structures. Committee members are government officials, a responsibility that sometimes overlaps with their responsibilities in the local government. For example, the Party Secretary of Industrial Park X is a member of the Party standing committee of X city. Because of the overriding priority assigned to economic performance, the close nexus between business and local government has meant that officials are under deep pressure to be on the side of the business when, for example, environment and/or labour regulations are implemented. This can lead to practical conflicts between the promotion of private accumulation and the guarantee of laws such as those concerning workers' rights. Some local governments have themselves been said to be active in either violating laws or trying to bypass them. As I am writing this, China's Xinhua News Agency reported that the vice-president of China's People's Supreme Court was sacked for corruption (No name 2009). As Lee points out, this fits into a larger pattern of 'decentralized legal authoritarianism', 'the twin strategy of decentralized accumulation and legalistic legitimation of authoritarian rule' (Lee 2007:10).

Migrant workers are the majority of the labour force in SEZs. China's governance of this population continues the Mao-era tradition of the *hukou* internal passport system. *Hukou*-based governance of internal migrants is based above all on a sharp divide between urban and rural residency status. Migrants' dual status as rural *hukou* holders and as outsiders to the locality has meant that they occupy the weakest position in the local labour market. In the 1980s and 1990s, the location of one's *hukou* increasingly became detached from one's actual day-to-day location. Consequently, internal migrants are officially neither rural nor urban. They do not reside in the place of their *hukou*. It is very difficult (except under certain conditions) to transfer one's *hukou* to one's new place of residence. 'The liminal space migrants occupy has meant that migrants are left on their own for welfare, but are subject to government coercion and charging of various fees in addition to capitalist labour discipline at workplace.' (Xu 2009: 43). In the lead-up to the present fiscal crisis, the harshness of this arrangement for access to medical, educational, and social services had begun to soften. But with the massive unemployment of migrant workers in the wake of the global financial crisis, it is doubtful whether workers' rights will be protected according to the LCL of 2007.

For the central government, economic growth was the unquestioned priority under the Hu-Wen leadership. But in the 1990s, social unrest began to mount across China. Some of the worst disruptions were (and are) thought to occur in SEZs in the Pearl River Delta. So the broad policy orientation, particularly pronounced with the transition to the Hu Jintao administration, shifts to give greater priority to social stability as well. The government has passed laws to bring labour unrest under control, and not merely by coercive means. That said, regulation is not merely about rule-making, but also about adjudication and implementation. The nature and proliferation of the SEZs have made it very difficult to enforce the new labour legislation. Further, the inherent problems with accountability along the global supply chain have meant that labour rights and environment protection and so on are still often sacrificed informally for capital's financial bottom-line.

International organizations provide norms and rules of conduct that can and do operate alongside official state legislation. As China participates in global supply chains, it at least has to appear to follow international norms, as long as these rules are presented as voluntary in character (for example, as industry 'best practices'). China has repeatedly engaged with international standards of this kind in a wide variety of policy fields as signs of modernity and of good international citizenship. The ILO and World Bank have been working particularly closely with the Chinese government on these terms.

International civil society organizations in China now run projects defending migrant rights, as they do in many other areas of social policy. But NGOs have to operate under communist government supervision. Further, their pressure on MNCs to protect labour rights and environment protection only touches on exceptional cases. Many more companies in SEZs remain under the domestic and international spotlight. In addition, the codes of conduct and corporate social responsibility programmes that MNCs adopt under international pressure are based on the self-regulating model, and can easily be compromised through the multiple layers of subcontractors in global supply chains.

In summary, in an increasingly marketized economy, the Chinese state increasingly turns to law, rather than coercive administrative measures, as the lead regulatory mechanisms in the labour market. Regulation means law/rule-making, implementation and adjudication. The Chinese government has been productive in making laws, but its record on implementation and adjudication has consistently faced structural barriers.

Temporary staffing agencies[2]

I use temporary staffing agencies as an example of some of the difficulties in regulation and accountability of SEZs and beyond. As Jamie Peck and Nik Theodore argue, the transnational staffing industry does not merely respond to national labour-market conditions, but rather is an *active collective agent* in re-regulating local labour markets. Temp agencies 'actively shape the growth in contingent labour through their role in labour-market intermediation, by selling employers the cost-cutting and labour-controlling virtues of workforce flexibility while mobilizing contingent workers and brokering connections to employers' (Peck and Theodore 2001).

Industry employment in SEZs – and in much of the rest of China – rests on a triangular employment relationship amongst employees, a corporate customer, and a private employment agency serving the corporation. As with temporary staffing agencies in the West, the private employment agency in China dispatches its employees to work for the corporate customer, and the corporate customer pays the agency a fee in exchange for the labour of the employees and the staffing service it receives.

Central to the staffing industry's growth has been its members' credentials as trusted mediators in the existing Chinese labour market context, with employment powerfully mediated by the state and personal networks. The staffing industry promotes ISO 9000 and private codes of conduct for its members to establish this trust in job applicants and client firms alike. The self-regulatory basis for instilling such trust is itself a move away from older bases for trust in China, based on personal and social connections (*guanxi*). This transition is broadly in line with the Chinese government's approach to active employment policy: 'workers must rely on themselves to seek jobs; the market mediates employment; and government promotes employment' (Ministry of Labour and Social Security 2003: 15). In this sense, then, the staffing industry contributes to turning the Chinese jobseekers into a contingent labour force, especially migrants and those laid off in the course of economic restructuring of the SOE sector. The industry's operations mesh with capital's powerful need for numerical flexibility in the labour force.

Here again, we see the SEZs providing an exemplary role. Temporary employment agencies first emerged in SEZs where labour supply comes from outside the zones, and labour demand comes from foreign capital. In other words, both labour supply and labour demand required mediated agencies to regulate the labour market. Temp agencies have since spread far beyond the SEZs. They include not only transnational temp agencies such as Manpower, Randstad, Kelly and Adecco, but also Chinese national and local temp agencies. Local governments have even set up temp agencies as a way to deal with workers laid off from local SOEs. In the latter case, we can see clear evidence of the blurred boundaries between the state and market in weakening protections for labour.

The temp agency industry was not regulated until the passing of the LCL in 2007: the Labour Law of 1994 did not cover it. There have been abuses within the temporary employment industry, and the national media and the national government have been willing to make highly publicized examples of some of the abusers.

The passing of the LCL is a revealing transition to the official regulation for this industry. In informative ways, it mobilized both domestic and foreign business and domestic and foreign labour. Key developments occurred after the public was invited to comment on the legislation's first draft. This consultative procedure is in itself a significant indicator of the country's move towards a 'rule-of-law' state; the loudest voices in the process certainly conform to the view that 'rule-of-law' tendencies in China today serve specifically developmental goals. The lobbying efforts of foreign business associations in China were quite telling, suggesting the extent to which the government was under new pressures that were opening up a new gap between it and these key circles. In particular, the American Chamber of Commerce in China and the European Chamber of Commerce lobbied strenuously against a regulated labour market. Their main expressed fear was that the LCL would increase labour costs, making them less competitive. Some even threatened to take their businesses to cheaper places such as Vietnam. Domestic capital also lobbied against the Law (US-China Business Council 2006).

The staffing industry associations lobbied especially strenuously against two articles in the draft. First, each labour dispatch company was to deposit no less than 5,000 yuan for each of its employees in a government-designated bank account. Second, when a dispatched worker had worked for one year with a corporate client of a dispatch firm, and if the corporate client intended to continue to use the worker, then the labour contract signed between the labour dispatch company and the employee was to be terminated, and the corporate client was to sign a labour contract directly with the employee instead, becoming the new employer.[3] The final version of the Law took out both articles. Now the labour dispatch company is obliged only to sign labour contracts of at least two years' duration with its employees. The lobbying efforts of the staffing industry have thus retained the overall pattern of high labour flexibility in China, albeit on a modestly higher standard.

However, the drafting of the LCL also mobilized domestic and international labour activists to lobby both the lawmakers and at the companies. Some high-profile firms also broke with the collective position of the major business associations. Under international pressure,

> Nike has virtually repudiated the efforts of the United States Chamber of Commerce in Shanghai (AmCham) to lobby against the law. And the

> E.U. Chamber of Commerce has reversed its opposition to the law and renounced its threat that its member companies may leave China if the law passed.
>
> (Global Labor Strategy 2007)

Of critical importance to workers' rights (and simultaneously to corporate fears of rising labour costs) is the Law's continued insistence on a written contract and more detailed provisions to enforce contract signing. Under the first draft, 'if an employer failed to enter into a written contract with workers, the law implied a non-fixed term contract between the employer and employee' (ibid.: 13–14). Transnational firms demanded and received a revision of this provision. In the end, the Law gave an employer in this instance a one-month grace period to sign (art. 10). The LCL distinguishes between three categories of contract: contracts with a fixed period, labour contracts without a fixed period, and labour contracts with a period to complete the prescribed work (art. 12). The business community was most fearful of the provisions on contracts without a fixed term (art. 14).

The Labour Contract Law also provides regulations governing the labour dispatch sector for the first time (arts 57–67). It recognizes the fundamental trait of modern labour dispatch arrangements: a triangular employment relationship (art. 58). It provides that

> the labour contract between the labour dispatch service provider and the dispatched workers shall be a labour contract with a fixed term of more than two years, and the remunerations thereof shall be paid by the labour dispatch service provider on a monthly basis. During periods when there is no work for the workers, relevant remunerations shall be paid to such workers by the labour dispatch service provider on a monthly basis at the minimum salary as prescribed by the people's government of the region where the labour dispatch service provider is situated.
>
> (art. 58)

The Labor Contract Law created much anxiety in business circles about the prospects of rising labour costs as a result of the Law's strict rules on the formation and termination of labour contracts. Consequently, on the eve of the Law coming into effect, there were numerous reports of companies trying to sever their employment relations with their employees through 'reverse labour dispatch': employees already hired directly by firms are 'asked' to sign labour contracts with a company-designated labour-dispatch company, and the workers are then dispatched by the latter to the original employer (Xue 2008).

It is still too early to gauge the impact of the LCL on the development of the staffing industry. It is important to emphasize that the Law is not meant to ban the industry, but rather legalize and regulate it. The result is meant to be that the industry can have some degree of accountability to the national government, as well as to the dispatched workers through their contracts. The intent of the government is to see the staffing industry develop into a modern service sector. Consistent with this goal, the Law favors larger labour-dispatch companies, primarily through a system of licensing and registration and raising the threshold of entering into business.

Conclusion

The global financial crisis brought home the inherent vulnerability of a Chinese economy based heavily on cheap labour and export-oriented growth. Since the late 1990s, there has been a push to shift from a made-in-China model to an invented-in-China model. However, building high-tech zones does not mean the end of cheap labour or the export-oriented economic development model. Rather this initiative is China's effort, in the first instance, to move up the global supply chain; and in the second instance, to avoid sole reliance on a cheap labour development strategy. Although moving up global supply chains might be able to make SEZs economically and socially more sustainable, there are still large numbers of migrant workers who will toil in low-quality manufacturing jobs either in coastal SEZs or gradually in SEZs in the interior. High-tech jobs are simply unavailable to the approximately 130 million migrant workers, although government encourages job training for migrants so that they can find better-paid jobs. Further, skilled workers and professionals who work in high-tech zones are also subject to flexible labour practice. Global corporations always look for skilled workers and professionals at the 'right price', and investors expect 'governments to fill the jobs with the right people, at the right place' (Ross 2006: 191).

SEZs will continue to exist in China as a distinct Chinese policy innovation tool to experiment with various policies that are considered appropriate to particular policy problems. The ultimate goal remains achieving economic growth in a market economy. In the early 1980s, as economic reform was just starting, foreign investment and decentralization of central power were deemed essential to achieve economic growth. SEZs were accordingly given special powers to experiment in these areas. Thirty years on, the economic growth model oriented strictly to GDP growth has brought with it mounting social problems that could potentially derail economic growth if they are not addressed. The Hu-Wen leadership thus shifted from a GDP-oriented economic growth model to a model building '*xiaokang* [roughly: modest-living] socialism and a harmonious society'. It is in this context that the 'NSEZ' model has been put on the government agenda. In regulating the labour market, the LCL of 2007 was passed with the goal of building a 'harmonious society'. It provides a legal framework for modest protection of workers. It is still too early to gauge the Law's effectiveness. However, recent reports of violations of labour rights, made worse by the onset of the global financial crisis, point to the consistent problems of legal implementation in China (Barboza 2009).

Notes

1 By 'made in China' I mean manufactured or assembled in China, with innovative design and marketing occurring elsewhere under non-Chinese control.
2 This section is based on a larger version of my article Xu (2009a).
3 Shanghai Rencai Zhongjie Xiehui (Shanghai Talents Intermediary Association), ed., *Baipishu* [*White Paper*], 2007:19.

Bibliography

Anagnost, A (2002) 'The corporeal politics of quality (*suzhi*)', *Public Culture* 16(2): 189–208.

Bakken, B (2000) *The exemplary society: Human improvement, social control, and the dangers of modernity in China*, Oxford: Oxford University Press.

Barboza, D (2009) 'Despite law, job conditions worsen in China', *New York Times*, 8 July, www.nytimes.com/2009/06/23/business/global/23labor.html?_r=2&ref=todayspaper

Bottelier, P (2007) 'China and the World Bank: How a partnership was built', *Journal of Contemporary China* 16(5): 239–58.

Crane, G (1994) 'Special things in special ways: National economic identity and China's SEZs', *The Australian Journal of Chinese Affairs* 32: 71–92.

Cui, W-H (ed.) (1988) *Heshang Lun [On River Elegy*] Beijing: Fine Arts Press.

Deng, Shangi (2005) *Institutional innovation and the development of nation-state: China's exploration*, Tianjin: Tianjin People's Press.

Foucault, M (1991) 'Governmentality', in G Burchell, C Gordon and P Miller (eds) *The Foucault effect: Studies in governmentality, with two lectures and an interview with Michel Foucault*, Chicago: University of Chicago Press, 87–104.

Gallagher, M (2005) *Contagious capitalism: Globalization and the politics of labour in China*, Princeton, NJ: Princeton University Press.

Global Labor Strategy (2007) *Undue influence: Corporations gain ground in battle over China's new labor law* (March), available at: http://laborstrategies.blogs.com/global_labor_strategies/files/undue_influence_global_labor_strategies.pdg

He, Jun (2009) 'Has the historic mission of "a laboratory for reform" ended?' [gaige shiyantian' de lishi shiming yijing wanjie?] Available at: http://club.163.com/viewElite.m?catalogoId=26175&entitled=26175_100ea2832790030

Hu, K (2008) 'Made in China: The cultural logic of OEMs and the manufacture of low-cost technology', *Inter-Asia Cultural Studies* 9(1): 27–46.

Keck, M and K Sikkink (1998) *Activists beyond borders: Advocacy networks in international politics*, Ithaca, NY: Cornell University Press.

Lawson, J (2008) 'Precarious labour, bankable profits', Paper presented at the annual conference of the Society for Socialist Studies, Vancouver, BC, Canada, 8 June 2008.

Lee, C-K (2007) *Against the law: Labor protests in China's rustbelt and sunbelt*, Berkeley, CA: University of California Press.

Lu, Ting (2008) 'Deng Xiaoping and the construction of Special Zones' [Deng Xiaoping yu tequ jianshe]: http://news.hexun.com/2008-07-11/107354045.html

Mackinnon, M (2009) 'Jobless, restless China: 20 million and growing', *Globe and Mail*, www.theglobeandmail.com/news/world/jobless-restless-china-20-million-and-growing/article972426/

Ministry of Labour and Social Security (ed.) (2003) *Zhongguo jiji de jiuye zhengce* [*China's active employment policies*] Beijing: China's Labour and Social Security Press.

Naughton, B (2007) *The Chinese economy: Transitions and growth*, Cambridge, MA: MIT Press.

No name (2009) 'Supreme court judge sacked for corruption,' *Xinhua*, 21 August 2009.

Ong, A-H (1999) *Flexible citizenship: The cultural logics of transnationality*, Durham, NC: Duke University Press.

Peck, J and N Theodore (2001) 'Contingent Chicago: Restructuring the spaces of temporary labor', *International Journal of Urban and Regional Research* 25(3): 471–96.

Piquet, H (2008) 'Chinese labour law in retrospect: Efficiency and flexibility legitimized' in A Laliberté and M Lanteigne (eds) *The Chinese party-state in the 21st Century: Adaptation and the reinvention of legitimacy*, London and New York: Routledge, 39–57.

Potter, P (1994) 'Riding the tiger: Legitimacy and legal culture in post-Mao China', *China Quarterly* 138: 325–28.

Pun, N (2005) *Made in China: Women factory workers in a global workplace*, Durham, NC: Duke University Press.

Ross, A (2006) *Fast boat to China: Corporate flight and the consequences of free trade lessons from Shanghai*, New York: Pantheon Books.

Shanghai Rencai Zhongjie Xiehui (Shanghai Talents Intermediary Association) (2007) *Baipishu* [*White Paper*].

Solinger, D (1999) *Contesting citizenship in urban China*, Chicago: University of Chicago Press.

Sum, N-L and N Pun (2005) 'Globalization and paradoxes of ethical transnational production: Code of conduct in a Chinese workplace', *Competition and Change* 9(2): 181–200.

US-China Business Council (USCBC) (2006) 'Comments on the draft LCL of the People's Republic of China': www.uschina.org

Xu, F (2009a) 'The emergence of temporary staffing agencies', *Comparative Labor Law and Policy Journal* 30: 431–62.

—— (2009) 'Governing China's peasant migrants: Building Xiaokang Socialism and harmonious society', in E. Jeffreys (ed.) *China's governmentalities: Governing changes, changing government*, London: Routledge, 38–62.

Xue, Song (ed.) (2008) 'Some companies set up their own labour dispatch companies to circumvent the labour contract law' [Bufeng Qiye wei guibi labodongfa zishi paiqiangongsi taobi yonggong zeren], available online at: www.cnss.cn/xwzx/zl2/ldhtf/rdjj/200802/t20080221_178295.html

Yu, X and L Li (eds) (1992) *The Rise of tides: The details of Deng Xiaoping's tour to the South* [*Dachao xinqi: Deng Xiaoping nanxun qianqianhouhou*], Beijing: China Radio and Broadcasting Corporation Press.

Zhang, X (2009) 'Zhongyang tongyi Chongqing she xinhinghitequ' [The central government agrees that Chongqing set up new Special Economic Zone] Available online at: http://forum.enorth.com.cn/thread_1497684_.html

Zweig, D (2002) *Internationalizing China: Domestic interests and global linkages*, Ithaca, NY: Cornell University Press.

4 A tale of two Chinese SEZs

From exogenous to sustainable endogenous growth?

Connie Carter

Introduction

In recent years, a debate has been taking place among some Chinese scholars and policy-makers in Beijing about the need to rebalance the Chinese economy so that it relies less on exogenous growth (through export of low-priced, labour-intensive, manufactured goods) and more on endogenous growth (through domestic investments focused on higher value-added production, skilled labour and domestic consumption).[1] Perhaps in an attempt to support this initiative, the claim has been made that the Wenzhou SEZ (Special Economic Zone) in Zhejiang province experienced predominantly endogenous growth and that it outperformed the Suzhou SEZ in Jiangsu province whose growth is largely exogenous. This claim remains unsubstantiated.

Therefore the main objective of the study discussed in this chapter was to substantiate or refute this claim. It was also expected that valuable lessons might be learned regarding China's options for more sustainable development policies and practice. Specifically, this study aims to discover whether it is true to say that the Wenzhou SEZ produced outcomes that are superior to and more sustainable than those achieved in the Suzhou SEZ. Second, if the basic hypothesis is true, the study seeks to identify the key factors that might account for Wenzhou's superior performance. Third, the study aims to uncover the role that law might have played in the socio-economic performance of the SEZs. Finally, it speculates on the sustainability of the chosen development path of each SEZ.

The study was undertaken during 2007–9. It was caught in the commercial peaks and troughs of abundant optimism followed by deep recession as the world economy lurched from boom to bust, led by the United States of America (USA), which is China's main market for consumption of low-priced manufactured goods. As I write this chapter, economists claim that the economy's deep dive, into the worst recession the world has experienced since the 1930s, has been halted so that a depression has been averted. However, on 1 January 2010, unemployment in the USA was still at an unprecedented 10 per cent, or nearly 17 million jobless. Furthermore, despite a seeming recovery in the stock markets, where, for instance the Dow Jones touched

10,500 on 2 December 2009, the jobless rate is expected to remain high. Commentators talk about a jobless recovery – which to some observers of the US economy must seem like an oxymoron. The situation is no better in the European Union (EU), whose member states form China's second largest export market.

Therefore, as previously lucrative world markets experience a deep recession and foreign demand plummets for China-made goods, further depressed by deep concerns about the safety, integrity and quality standards of those goods, China's manufacturing base is facing its biggest challenge since 1979 when the SEZ-driven FDI (foreign direct investment) experiment was announced by the Chinese government. It was probably not the best year for China to experience such humbugs since 2009 marked the sixtieth anniversary of the founding of the People's Republic with its allegiance to communism and a closely controlled planned or command economy. But 2009 was also the thirtieth anniversary of the start of the open-door policy with its focus on the SEZ experiment and China's move towards an open market economy, or capitalism. However, 2009 might also mark another essential turning point for China: from an FDI, export-driven, 'made in China' economic development model to one that is domestic-led and domestic-invested, where a substantial percentage of the 'made in China' goods are also 'invented in China', and 'consumed in China'.

Of course, this domestic-led, domestic-invested model is already enjoying success in the Wenzhou SEZ, or so some Beijing policy-makers and scholars would have us believe. However, it is fair to note, at the outset, that this study was unable to substantiate that claim. Furthermore, it seems to be a Chinese conundrum that, like in their well-known practice of mis-measurement or mis-reporting of many domestic statistics, especially at the provincial and municipal levels, some Chinese policy-makers tend to conflate aspirations with facts.[2] Sometimes they simply confuse aspirational goals with achieved or achievable goals. In a way, this practice is nothing new and the phenomenon can be witnessed in several spheres of Chinese society: for example, many Chinese laws begin life as vague, programmatic or aspirational goals. The Equity Joint Venture Law 1979, discussed below, is a good example of this. The important point to note, and one that is worth celebrating, is that some Chinese policy-makers and scholars seem to have recognized China's need to rebalance or reinvent its economic development model. Indeed, having a vision of the future and a willingness to experiment and be tolerant of ambiguity seems to be characteristic of many Chinese policy-makers.

But it is not only Chinese scholars and policy-makers who have recognized that China is ripe for policy changes in this area; some Western economists also argue that China's economy is poised for a fundamental structural adjustment (Ferguson and Schularick 2009; Klein 2008; Krugman 2009; Pettis 2009: 8–13). Thus the thirtieth anniversary of communist China's first step to opening up to the Western world, coinciding as it does with the West's first major recession in sixty years, might spur China's policy-makers to revisit the rebalancing story and seek to strengthen the tenuous links between sustainable economic development and its own rapidly rising domestic middle class. It might be time to shelve its exogenous SEZ-driven economic development model and encourage a more sustainable model which China must also develop in order to rescue the millions of laid-off factory workers and millions of migrant labourers who are left jobless as export-driven factories close and the rate of building construction slows.[3] Obviously, the construction frenzy prior to the 2008 summer Olympics ended with a thud and due to the recession in the West, the anticipated post-Olympics dividend with masses of construction-craving FDI never materialized. The majority of jobless migrant workers have therefore been returning to the countryside, which remains tough, unforgiving and largely unchanged from when they left years earlier to seek their fortunes in the SEZs and other coastal areas that promised economic prosperity and improved quality of life. And to be sure, improved quality of life and prosperity are the prime motivators for China's job-seeking citizens both in the rural and urban areas. These, rather than bare gross domestic product (GDP) or gross national product (GNP) figures, also become the measures of success for government policies – including SEZ policies.

GDP and GNP are crude and sometimes unreliable tools for measuring and describing the performance of a nation if the quality of life and well-being of its people are to be taken into account. This charge is even more apt when the measure concerns the GDP of a specific region or area within a nation. Therefore, in its methodology, this research seeks to go beyond the usual quantitative analyses of GDP and GNP. Instead it attempts to compare the prosperity or general betterment of the people in the two SEZs by examining the extent to which social and environmental effects were enhanced positively or negatively by economic development in each zone. In other words, cognizant of the GDP measures for the two SEZs, this study seeks to answer this question: to what extent did higher GDP result in increased living standards for the people of the two SEZs? To help deconstruct 'increased living standards', the United Nations' (UN) Human Development Index (HDI) was adapted and used to ascertain performance in areas such as health care, education and skills training, wages and labour conditions, life expectancy, environmental protection, and ownership of capital goods (such as cars, mobile phones and access to the Internet).

However, as an essential theoretical background to this study, it is acknowledged that China as a whole seems to have progressed quickly through the Investment Development Path (IDP; Dunning and Narula 2004), which theorizes that there exists a systematic relationship between the degree of internationalization of an economy (measured by inward and outward direct investment) and its degree of economic development (measured by gross domestic product per capita). It is through this IDP lens that observations and analyses of development in the two SEZs are made – together with the added enquiry into the well-being and prosperity of the local people.

China as a whole seems to have followed stage one of the IDP, where exports are comprised of low-skilled, labour-intensive products, and imports are mainly standard manufactured goods and assembly kits. Similarly, as discussed below, the development of Suzhou after 1994, when the SEZ was established, seems to have followed this path. Predictably, the government's role was providing the legal and commercial infrastructure together with location and fiscal incentives to spur economic development. Arguably, Wenzhou did not follow this path, since, as discussed below, the small family-held, workshop-based economy did not export its products but supplied other provinces of China, especially those in the interior, which were marked by scarcity and shortage of all kinds of consumer goods. Stage two of the IDP theory reflects market-seeking FDI or an import-substitution phase when government focuses on upgrading local labour capabilities, developing a capital market, an accountable, commercial banking system and securing a favourable business environment for both foreign and domestic players. The Suzhou mode of development also followed stage two of the IDP, albeit with the Singapore government providing the templates for labour market upgrading as well as the commercial and environmental infrastructure (Carter 2003: 271–86). In the Wenzhou mode, no such stage two characteristics were observed. However, there was a clear agglomeration phase when small family-owned single-product manufacturers pooled their resources and became industrialized SMEs (small and medium-sized enterprises). Stage three of the IDP theory exhibits a growing and more professional domestic market, with domestic firms seeking to supply the products that foreign investors produced earlier. To counteract displacement, foreign firms seek to move into higher value-added products and services, but indigenous firms also begin to exploit foreign markets and increase their own competitive advantages. There is little evidence of the presence of this characteristic in either Suzhou or Wenzhou. In Suzhou, many of the foreign joint ventures were replaced by wholly foreign owned enterprises (WFOEs) as soon as the law facilitated this kind of business association, and their aim was mainly to exploit foreign markets using the premiums gained from low wages. Indeed, many enterprises in Suzhou started life as export-led WFOEs. As discussed below, this was not the case in Wenzhou where the focus continued to be production of small, inexpensive, single items predominantly designed for the domestic market. Stage four of the IDP theory requires domestic firms to begin exploiting foreign markets by participating in outbound FDI through cooperative ventures, agglomerations or networks of related activities and regionalization. At this stage, the role of government is upgrading the legal and commercial infrastructures and nurturing entities to become more innovative and entrepreneurial. Evidence abounds that the central government is doing that, and both Suzhou and Wenzhou seem to reveal evidence of moves towards greater innovation and accelerated outbound FDI. However, whereas many of the Suzhou-based companies are foreign owned, those in Wenzhou are predominantly domestic owned agglomerations, cooperative ventures and networks. Surprisingly, at this stage, there is a tendency for the outcomes and performance of companies in Suzhou and Wenzhou to converge; so much so that the effects of the recession in 2008–9 seemed to be hitting some Wenzhou companies as hard as or harder than companies in Suzhou exporting similar goods. For instance, in 2008, the pre-Christmas sale of toys from Zhejiang to the West crashed, causing many factory closures. In fact, according to one estimate, about 56 percent of all toy factories in Zhejiang closed in 2009 (*Far East Economic Review* 2009: 12) while others directed their efforts to the domestic market and to Africa, South America and other Asian countries.

Clearly, China as a whole, as represented by SEZs such as Shenzhen, Xiamen, Tianjin, Suzhou, and so on, has progressed along stages one and two of the IDP, and in many cases, stages three and four are being encountered. From being regarded as the world's factory, policy-makers are seeking to transform China into an attractive, innovative location where higher value-added activities thrive. That is stage three. In addition, China has an ambition to broach stage four of the IDP, where outward FDI typically surpasses inward FDI. It is this part of the equation that might be thwarted because although China has many emerging transnational companies (TNCs) with investments in many parts of the world, it is not clear that this outward FDI path is sustainable. The external economic downturn and the internal social and environmental infrastructures might not support this strategy. Finally, although it seems clear that China's early development followed the trajectory and patterns suggested by FDI theories, especially the IDP theory discussed above, and that the Suzhou SEZ also followed and is following the IDP, it is not absolutely clear whether Wenzhou's development departed significantly from that path and therefore exhibited better performance than Suzhou as some policy-makers would have us believe. To gain a degree of clarity on this position is one of the purposes of the discussion that follows.

The chapter is divided into five parts, of which this introduction is the first. The second part explores the historical development of China's SEZ policy and practice. The third examines the legal basis for the founding and operation of the Wenzhou and Suzhou SEZs. The fourth compares the social and environmental performance of the two SEZs using an adapted version of the UN Human Development Index. The final part concludes, arguing that peoples' lives do not seem to have been bettered significantly more in the Wenzhou SEZ than in Suzhou. Indeed, in all areas, except per capita income and car ownership, the Suzhou SEZ seems to have outperformed Wenzhou. However, the data are incomplete and perhaps unreliable. It has been almost impossible to gain access to meaningful information about social infrastructural issues including key areas of enforcement of labour rights and environmental protection in Suzhou and Wenzhou. Therefore further research in this area is highly desirable. For a discussion of China's attempt to improve environmental management through SEZs, see Krusekopf (this volume) and for labour market and social equity issues, see Xu (this volume).

Development of China's SEZ policy and practice

The concept of SEZs was introduced into China in 1979. The idea was modelled on export processing zones (EPZs) from other developing countries and they 'were originally envisioned as areas where foreign investment would be both permitted and controlled in an effort to gain national economic advantage from world markets' (Crane 1994: 71). This move represented a gigantic shift in China's policy and practice regarding foreign trade and economic development in a country whose leadership, until then, had regarded intercourse with private foreign capital as diametrically opposed to its socialist development ideals. For in 1949, when the new republic through the Chinese Communist Party (the Party) adopted Marxist-Leninist ideology, it was thought that export of capital was the core of imperialism and that MNCs (multinational companies) were doubly parasitic in that they exploited the working class of their own countries as well as those in developing countries. It might seem surprising but it is quite understandable to note that until the opening-up policies were announced in December 1978 by Deng Xiaoping, 'there had been no foreign investment [in China] from non-Communist nations since the early 1950s, when foreign investors were forced to leave China' (Lubman 2006: 11).

Thus acceptance of an *experiment* with the concept of SEZs, whose very existence is premised on foreign direct investment (FDI) from capitalist MNCs, must be viewed in the context of the gigantic changes made in China at the end of the 1970s. Major changes started when the Party confirmed in December 1978 that Deng Xiaoping would succeed Mao Zedong as China's paramount leader[4] (Osborne 1986: 82). It was Deng and his team who envisioned and introduced the policies that would allow China to embark upon the huge economic reform programme and experiment.

The SEZ experiment was accepted on the understanding that FDI would be controlled and regulated at all levels, especially in the six areas which the government deemed would exert a huge impact on the Chinese economy. The six areas were: one, access to domestic markets (of which there would be very little); two, accrual of foreign currency (the more the better); three, inclusion of domestic content in all manufactured goods (the more the better); four, profits and repatriation of profits (grudgingly allowed); five, technology transfer (the more the better, and the more advanced the better); six, knowledge transfer (the quicker the better).

The development of China's SEZ policy and practice is a story of the way in which China progressed in its effort to administer and control those six areas at the national, regional and local micro levels. Ideally, this study should review each area during the period from the birth of SEZs in 1979 to the present. However, lack of space dictates only highlights in key areas during formative periods. In effect, the leaders used a system of carrots and sticks to entice and curtail FDI by limiting it to particular modes of entry, particular industries and specific geographic areas; thus the founding of the SEZs.

Despite the mixed views and ideological differences among the three distinct groups that co-existed in China's leadership during the late 1970s,[5] the Deng team forced the Party to abandon the Maoist 'class struggles' and put an end to China's self-imposed isolation from the world. Instead, Deng's team pledged to modernize the country by opening it to the world in a controlled way. First, Deng announced the Four Modernizations or four national development goals which were designed to transform China from a socialist planned economy to a (socialist) market economy. The Four Modernizations are agriculture, defence, industry, and science and technology. The modernizations were validated in the new programmatic Chinese Constitution 1978 and in the ten-year plan (1976–85).[6] Second, it was made clear that modernization would require not only an open-door policy, to be effected initially through the SEZ experiment, but also law – 'socialist law with Chinese characteristics'. Indeed, at that time, any kind of law would probably suffice. During the early post-Mao period, China was emerging from a decade of chaos, the so-called Cultural Revolution (1966–76), a time when 'the very concept of law was denounced as an alien bourgeois notion' (Gellhorn 1987; Lubman 2006).

Securing law and order in the chaotic society that emerged from the Cultural Revolution was at the top of Deng's agenda. It is noteworthy that provisions for restoring the courts and procuracy as well as a new Criminal Law and Criminal Procedure Law were all included in the raft of laws that were enacted in early 1979. More surprisingly, one of Deng Xiaoping's first steps to introducing FDI into China involved the enactment of a very brief, provisional and programmatic Equity Joint Venture Law in 1979. This law was only three pages long but it set out the basic principles for enabling joint ventures between foreign and domestic enterprises or persons. In other words, the Law signaled the terms under which China would 'selectively absorb the good things and boycott the bad things from abroad' (Liu 1985: 126). At the core was reliance upon extensive central government participation in and regulation of the economy and of society itself. One thing seemed clear at the outset: China was going to retain extensive control over foreign capital and all investments within its borders while seeking to derive substantial benefits from them. Among the benefits sought, the anticipated spillover effects would require the package to include: jobs, foreign currency, technology transfer, management expertise, training of the unskilled, product-to-market expertise, including marketing and distribution know-how, banking and financial services, and umpteen other knowledge-based assets that underpin the functioning of Western and emerging Asian market economies.

Deng's second step in implementing his vision was the establishment of four special economic zones (SEZs) in areas along China's south coast. These were to be the FDI vehicles, the learning laboratories where China's economy would be transformed from a planned to a 'socialist' market economy (Chan et al. 1986; Sit 1985; Sklair 1991). The zones were chosen for their ideal geographic locations, close to Hong Kong, Macau and Taiwan, three successful centres of Westernized market-driven economies, all of which China claimed were part of its territories.[7] These locations also provided access to modern transportation infrastructure. However, the biggest prizes were a host of investment-minded Chinese diaspora just outside China's coast and, on the inside, cheap labour or labour that was willing to migrate to the coast. Thus the Shenzhen SEZ was opened in May 1980. It was a small village on the mainland in Guangdong province just opposite Hong Kong. In the same province, Zhuhai SEZ and Shantou SEZ followed; all were established under the provisions of the August 1980 National People's Congress Regulations for SEZs in Guangdong Province. Next, Xiamen SEZ was established in Fujian province, just opposite Taiwan.

In truth, the initial establishment of the SEZs was a timid experiment in economic liberalization. There was even an experimental SEZ prior to the establishment of the four above-mentioned experimental SEZs: tiny Shekou, which was under the administration of the Shenzhen municipality, was the 1979 forerunner. It opened in January 1979. Initially, it was developed separately from Shenzhen as a public-public SEZ partnership between the China Steamship and Navigation Company, a Hong Kong-based agent of the PRC's Ministry of Transportation and the Ministry itself. Shekou focused on maritime and shipping activities but after its initial success, it was soon incorporated into the larger Shenzhen SEZ experiment. The sub-tropical island of Hainan was added as a sixth experimental SEZ. Owing to fraudulent real estate transactions and misallocated investments in hotels and golf resorts, it became an early monument of how not to conduct FDI. However, in 1988 it was granted provincial status and the whole area was designated an SEZ and given a fresh start.

In 1984, fourteen other coastal cities were designated as foreign investment enclaves. Wenzhou in Zhejiang province is numbered among this second tranche of approved locations. Throughout the period, ideological debates among the reformers (Deng's group) and the conservatives and radicals in the Party leadership would act as potent catalysts for policy changes – especially during the turbulent 1980s and early 1990s. The topic for debate was always how much and how fast economic liberation should be and how much control China would retain in order to ensure its absolute sovereignty and to keep 'unhealthy influences' at bay. Some even feared that SEZs would become modern concessions or treaty ports.[8]

In 1988, some areas along the Yangtze River established themselves as 'special zones'. They did not adopt the SEZ nomenclature but all *acted* in the same way as SEZs: proffering policies that gave foreign investors local tax incentives to locate in the area, greater independence in conducting foreign trade activities and enabling huge construction projects (sometimes on rural land designated for farming), joint ventures between Chinese and foreign enterprises, the manufacture of products solely for export and for gaining the coveted foreign currencies in exchange, and abiding by market-driven forces in their operations.

By 1990, many new zones and 'clusters' were established along the Yangtze Delta. This included the Pudong New Area, which became an infrastructural showpiece that was destined to transform Shanghai. In addition, also in 1990, fifteen free trade zones (FTZs), thirty-two state-level economic and technological development zones (ETDZs) and fifty-three high-tech clusters were established.[9]

The pioneer phase of zone fever is considered to be from 1979 to 1992. During this period many towns, villages and cities in China mushroomed into special zones of one kind or another, either in part or *in toto*. The establishment of each was often without legal or other central government support. For instance, *approval* of the enclave in Wenzhou dates back to 1984, but zone-like activities preceded that date, for as Hu Zuguang (2008: 4) writes:

> the local government of Wenzhou had neither [the] intention nor [the] ability to guide the institutional change in Wenzhou, but they took the attitude of doing nothing against human nature. ... Wenzhou City Party Committee and the city government at that time were wise enough to know that it has [*sic*] no financial ability to help the local people to pioneer a way of development, but at least they should not block the way for the Wenzhou people in seeking wealth and happiness.

That sentiment seems to have been common currency in many parts of China during the turbulent 1980s and early 1990s. One reason could be the fact that establishment of SEZs was, in reality, an experiment in the transition from a closely controlled command economy to a market economy. This experiment supported many communities that were eager to seize the opportunity to free themselves of the burdensome ways and quirkiness of the communist command economy. Similarly, when people saw the economic success of the official SEZs such as Shenzhen, Zhuhai, Tianjin and Xiamen, they wanted to try to replicate that success in their regions.

New impetus was given to SEZ development after Deng Xiaoping's now infamous 'southern tour' in 1992. For instance, in 1992–93, the central government established eighteen national or state-level economic technology and development zones (ETDZs) and adjusted the economic policy in order to accelerate economic reform. This was also when the term '*socialist* market economy' was officially adopted as a strategic goal and a politically calming mantra.

During the next decade the central government tried to rein in some of the tax incentives and preferences through legislation (Litwack and Qian 1998). Nevertheless, many new zones were born, some legitimate, some not. One of the legitimate, Suzhou in Jiangsu province (see below), was a state-to-state partnership between China and Singapore (Carter 2003: 271–86). It was the only state-to-state partnership to establish an SEZ in China. That was probably also its Achilles' heel, as the provincial level authorities seemed to object to the decision being made over their heads by China's leader Deng Xiaoping and Singapore's Lee Kuan Yew. The Suzhou SEZ, though labelled an industrial park, was given multiple powers and authorities, many of which were similar to or higher than the administrative powers of Jiangsu province (ibid.). Subsequently, the SEZs that were referred to as 'state-level' enclaves simply meant that they were established and operated under the auspices of national rather than provincial or municipal authorities (China Association of Development Zones). The Suzhou SEZ remained the only state-to-state SEZ experiment within China. However, in recent times that model has been taking on new life in African countries (Blair 2007: 24) and in Pakistan, where China's thirst for natural resources and export markets has spurred state-state SEZ experiments of its own. China has also ignored the latest trend in SEZ development, which, according to the World Bank (2008) has been that the majority of the SEZs in developing and transitioning economies have been developed and operated by private sector partnerships, thus reducing the burden on host countries' scarce resources (ibid.: 2).

According to China Statistics, by 2004 there were 6,686 special zones in the People's Republic. Of these, 207 are operated at the national level and the others are either operated at provincial or lower level (China Statistical Yearbook 2006). A year earlier a joint campaign was conducted among several ministries, including the Ministry of Land and Resources, the Ministry of Construction, the Ministry of Commerce and the National Development and Reform Commission in order to take stock of, clean up and reduce the multitude of areas calling themselves 'special zones', many of which operated in nefarious ways.

In April 2006, following the nationwide inspection, the campaigners announced that there were then a total of 1,115 legitimate zones in operation in China. Of these, 54 were ETDZs (Economic and Technological Development Zones), 53 were Advanced and New Technological Development Zones, 46 were Export Processing Zones, 14 were Free Trade Zones, 5 were Bonded Logistics Zones, 33 were other National Level Special Zones, and 910 were SEZs – Special Economic Zones operated by provincial or lower level administrative entities (Investment Guide to Special Zones in China 2006).

This proliferation of 'special zones' and SEZs by other names was startling. It is also surprising but understandable that the China Association of Development Zones (CADZ) warns that *investors* should ensure that the zones in which they wish to settle have the appropriate *central government* approval for the *locally* proffered incentives (emphasis added; ibid.: no page). In any event, the whittling down of the number of 'special zones' from 6,686 to 1,115 is very significant – though it is unclear what exactly has happened to the 5,000-odd zones that are no longer considered 'special'. It is also noteworthy that the website of the CADZ (no page) reports that the Ministry of Land and Resources et al. closed only 4,735 development zones or 70 per cent of the total in 2006. The discrepancy between these figures and those given by China Statistics is not unusual in China, where each authority seems to have its own discrete measuring tool. In both cases the number of closures is remarkably high. Besides, these closed zones could be the ones for which the CADZ warning is needed. It could also be that China has decided that the country has reached such a high level of economic liberalization that the experimental SEZs are no longer necessary. However, a more likely scenario is that China might have been attempting to comply with its World Trade Organization (WTO) obligations regarding subsidies.[10] For under the provisions of the WTO-covered Agreement on Subsidies and Countervailing Measures (SCM Agreement) certain export-oriented subsidies are prohibited (Muchlinski, this volume; Torres 2007: 217). According to the World Bank's interpretation (World Bank 2008: 54):

> SEZ regimes are consistent with the WTO so long as benefits are not contingent on export performance, use of local content, or maintenance of a foreign exchange balance; or primarily benefit a specific firm, industry, or other interest. Zone regimes that have specific incentives linked to export performance – such as minimum export requirements, subsidized rent or utilities, or a lower tax on export income – are not compatible with WTO mandates and need to be altered.

A close examination of company-level joint venture contracts with SEZ incentives and provisions of the early Joint Venture Law and Regulations reveal that China has been notorious for specifying use of local content, maintenance of foreign exchange balance, and giving foreign investors incentives linked to export performance.[11] So if the intention is to minimize these practices by the reduction of the areas in which they occur, China is to be commended. However, to judge by the United States Trade Representative (USTR), China's WTO compliance is mixed, for while there have been great strides in some areas,

> China continues to pursue problematic industrial policies that rely on trade-distorting measures such as local content requirements, import and export restrictions, discriminatory regulations and prohibited subsidies, all of which raise serious WTO concerns.
>
> (USTR 2006: 3)

It should be noted that the overall official policy trend on SEZs in China is not only to reduce their number but also to reduce substantially or stop some of the large tax incentives that were commonplace in the early days. Indeed, as Litwack and Qian (1998) argue, many of China's 1990s tax and economic reforms aimed to gradually phase out some of the preferential tax breaks available in SEZs rendering these zones less special. However, as many Sinologists will tell you, although China appears to have a powerful centralized government, in reality a substantial amount of operational power resides in the provinces and municipalities.

Legal basis for establishing and operating SEZs

Law reform and FDI policies have progressed hand-in-hand as enabling tools for the bigger agenda of China's modernization. Both have been driven by China's appetite for growth and economic reform (Gellhorn 1987; Lubman 2006; Potter 2001). It would appear that law was as instrumentalist in China as it has been in many other parts of Asia (Carter 2002: chs 5–7). However, whereas China's economy has succeeded mightily, the verdict is still out on the success of law. For instance, China's move to the Western notion of the rule of law continues to be elusive and remains, at best, 'rule *by* law' (Chen 1999; Peerenboom 2004). This section examines, in broad strokes, key characteristics of the legal environment as it developed for FDI and SEZs in China since 1979.

At the outset, it should be noted that by far the most pervasive characteristic of early FDI-related law in China is its tentativeness: nearly all legislation both national and provincial was usually labelled 'provisional' or 'interim'. This is in harmony with the overall experimental tone of China's economic reform and opening-up policy, even if it was not conducive to the certainty and stability required by investors. Next is the fact that all over China, the tendency is for policy – especially Party policy – to trump the word and spirit of the law. Commentators usually cite criminal cases to support this proposition but it is also pervasive in civil law, especially in intellectual property (IP) cases where local protectionism is rife (Clarke 1991; 1992). The third important factor is the huge discretion that is given to officials who interpret the law, whether in its implementation or its enforcement, and the subservience of the judiciary to the executive and legislative powers. These characteristics hamper both implementation and enforcement, and are major sources of frustration and uncertainty among foreign investors and Chinese business people alike. In addition, the provisions of national laws and laws or regulations enacted in the SEZs or at provincial or municipal levels do not always coincide; in fact, in many cases they may conflict. In the following section, an analysis of the main FDI and SEZ-enabling legislation will illustrate these characteristics.

Unlike in India (Harding, this volume) and in Russia, there is no national SEZ Act in China. However, at the national level, three laws influenced the early development of FDI and indirectly of SEZs in China since in the early years FDI was only allowed in the SEZs. These are the [Equity] Joint Venture Law 1979 (amended in 1990); the Joint Venture Implementing Regulations 1983, and Provisions for the Encouragement of Foreign Investments 1986 (White 2003).

The three-page, fifteen-article Joint Venture Law 1979, was not impressive, but in the context of China, it was an innovative piece of legislation. Article 1 set out the objective:

> With a view to expanding international economic co-operation and technical exchange, the People's Republic of China permits foreign companies,

> enterprises, other economic organizations or individuals (hereafter referred to as 'foreign joint venturers') to join with Chinese companies, enterprises or other economic organizations (hereinafter referred to as 'Chinese joint venturers') in establishing joint ventures in the People's Republic of China in accordance with the principle of equality and mutual benefit and subject to approval by the Chinese Government.

The objective was wide but clear, the focus would be to expand 'international economic cooperation and technical exchange'. This set the stage for what was required and a very general, vague idea of how joint ventures would be formed. There would be a contract in 'the principle of equality and mutual benefit' which would be subject to government approval. Many foreign investors found the 'equality and mutual benefit' phrase problematic since its meaning was unclear – especially when viewed in light of the articles outlining equity stakes and liability.

Article 2 clearly extended legal protection to foreign investment and even legitimized the notion of making a profit in communist China:

> The Chinese Government protects, in accordance with the law, the investment of foreign joint venturers, the profits due to them and their other lawful rights and interests in a joint venture, pursuant to the agreement, contract and articles of association approved by the Chinese Government.

In later years, the 'pursuant to the agreement. ... approved by the Chinese Government' phrase would take on a life of its own as the government exercised its power to interpret the agreement, contract and articles innovatively and usually in favour of the Chinese 'joint venturer' which, in those days, was nearly always a state-owned company (SOE).

Article 4 called for a minimum of 25 per cent equity stake to be held by foreigners but gave no maximum. It also stipulated that 'A joint venture shall take the form of a limited liability company', although, as yet, there was no company law in China[12] and therefore no specific provisions defining the term 'limited liability'. To solve the company law conundrum, the Shenzhen SEZ issued its own 'Tentative Provisions of Shenzhen Municipality on Companies Limited by Shares' in 1992. Shanghai Municipality also issued its own 'tentative provisions' which were identical to those in Shenzhen. However, the lack of clear national company law provisions, together with the on-going discussion regarding the meaning of contracts being formed in 'the principle of equality and mutual benefit' challenged many foreign would-be 'joint venturers' (*sic*).

Furthermore, Article 7 of the Joint Venture Law 1979 provided that:

> A joint venture that possesses advanced technology by world standards may apply for a reduction of or exemption from income tax for the first two to three profit-making years.

This is a good example of the statute's vagueness of language and openness to discretionary interpretation. First, is the tax holiday for two years or three years? Second, does the joint venture get a tax reduction or a total exemption from income tax? Third, under what conditions are 'profit-making years' to be decided? And finally, what exactly is 'advanced technology by world standards'? Who decides?

Article 2 stipulated that 'all the activities of a joint venture shall be governed by the laws, decrees, and pertinent rules and regulations of the People's Republic of China' – thus enshrining the general principle that joint ventures would be subject to Chinese law. Efforts on the part of foreign companies to include a contractual clause regarding dispute settlement under another jurisdiction were always defeated.[13] Article 15 of the 1983 EJV Implementing Regulation effectively put an end to such contractual negotiations by stating unequivocally that: 'the conclusion, validity, interpretation and implementation of joint venture contracts and the resolution of disputes thereunder shall be governed by Chinese law'.

Joint ventures were deemed to be 'Chinese legal persons' (*zhongguo furen*) once and for all. However, they must also have been deemed 'special' Chinese legal persons since they were subject to laws which did not apply to Chinese domestic companies, which at that time were state- or provincial-owned entities. That is why some scholars argue that companies that existed in, for example, Wenzhou, were essentially 'illegal' entities. However, this was not unusual in China, where there was also a Foreign Economic Contract Law for contracts between foreigners and Chinese companies,[14] and a different Economic Contract Law for contracts between Chinese people and state entities. It was not until 1996 that China enacted a unified Contract Law to serve everyone: Chinese legal persons, Chinese individuals, foreigners, and SOEs alike.

Finally, the Equity Joint Venture Law did not specifically state whether the joint ventures should be domiciled in SEZs and it lacked guidance on many other legal and operational matters. However, all of the eighty-three joint ventures that were formed by the end of 1983 were based in SEZs. And this became the norm for joint ventures as well as wholly foreign owned enterprises from 1986 when that form of business organization was allowed.

By then a labyrinth of regulations, most of them also vague and programmatic, had been added in an attempt to clarify issues about the labour force – specifically for those working in joint ventures,[15] foreign exchange,[16] taxation of joint ventures,[17] exports, and so on. Many foreign investors were sceptical; however, the long-term promise of what became known as 'the China market' – that is, the domestic market with its 1.3 billion people – lured foreigners to invest in SEZs. By 1988, the number of pledged FDI joint venture projects was 8,539, valued at $9.88 billion (Pearson 1991: 71). As is well-known, economic growth in China progressed mightily during the next two decades. However, as Chinese statistics are notoriously unreliable, it is not known whether the usually touted national average of more than 10 per cent growth per year is credible; let alone the 28 per cent average for Shenzhen. According to China Statistics, by 2007, the amount of FDI flowing into China had reached $2.11 trillion. And the legal environment had become much more sophisticated, with statutes regulating many forms of business organizations including sole proprietors, partnerships, representative companies, corporations and wholly foreign-owned enterprises.

The Joint Venture Implementing Regulations, 1983, played a huge role in clarifying the provisions of the short, programmatic Joint Venture Law 1979. It helped to build confidence among foreign investors as it included provisions about repatriation of profit, technology transfer, foreign exchange, and local content and export obligations. At the same time, the promulgation of China's first westernized Trademark Law (1982), two Contract Laws (1982, 1985), a Patent Law (1985), Company Law (1993) and an Accounting Law (1985) helped to improve the business environment enormously by providing a degree of certainty and clarity.

However, towards the end of 1985 and in 1986, the Chinese government drastically reduced domestic spending of foreign exchange. This also limited the ability of foreign investors to import parts for production, gain money from the sale of joint venture goods and repatriate any profits. Complaints among foreign investors were strong and lobbies powerful. For example, AMC – American Motor Company – the joint venture partner in the maker of the Beijing jeep, was among the most vocal; as were several US business associations with interests in China. Growth rates plummeted and lack of confidence crept in among investors. Thus the State Council promulgated the 1986 Provisions for the Encouragement of Foreign Investment – designed to do just that. The 1986 General Principles of Civil Law (GPCL 1986) was also promulgated. It was one of the most significant pieces of legislation in China, allowing that for the first time, Chinese law formally recognized the rights and obligations of the people in China. This national legal framework was accompanied by China's accession to several international treaties designed to protect, for instance, intellectual property rights.[18] As early as 1985, China had sought to rejoin the GATT (General Agreement on Tariffs and Trade) and in doing so started to prepare its legal and commercial environment for membership. Thus, at the national level, a legal structure started to take shape from the middle of the 1980s which accelerated in the 1990s and culminated in 2001, when China acceded to the World Trade Organization.[19]

Special regulations at the provincial and municipal levels were also passed to facilitate the establishment and operation of SEZs. These mainly complemented the national-level laws, although there were instances where the provincial rules opposed the national law or where national laws were nonexistent, as in the Company Law example discussed above. The provincial authorities were keen to promulgate laws and regulations to suit their own purposes. For instance, in Guangdong province, there were provisional regulations for governing wages,[20] technology transfer,[21] and what the government termed 'internal linkages',[22] and entry and exit rules for the SEZs.[23] The latter regulation also included rules about migrant workers, who formed the primary workforce in the SEZs. It seems that many of the regulations created in Guangdong province were replicated in Zhejiang and sometimes also in Suzhou when the Singapore 'software' was found lacking. But in general, the specific national laws as discussed above applied to FDI and the SEZs, which were the only places where FDI was permitted in China.

Socio-economic and environmental performance of the two SEZs

On paper, the Wenzhou SEZ was approved in 1984. However, two clarifications are necessary. First, Wenzhou was not established as an SEZ but as an ETDZ: an economic and technological development zone in which foreign investors and local enterprises could gain preferential treatment similar to those being enjoyed in the SEZs. Second, Wenzhou did not start work on establishing itself as an ETDZ for several years owing to inadequate transportation and communication infrastructures. It should be noted that one major difference between SEZs and ETDZs is that while the former are granted administrative independence, the latter are controlled by the regional or provincial government. So the work of implementing the special zone in Wenzhou was a purely local initiative. Therefore, although it is true that Wenzhou was one of the fourteen coastal cities which premier Zhao Ziyang announced as special zones in May 1984 following Deng Xiaoping's visit to Shenzhen, Zhuhai, and Xiamen SEZs (*14 Coastal Cities of the PRC Handbook 1985*), in reality Wenzhou's official establishment lagged far behind the other SEZs. According to the Coastal Cities Handbook, the plan was that the fourteen cities, together with the four original SEZs, dotted along China's southeast coastline, were to form China's official front to the outside world (ibid.: 26–29).

However, Wenzhou had other plans. Its modern economic development had started earlier, from about 1978, and from a very low base. Located on the southern coast of Zhejiang province, not far from Taiwan, Wenzhou, like Xiamen in neighbouring Fujian province, was considered unsuitable for serious industrial investment since they were too close to the 'frontier of war'.[24] From 1949 to 1978, the average amount of per capita investment per year in the mountainous Wenzhou region was less than 2 dollars (Hu 2008: 3). Perhaps the seemingly deliberate underdevelopment of the area sharpened the resolve of the Wenzhou population, because when the national reform programme was introduced in 1978, it unleashed a flurry of spontaneous, small entrepreneurial activities among the locals who thereby invented a private economic sector in Wenzhou (ibid.).

Thus, as Professor Hu Zuguang points out in his analysis of development in Zhejiang and Jiangsu provinces, the Wenzhou mode of development is based on small firms with private ownership which were not strictly legal in the early reform days (Hu 2008: 4). Instead, these firms benefited from the 'don't ask, don't tell' or 'no argument' attitude advocated by Deng and his reformers who sought every possible way of moving away from the Mao-inspired collectives and households which had stifled entrepreneurship and initiative. The small family-owned firms in Wenzhou specialized in home-made textiles and basic low-technology household goods such as brooms, zippers, plastic and ceramic kitchenware, plastic toys, shoes, disposable lighters, disposable pens, pencils and so on.

As these businesses grew in number and became successful as small and medium-sized enterprises (SMEs), owned and operated by family members, the issue of their legality became more problematic. However, that was solved by the Wenzhou government's policy of 'borrowing title'. That is, these successful small private firms were allowed to use the name of a state-owned firm or collective enterprise and operate under the title of 'public ownership' (ibid.). Of course, the private enterprises paid a fee to the government for the use of this discretion (ibid.). As expected, there are no statistics, and as for data regarding the number of firms involved and their profitability, there are none. A field trip to Wenzhou in 2009 corroborated Professor Hu's postulate, but it was impossible to quantify the incidence or scope of such enterprises, mainly because several interviewees seem to have developed loss of memory.

According to Professor Hu, later on the Wenzhou government further exercised its right to interpret the rules and encouraged the spirit of cooperation by constantly merging two or more of the family-owned SMEs into larger conglomerates so as to imitate the 'behaviour of collective ownership' (ibid.). Implementation of these lenient policies encouraged the private economy's growth in Wenzhou in those early years. There is no evidence of foreign capital entering the chain. However, Wenzhou's privately owned SMEs, town and village enterprises (TVEs) and collectives manufactured and sold goods that were in demand locally within Zhejiang province and in other provinces in China. Together they formed an agglomeration economy, and became specialists in certain basic commodities which were scarce in other markets in China. In those days, it was easy to choose what to produce since Chinese society was marked by scarcity. When the central government and the Party further liberalized the economy by choosing to promulgate laws to regulate contractual or cooperative joint ventures,[25] companies (1993), partnerships (1997) and so on, and by exercising flexibility in their initial conceptualization of the open-door policy, the economy in Wenzhou increased dramatically. From a GDP in 1978 of only RMB1.32 billion, GDP catapulted to RMB183.44 billion in 2006. Thus obviously there was a huge growth in GDP. The issue is: how did this vast increase in GDP affect the well-being and betterment of the local population? And how does this compare with development in Suzhou? These issues will be addressed in the next section, but first a look at Suzhou's development.

The situation in Suzhou is almost the opposite of that in Wenzhou. Suzhou is part of the larger area called Sunan in south Jiangsu province, which counts Shanghai, China's largest industrial and financial city, as its neighbour. Suzhou, which is an old imperial capital, is only 80 km west of Shanghai. With its new transportation infrastructure, Suzhou is just an hour's drive from Shanghai and is located conveniently along the busy railway line connecting Shanghai to Nanjing. Because of its close proximity to Shanghai, Suzhou has nearly always enjoyed excellent economic development, supported by government contracts and collective ownership. This was the case even during the darkest, most unproductive and wasteful years of Mao Zedong's rule. Besides, compared with mountainous Wenzhou, Suzhou boasts fertile agricultural land and traditionally Suzhou's farmers have been among the most successful in China. Indeed one criticism of Suzhou's modern development path is that arable land has been harnessed to serve industrial development at the expense of agricultural production.

The part of the Suzhou development story with which this study is concerned is the 144 square kilometers of land carved out by the Chinese government to form the special China-Singapore Suzhou Industrial Park (CS-SIP). This alliance was negotiated and finalized shortly after Deng's 1992 trip to the south in which he openly praised Singapore's 'good social order' and its management style (Carter 2003; Pearson 1991). Although not registered as a treaty and therefore not a public document, the undisclosed agreement between the two governments was signed in February 1994 in the wake of the 'leftists' concerns about the runaway excessive capitalistic nature of the Hong Kong-dominated Shenzhen SEZ (Crane 1990: 3). The concerns involved ideological condemnations of capitalist and laissez-faire excesses as well as the Party's anxieties about the loss of traditional Chinese values. It was thought that Singapore was able to control these issues better than Hong Kong. In any event, among the Chinese leadership, both Hong Kong and Singapore were held in high esteem as icons of modernity; either could be a suitable model for the future China. Collaboration with Hong Kong was considered easier owing to its closer proximity to mainland China, and from 1997, when it also became a part of China – a so-called SAR: special administrative region – the ties would be indisputable as the ex-British colony was returned to China (White Paper 1984). However, another huge advantage was that both Hong Kong and Singapore possessed wealthy and well-motivated Chinese diasporas who were eager to invest in their ancestral homes in south and southeast China.

The expressed initial intention of the state-to-state joint venture partners was to develop a modern 70 sq. km town capable of supporting 600,000 people. In its scope and features, phase one would essentially replicate Jurong, a Singapore model town-cum-industrial park that was built in the 1980s (Carter 2003). However, the Singapore town came with a software package which included assistance in:

- land use planning and development;
- environmental planning and regulation;

- building construction management;
- planning and management of industrial estates;
- management of new towns and public utilities;
- labour management, and
- social security.[26]

According to Singapore's Economic Development Board the bilateral agreement 'involves a software transfer co-operation project between the two countries' (EDB pamphlet 1995, no page). Furthermore, 'software transfer refers to the sharing of Singapore's successful public administration and economic management experiences … so that [the Chinese] authorities can formulate and implement pro-business policies in the China-Singapore Suzhou Industrial Park' (ibid.). In an analysis of these issues supported by field work about implementation of the agreement, I have argued elsewhere that the Singapore 'software transfer' is a euphemism for 'law' (Carter 2003: 271–86). It is clear that the Suzhou SEZ implemented and benefited from the national FDI-enabling laws of China as discussed above. But it also benefited from major foreign legal transplants in the form of Singapore-derived regulations designed to enhance the SEZ's overall administration as well as its socio-economic and environmental well-being. Of particular interest are labour and environment regulations, both of which received special attention in terms of procedures for implementation and enforcement in the Suzhou SEZ. China's first national Labour Law was enacted in 1994 and came into force 1 January 1995. Although article 1 boasted that it was made in the spirit of China's Constitution to support the socialist market economy, it is thought to have been influenced greatly by provisions in the Singapore Labour Law.

In May 2009 the Suzhou SEZ celebrated its fifteenth anniversary. My visit confirmed the huge physical and environmental success of the main project – it is a showcase that is second to none in China. A spokesperson at the administrative office also confirmed that the Suzhou SEZ hosts visitors from all over the world and it is held as the model for China's own SEZ transplants into other parts of Asia (Pakistan, for instance) and for development aid to countries in Africa.

With success comes conflict, and the division of the shares invested by the original partners has been altered so that a Chinese consortium instead of the Singapore authorities now owns the lion's share of the Suzhou SEZ. From the original shareholding in the ratio of 65 to 35 to Singapore and China respectively (Carter 2003: 277), Singapore's share in 2009 was a modest 28 per cent. Some foreign observers who wish to remain unidentified say that China ousted Singapore as soon as the SEZ became a profitable venture. Neither Chinese nor Singaporean authorities will discuss the reason for the dramatic change, so it is difficult to draw any meaningful conclusion. However, even the Suzhou New District Hi-Tech Industrial Co. Ltd, which was an original competitor of the Suzhou Industrial Park, now owns

Table 4.1 Comparing social and environmental performance in Wenzhou and Suzhou SEZs

	2002		*2003*		*2004*		*2005*		*2006*		*2007*	
	Suzhou	*Wenzhou*	*Suzhou*	*Wenzhou*	*Suzhou*	*Wenzhou*	*Suzhou*	*Wenzhou*	*Suzhou*	*Wenzhou*	*Suzhou*	*Wenzhou*
1 General information												
Population (million)	5.83	7.39	5.90	7.42	5.98	7.46	6.06	7.50	6.15	6.15	6.24	7.64
GDP in total (billion RMB)	208.0	105.5	280.2	122.0	345.0	140.2	400.0	160.0	482.20	183.43	570.00	215.70
Unemployment rate	4.08%	3.7%	3.93%	3.1%	3.69%	2.7%	3.42%	2.3%	3.22%	2.5%	3.0%	2.4%
Per capita income (urban area, RMB)	10,617	14,591	12,361	16,035	14,451	17,727	16,276	19,805	18,532	21,716	21,260	25,740
Per capita income (rural area, RMB)	6,134	5,091	6,750	5,548	7,460	6,020	8,300	6,845	9,316	7,543	10,300	8,591
Private enterprise contribution	19.5%	96.0%	25.7%	91.8%	27.3%	91.4%	29.5%	89.2%	30.8%	88.9%	30%	80.7%
2 Capital goods ownership – in total												
Car ownership (thousand) (urban area)	104.0	154.7	158.4	200.0	355.3	401.2	449.4	492.2	559.4	606.3	697.9	748.1
Mobile phone (thousand) (urban area)	2,660.3	2,383.0	3,592.1	3,416.3	4984.0	N/A	5,980.0	4,882.6	7,300.0	6,816.3	9,180	7,447
Internet (thousand)	N/A	W	578.9	755.8	589.1	N/A	6,264	8,476	777.4	980.5	1,050	1,140
3 Education and technology												
Public budget for education (percentage of annual GDP)	N/A	N/A	N/A	N/A	N/A	N/A	N/A	N/A	N/A	N/A	N/A	5%

Continued

Table 4.1 Continued

	2002		2003		2004		2005		2006		2007	
	Suzhou	*Wenzhou*	*Suzhou*	*Wenzhou*	*Suzhou*	*Wenzhou*	*Suzhou*	*Wenzhou*	*Suzhou*	*Wenzhou*	*Suzhou*	*Wenzhou*
R&D (percentage of the GDP)	N/A	N/A	N/A	N/A	N/A	N/A	N/A	0.53%	1.5%	0.68%	N/A	0.85%
Population in primary/ elementary school	663,500	990,965	633200	972,854	602,500	948,197	581,000	916,976	554,000	907,948	560,600	908,080
Population in secondary school	184,000	194,976	222,600	218,775	236,500	576,644	252,600	361,795	243,700	257,725	241,900	250,304
Population in post-secondary or tertiary education (college/university)[1]	104,500	31,969	111,000	39,868	126,000	45,330	113,500	49,947	130,600	56,811	152,400	59,214
Entrance rate to post-secondary education[2]	41.06%	21.7%	45%	24.30%	50.14%	28.00%	51.53%	32.6%	52.3%	34.8%	53%	37%
Patents	2,300	2,477	2,593	2,770	2,750	3,224	4,855	3,116	4,855	3,816	8,500	5,316
Famous brands (so far in total)	N/A	7	N/A	7	N/A	10	22	32	22	32	43	80
4 Health												
Number of doctors per 1,000 population	1.98	1.37	2.20	1.59	2.15	1.59	2.11	1.64	2.195	1.939	2.564	2.045
Health care cover rate (rural area)[3]	N/A	N/A	N/A	N/A	95%	N/A	N/A	N/A	96.1%	76.91%	96.5%	83.35%
5 Legal sophistication[4]												
Number of civil cases brought (in total)	N/A	10,744	N/A	10,670	N/A	12,900	N/A	14,456	N/A	15,272	N/A	15,268
Number of criminal cases	N/A	6,010	N/A	5,093	N/A	6,031	N/A	5,983	N/A	4,271	N/A	4,599

Number of administrative cases	N/A	557	N/A	688	N/A	1,158	N/A	1,165	N/A	1,086	N/A	902
Mediation	N/A	20,500	N/A	21,500	N/A	20,700	N/A	21,000	N/A	20,263	N/A	18,763
Notarization	N/A	62,600	N/A	82,400	N/A	90,200	N/A	88,000	N/A	81,209	N/A	83,868
International notarization[5]	N/A	94,000	N/A	78,700	N/A	78,100	N/A	85,000	N/A	65,954	N/A	70,371
6 Environmental issues												
National parks	N/A	N/A	N/A	3	N/A	3	N/A	5	N/A	5	5	5
Provincial parks	N/A	N/A	N/A	12	N/A	12	N/A	11	N/A	11	9	11
Air quality reaches level 1 (days)	N/A	75	N/A	69	N/A	109	43	82	43	82	32	53
Air quality reaches level 2 (days)	N/A	356	N/A	361	305	355	324	355	324	355	326	308
7 Life expectancy at birth	77.5	N/A	N/A	N/A	N/A	N/A	N/A	N/A	N/A	N/A	78.9	74

Notes:

[1]More colleges and universities are located in Suzhou (18) than Wenzhou (5).

[2]In Wenzhou, parents tend to let their children join in the family business as soon as they can. Experiential learning is held in higher esteem than formal education.

[3]Health care in rural areas started around late 2003 and early 2004, see the official website of the Rural Health Care, www.cncms.org.cn/

[4]The number of administrative cases is considered an indicator of the openness and liberalization of the society, but statistics on Suzhou's legal sophistication are unavailable.

[5]International notarization denotes high activity in international trade.

5 per cent of the main developer: the China-Singapore Suzhou Industrial Development Co. Ltd (CSSD).

Another view could be taken. This concerns the anticipated spillover effects between foreign companies in the Suzhou SEZ and Chinese companies during the decade 1996–2006 when the Suzhou SEZ grew and performed mightily. Disappointingly, studies suggest that there were no significant spillover effects. Indeed, in an econometric study of SOEs in both Zhejiang (Wenzhou's province) and Jiangsu (Suzhou's province) employing seven economic models, Professor Hu (2008: 28) concluded that

> [f]rom the seven models, we can see that the models are either not fitting well or fitting well but spillover effects [are either] zero or even negative. The results indicate that there is virtually no spillover effect from FDI for state owned firms either in Zhejiang or Jiangsu.

The main reasons for this surprising result seem to be the fact that foreign companies had grabbed the chance of registering themselves as wholly foreign owned enterprises, as soon as the law permitted this form of business association, thus leaving behind the cumbersome equity joint venture organizations in which foreign companies were forced to make alliances and share all kinds of expertise and technology with Chinese SOEs. In the 1980s and early 1990s when joint ventures were prescribed and were the only form of business organization, Chinese employees worked closely with their foreign counterparts and benefited from exchange of ideas and experience as well as formal and informal in-house training. When these employees left and joined Chinese companies, they obviously took their newly acquired knowledge and experience with them – to the benefit of the Chinese SOEs inside or outside the SEZs. Furthermore, by the late 1990s and into the twenty-first century, many Chinese SOEs had also acquired technological skills and expertise of their own so the need for spillovers became less pronounced. It is also a fact that many Chinese SOEs operate in monopoly areas or protected industries where joint ventures and cooperation with foreign companies are inappropriate. For the same reason, there are also few supply chain relationships between foreign and domestic firms within the SEZs. Many suppliers are located in a ring just outside the SEZs. It has been claimed that this so-called 'doughnut' structure allows the companies outside the SEZs to supply the foreign companies inside the SEZs but without having to conform with the cumbersome rules and regulations that exist inside the SEZs. Suzhou is no different. However, it is possible that Hu's findings of spillover effects might have been different if the Chinese companies researched were private corporations and partnerships instead of SOEs. Although the data and information are scarce, it is hoped that more research into spillover effects between private Chinese corporations and FDI will be conducted in future. It is clear that FDI (both inward and outward) is the single most important vehicle for bringing goods and services to foreign markets and for integrating national production systems. Thus an understanding of how these systems work in China will be crucial to balancing future development.

So if there were no significant FDI spillover effects between foreign and Chinese companies in the SEZs in Zhejiang and Jiangsu, what about social and environmental performance in the SEZs? Did the residents of Wenzhou SEZ actually enjoy greater betterment of their lives than those of Suzhou during the SEZ years? This comparison is supported by the data shown in Table 4.1, which were collected using an adapted version of the UN Human Development Index (HDI).

Most researchers know that collecting data in China can be difficult since authorities do not always willingly share social and environmental data, which they often consider to be sensitive. However, the difficulty that faced this project was not lack of cooperation but the nonexistence of relevant data, especially data for the early decades of the SEZs' existence. There was no opportunity to register, for example, local conditions prior to the establishment of the SEZs as a base point for comparison. In fact, the data required for the 1980s and 1990s in the case of Wenzhou were unavailable, perhaps totally nonexistent. And, as for Suzhou, some data existed from its opening in 1994 but since this study attempts to compare the two SEZs, comparisons can only be made for the years for which data are available for both places. Table 4.1 below therefore shows the performance of the SEZs for the five years from 2002 to 2007.

It should be noted that the statistics for Suzhou SEZ incorporate a wider area than the original China-Singapore Suzhou Industrial Park. This is because the original area has been combined with the competing township called the Suzhou New District and other areas developed by the municipal government minutes away from the original industrial park. To the extent that the parameters for growth were also predominantly exogenous in the new areas, and Singapore software was also transferred there, it matters not that the area is extended geographically. But it does explain many details in the data shown in Table 4.1, for instance, the larger population figures than those envisaged in the original plan of the Suzhou SEZ project. However, even the extended Suzhou SEZ remains an essentially homogeneous target when compared with Wenzhou's claimed mode of development.

The parameters for GDP, per capita income both for rural and urban areas, unemployment rate and population are compared in the table. They show that Wenzhou's population is larger than Suzhou's. Per capita income in the *urban* areas of Wenzhou was higher than in Suzhou throughout the period under study, while per capita income in the rural areas was higher in Suzhou. The numbers are not surprising, Suzhou's fertile farmland outperformed Wenzhou's mountainous production; and Wenzhou's urban areas had been practising (small scale) industrial production for several years before Suzhou SEZ joined in industrialization. Therefore, prima facie, the per capita income confirms that Wenzhou outperformed Suzhou in financial measurement. However, in the other areas researched, which we can call the outcomes of prosperity, such as level of education, technology usage, health care, ownership of capital goods, legal sophistication and environmental protection, based on the data available, Suzhou has outperformed Wenzhou.

Based on these findings, there is no evidence that Wenzhou outperformed Suzhou in the parameters studied, except urban per capita income and car ownership. The reason for the higher performance in car ownership might not be purely a reflection of affluence but the practicality of getting their products to market. The higher number of people under primary/elementary education reflects the bigger population in Wenzhou, but it is the number undergoing post-secondary education at universities and colleges that is interesting, and here Suzhou outperforms Wenzhou mightily. There are also eighteen higher education institutions in Suzhou compared with only five in Wenzhou. Similarly, the number of cultural institutions appears to be far fewer in Wenzhou than in Suzhou. This would also suggest greater attention being paid to quality of life issues rather than mere economic prowess.

The level of information available about environmental protection was disappointingly low.[27] So too was the level of information about the legal sophistication of Suzhou. For instance, the data regarding the number of civil and criminal cases brought in Suzhou were simply unavailable for the period under review.

An attempt to use the Gini coefficient as indicators of inequality was abandoned – at least temporarily – owing to lack of relevant data.[28] The plan is to visit China again and conduct in-depth interviews for qualitative data among corporate managers and bureaucrats at the SEZs, and to seek additional quantitative data on areas such as infant mortality (per 1,000 births), adult literacy rates, labour rights and environmental protection.[29]

Conclusion

Based on the relatively incomplete data available, there is evidence that Wenzhou SEZ outperformed Suzhou SEZ in GDP during the period researched but there is no clear evidence that Wenzhou outperformed Suzhou in key aspects of the standard of living or betterment in the lives of people in the SEZ. What seems also clear is that the scope and rate of development or growth in both SEZs appear to be converging in most areas. It is not impossible that further study would reveal greater differences in the more nuanced areas which we can call 'quality of life', especially areas such as quality of the environment, health care, education, recreation and cultural activities. If this is so, then it might also be fair to conclude that under the circumstances, the Wenzhou model, based predominantly on endogenous growth, should be nurtured in China. This is because Wenzhou's performance level is sufficiently close to Suzhou's performance to warrant this choice – given the current imbalances in world trade and the weak prospects for China's continued mass export of low technology products to Western countries. In addition, as discussed above, since studies suggest that there are no significant spillover effects in either the Suzhou or the Wenzhou model, there are no good reasons to continue the unbridled production of cheap goods for export.

Therefore, a move to nurture the Wenzhou model with its predominantly endogenous growth should be particularly useful now that the export-oriented pillars on which Suzhou's exogenous growth rests are becoming increasingly unstable. The other part of the equation requires a significant increase in the domestic consumption of the China-made goods and greater emphasis on creating a more equal and sustainable society within China by offering social welfare benefits of health care, education, training, pensions, good air and good water quality, safe, healthy housing and so on.

It has been said that household consumption in China stands at just 35 per cent of gross domestic product (GDP). That is the lowest share for any major economy in the world. By comparison, household consumption in the United States is twice that amount. In rebalancing its economic development model, China will have the luxury of encouraging its population to become valued consumers and beneficiaries of their own hard labour instead of being mere producers of goods for foreign consumption. In so doing, China could reinvent its economic development model by ensuring social security rights for the 130 million people, including migrant workers and the aged, who are currently treated almost like stateless individuals. That investment alone would go a long way to securing premier Hu Jingtao's harmonious society, rebalancing the notoriously uneven development and making economic development more sustainable.

Notes

1 See, for example, 'Outline of the National Intellectual Property Strategy' issued by the State Council on 5 June 2008: www.sipo.gov.cn/sipo_English/news/iprspecial/20080621_407693.htm (accessed 20 January 2010). Several leaders have noted the need to transition from 'made in China' to 'invented in China'. However, the first concrete step is probably the 'Scientific and Technological Progress Law' promulgated in July 2008. See also Editorial, *Far Eastern Economic Review*, November 2008, 5; Hugo Restall: Can Asia Consume a Way Out of Crisis? Ibid.: 6–10.

2 For an analysis and discussion of distortions in China during the reform process, see Young (2000).

3 See 'China factory output dips further': http://news.bbc.co.uk/1/hi/business/7810414.stm; Professor Willy Lam claims that close to 33 million urban residents lost their jobs in the second half of 2008: 'Hu Jintao's great leap backward', *Far East Economic Review*, Jan/Feb 2009, 20. There are an estimated 120 million (internal) migrant workers in China (see Xu, Chapter 3 in this volume); however, it is unclear whether Lam is equating 'urban residents' with migrant workers or whether unemployed migrant workers are in addition to unemployed urban residents.

4 Following the death of Mao Zedong, the demise of the Gang of Four in 1976, and of Hua Guofeng in 1978, it became more and more clear that Deng Xiaoping would emerge as China's leader. The key declarations were made during the third plenary session of the Eleventh Central Committee of the Communist Party of China which was held in late December 1978.

5 The three groups which had been influential at varying times in China's leadership and the bureaucracy since the 1949 revolution are: the radicals, the conservatives and the reformers. The policy pendulum swung, and policies were created and changed according to the ideas advocated by each of the three groups or by an alliance of two against the other. For a discussion, see Pearson (1991: 20–25).
6 The ten-year plan was announced during the first session of the Fifth National People's Congress in 1978.
7 In 1984 Deng Xiaoping successfully negotiated the return to China of the British crown colony, Hong Kong, see White Paper 1985. At the 1997 handover, Hong Kong became a Special Administrative Region (SAR) under the Chinese government. Macau, a former Portuguese colony, was handed back to China in 1999. The official status of Taiwan is still pending. However, after its state recognition was withdrawn by United Nations bodies such as the IMF, World Bank, etc., it is now de facto only a customs region, and China's claims that it is an autonomous province might yet be fulfilled.
8 For a discussion on concessions and treaty ports in China, see Bickers 1999.
9 See www.us-embassy-china.org.cn/fcs/china
10 After almost fifteen years of negotiations, China joined the WTO in December 2001.
11 See discussion below in the third section on the legal basis for establishing and operating SEZs.
12 China's first company law was promulgated in 1993.
13 One example is the joint venture contract negotiation between Schindler Holdings and the China Construction Machinery Corporation in 1980. The draft document allowed that an unresolved dispute should be 'brought in principle before the ordinary court of the domicile of the actual defendant'. The non-Chinese courts would be Swiss and British. In the final contract, this clause was replaced by a Chinese governing law clause. For a discussion, see Pearson 1991: 106. See also Moser 1987: 105.
14 See "Law of the People's Republic of China on Economic Contracts Involving Foreign Interests", promulgated in 1985. Translated in *China Business Review* 12(4) (July-August 1985): 54–55.
15 See, e.g. Regulation of the PRC on Labour Management in Joint Ventures using Chinese and foreign investment, 1980, promulgated by the State Council on and effective as of 26 July 1980. See also 'Interim Provisions Concerning Ideological and Political Work for Chinese Staff and Workers in Chinese-Foreign Equity and Cooperative Joint Ventures', August 1987.
16 See 'Detailed Rules for Foreign Exchange Control for Enterprises with Overseas Chinese Capital, Enterprises with Foreign Capital and Chinese-Foreign Joint Venture Enterprises', August 1983.
17 Detailed Rules and Regulations for the Implementation of the Income Tax Law of the PRC Concerning Joint Ventures using Chinese and Foreign Investment', promulgated 14 December 1980'.
18 Among the IP treaties China has ratified are: the Paris Convention for the Protection of Industrial Property in force since 1970; the Berne Copyright Convention in force since 1970; the Nice Agreement Concerning the International Classification of Goods and Services for the ... Registration of Marks; the Rome Convention for the Protection of Performers, Producers of Phonograms and Broadcasting, in force since 1961; the Madrid Agreement Concerning the International Registration of Marks, 1891 as amended in 1989; Protocol Relating to the Madrid Agreement Concerning the International Registration of Marks, 1989, which came into force on 1 December 1995 when China, as member number 5, ratified the treaty; and, of course the Agreement on Trade-related Aspects of Intellectual Property Rights in force since 1995.

19 WTO; See 'Accession of the People's Republic of China', WTO Doc. WT/L/432 (23 November 2001).

20 Provisional Regulations on Wages in the Enterprises in SEZs in Guangdong Province, Standing Committee of the 5th Guangdong Provincial People's Congress, 17 November 1981 in Chu et al. 1982: part 9.

21 Provisional Regulations of Shenzhen SEZ on Technology Introduction', 8 February 1984.

22 Provisional Regulations for Shenzhen SEZ on certain policies for 'Internal Linkage' enterprises, cited in Pearson 1991: 319.

23 Provisional entry/exit rules for the SEZs in Guangdong province, in Chu et al. 1982: part 14.

24 The phrase 'frontier of war', referring to Wenzhou's close proximity to Taiwan, is from Hu Zuguang (2008) at 3. I have lived in Xiamen and noticed that scholars at Xiamen University often used the same phrase about Xiamen and its proximity to Taiwan.

25 The Law on Contractual Joint Ventures, 1988. This form of joint venture was most popular among Chinese expatriates from Hong Kong, Taiwan and Macau. The law merely legitimized the practice.

26 See Singapore Economic Development Board literature 1994–1998 on file with author. These points are from a 1995 pamphlet, no page.

27 For a comprehensive discussion, see Richardson 2004: 161–64.

28 For a discussion of the growing inequality gap between cities with SEZ-driven policies and those without, see Jones et al. 2003: 186–200.

29 For discussion of similar issues, see Dollar (2007); Gustafsson et al. (2008); Shah and Shen (2006).

Bibliography

Blair, D (2007) 'Why China is trying to colonise Africa', *Daily Telegraph*, 31 August 2007, 24.

Bickers, R (1999) *Britain in China: Community, culture and colonialism, 1900–49*, London: Manchester University Press.

Carter, C (2002) *Eyes on the Prize: Law and Economic Development in Singapore*, London: Kluwer Law International.

—— (2003) 'The clonability of the Singapore model of law and development: The case of Suzhou, China', in Christoph Antons (ed.) *Law and development in Asia*, London: RoutledgeCurzon, 271–86.

Chan, T, E Chen and S Chin (1986) 'China's special economic zones: Ideology, policy and practice' in YC Jao and CK Leung (eds) *China's special economic zones: Policies, problems and prospects*, Oxford: Oxford University Press, chapter 5.

Chen, Jianfu (1999) *Chinese law*, London: Kluwer Law International.

China Association of Development Zones (CADZ), www.cadz.org.cn.en (accessed 20 January 2010).

China Statistical Yearbook 2006, National Bureau of Statistics, available at www.stats.gov.cn/tjsj/ndsj/2006/indexeh.htm

Chu, F, M Moser and O Nee (1982) *Commercial, business and trade laws*, Hong Kong: Oceana Publications.

Clarke, D (1995) 'The execution of civil judgments in China', *China Quarterly* no. 141 (March): 70.

—— (1992) 'Regulation and its discontents: Understanding economic law in China', *Stanford Journal of International Law* 28: 283.

—— (1991) 'What's law got to do with it? Legal institutions and economic reform in China', *Journal of Chinese Law* 10: 1.

Crane, G (1994) 'Special things in special ways: National economic identity and China's Special Economic Zones', *The Australian Journal of Chinese Affairs* 32:71–92.

—— (1990) *The political economy of China's special economic zones*, Armonk, NY: ME Sharpe.

Dollar, D (2007) *Poverty, inequality and social disparities during China's economic reform'*, http://china.usc.edu/App_Images//Dollar.pdf

Dunning, J (1997) *Alliance capitalism and global business*, London: Routledge.

Dunning, J and P Narula (2004) *Multinationals and industrial competitiveness*, Cheltenham: Edward Elgar.

Fan, Maureen (2008) 'Hu sees China losing its competitive edge: President cites reduced global demand', *Washington Post Foreign Service*, 1 December 2008, A12.

Far East Economic Review (2009) November, no. 11.

Ferguson, N and Moritz Schularick (2009) 'The end of Chimerica', Harvard Business School Working Paper 10-037.

Gellhorn, W (1987) 'China's quest for legal modernity' *Journal of Chinese Law* 1(1): 1–22.

Gustafsson, B, Li Shi and Terry Sicular (eds) (2008) *Inequality and public policy in China*, Cambridge: Cambridge University Press.

Hu, Zuguang (2008) 'Comparing development of Zhejiang and Jiangsu', Zhejiang Gongshang University, Hangzhou 310018, China, manuscript on file with author.

Investment Guide to Special Zones in China (2006) Hong Kong: CCH, Wolters Kluwer

Jones, D, C Li and A Owen (2003) 'Growth and regional inequality in China during the reform era', *China Economic Review* 14(2): 186–200.

Klein, B (2008) 'How low will Asia go?' *Far East Economic Review*, 23 October, 12.

Krugman, P (2009) 'China needs to spur local demand', *China Daily*, 12 May, 1.

Lam, W (2009) 'Hu Jintao's great leap backward', *Far East Economic Review*, Jan./Feb., 20.

Litwack, J and Y Qian (1998) 'Balanced or unbalanced development: Special economic zones as catalysts for transition' *Journal of Comparative Economics* 26(1): 117–141.

Liu, Peng (1985) 'We must revise our understanding of the open door policy' (*Liaowang*) (*Outlook*) cited in JPRS-CEA-85-038 (18 April) 126–28.

Lubman, S (2006) 'Looking for law in China' *Columbia Journal of Asian Law* 20(1): 11.

Moser, M (1987) Foreign Trade, Investment and the Law in the People's Republic of China, Oxford: Oxford University Press.

Osborne, M (1986) *China's special economic zones*, Geneva: OECD.

Park, J (1997) *The special economic zones of China and their impact on its economic development*, London: Praeger.

Pearson, M (1991) *Joint ventures in the People's Republic of China*, Princeton, NJ: Princeton University Press.

Peerenboom, R (ed.) (2004) Asian discourses of rule of law: Theories and implementation of rule of law in twelve Asian countries, France and the US, London and New York: RoutledgeCurzon.

Pettis, M (2009) 'China's great demand challenge', *Far East Economic Review*, Jan./Feb., 8–13.

Potter, P (2001) *The Chinese legal system: Globalization and local legal culture*, New York: Routledge.

Richardson, B (2004) 'Is East Asia industrializing too quickly? Environmental regulation in its special economic zones', *UCLA Pacific Basin Law Journal* 22(1): 150–244.

—— (2004a) 'Uneven modernisation: Environmental regulation in China's special economic areas', *Asia Pacific Law Review* 12(2): 115.

Shah, A. and Ahunli Shen (2006) *The reform of intergovernmental transfer system to achieve a harmonious society and a level playing field for regional development in China*, World Bank Working Paper 4100.

Sit, V (1985) 'The special economic zones of China: A new type of export processing zone?' *The Developing Economies* 23(1) (March): 68.

Sklair, L (1991) 'Problems of socialist development: The significance of Shenzhen Special Economic Zone for China's open door development strategy' *International Journal of Urban and Regional Research* 15(2) Special Issue: 'Urbanisation in the Hong Kong-South China region', p. 197.

Torres, R (2007) 'Free Zones and the World Trade Organization Agreement on Subsidies and Countervailing Measures' *Global Trade and Customs Journal* 2(5): 217.

USTR (United States Trade Representative) 2006) 'Report to Congress on China's WTO compliance', United States Trade Representative, 11 December 2006, 3, www.cfr.org/publication/15073/report_to_congress_on_chinas_wto_compliance_2006.html

Wesley-Smith, P (1983) *Unequal treaty 1898–1997: China, Great Britain and Hong Kong's New Territories*, Hong Kong: Oxford University Press.

White, G (2003) 'Enter the dragon: Foreign direct investment laws and policies in the PRC' *North Carolina Journal of International Law and Commercial Regulation* 29: 35–58.

White Paper (1984) 26 September, *Joint declaration of the government of the United Kingdom of Great Britain and Northern Ireland and the government of the People's Republic of China in the question of Hong Kong*, London: HMSO.

World Bank (2008) *Special economic zones: Performance, lessons learned, and implications for zone development*, Washington, DC: World Bank Group/ FIAS.

Young, A (2000) 'The razor's edge: Distortions and incremental reform in the People's Republic of China', *Quarterly Journal of Economics* 115(4): 466–84.

5 Special economic zones and improved environmental management in China

Charles Krusekopf

Introduction

Special economic zones (SEZs) have an opportunity to play an important role in improving environmental management practices and conditions in China. Due to their well educated, affluent populations and ties to international firms and markets, SEZs are well positioned to become leaders in environmental fields such as the development of pollution control technologies, green product design, environmental finance and other environmental services. A focus on environmental management offers a double benefit for SEZs, helping to improve the local environment while also supporting economic development plans. The market for environmental services and products is growing rapidly in China and around the world, and a focus on environmental management and services supports the efforts of SEZs to build their knowledge and service base and move away from a reliance on manufacturing. SEZs can support the development of the environmental service industry by setting high local environmental standards, exploring innovative policy approaches, and supporting research and education efforts.

China created SEZs in the 1980s to attract foreign direct investment (FDI) and experiment with new regulatory, legal and institutional structures. The zones were highly successful in attracting investment and promoting economic growth. However, the rapid development of the SEZs created a number of challenges, in particular severe environmental pollution problems in and around the SEZs. The SEZs have taken actions to address pollution and have been cited as leaders in environmental management; however, the scale and complexity of the pollution challenges facing both the SEZs and China have increased with the country's rapid development (Luan et al. 2007; Ministry of Environmental Protection, China, n.d.). China has pledged to improve environmental conditions in the country, including a commitment to reduce carbon emissions per unit of economic output by 40–45 per cent by 2020 from 2005 levels (Jing 2009). New technologies and approaches will be necessary to allow China to achieve its dual goals of economic growth and stronger environmental protection.

Since the original designation of four coastal cities in China as SEZs in the early 1980s, the term 'special economic zone' has been used in a variety of ways to refer to specially designated economic development areas. SEZs have been defined as, 'geographically or juridically bounded areas designated by governments for foreign investment and export-oriented industrialization, to which are conceded favourable investment and trade conditions, and reduced red tape' (Richardson 2004: 4). The definition of an SEZ can be stretched to potentially include thousands of areas across the country; however, this paper focuses its attention on the four original SEZ cities, Shenzhen, Shantou, Zhuhai, and Xiamen, plus Hainan Island, which was named an SEZ in 1984. In its references to these locations, the paper considers the entire city, and not just the actual SEZ, which is a special trade zone within the larger boundaries of the city. The trade zone contains the concentration of industry and foreign investment, but the larger city includes residential and commercial areas that are inevitably linked to the industries within the zone. Efforts are also now underway to expand the trade zones to encompass the entire city boundaries, which would unite the two entities and expand the geographic area where special tax and other incentives are offered (Xinhua 2009a). The original SEZs, in particular Shenzhen and Xiamen, remain among the largest and most developed SEZs in the country, and are often looked to by leaders at the national and local levels for new ideas and innovations. They have also served as models for newer SEZs such as those in Suzhou and Tianjin and several 'green development zones' that have been proposed or developed (RightSite Team 2009).

SEZs have a number of key characteristics that make them good candidates to serve as leading players in developing and demonstrating environmental management improvements. For example, SEZs have strong ties to international companies and countries that have advanced environmental management practices, creating networks that will facilitate the import of technology and know-how. SEZs can become a testing and development ground for new environmental technologies and services, a business field that is expanding rapidly in China and around the world. Internally, there is strong pressure from the residents of SEZs to improve the local environment. The increasingly mobile, educated population of China will seek to locate in cities that have a high quality of life. Environmental conditions are one of the most important issues that people consider when deciding where to live. Knowledge industries, which are not tied to specific geographic locations, often locate in areas with a high concentration of well educated workers. The quality of life in SEZs will play an important role in whether knowledge workers and companies locate in SEZs, as they will help attract knowledge workers and industries, and assist in the development of new market opportunities.

China's central government has emphasized the importance of improving environmental protection for the well-being of its citizens and for the ability to continue to develop rapidly in the future (State Council of China 2006). The Chinese government has stressed that economic growth should not come at the expense of the environment (Hanson and Martin 2006: 3).

However, environmental management in China is largely the responsibility of local and provincial governments, whose primary focus has been on economic growth (Economy 2005: 22; Palmer 2007: 16). Environmental protection bureaus at all levels of government suffer from a lack of resources and authority. For example, China's Ministry of Environmental Protection has substantially fewer personnel and resources than the US EPA, but must oversee more enterprises and a far larger population (Palmer 2007: 211). The primary policy approach in China has been one of command and control, but enforcement of regulations is often lax and penalties for violations are low (Palmer 2007: 232). Despite repeated calls for environmental improvements from the public, government and international observers, pollution levels for many pollutants in China continue to rise and the environment has been severely degraded (Economy 2005: 102; Palmer 2007: 205).

Environmental challenges of SEZs

All Chinese cities, including the SEZs, face serious environmental problems due to their growing and inefficient use of water and power, lack of water treatment, problems in hazardous chemical use and disposal, lack of effective recycling and solid waste management, and deteriorating air quality. Environmental problems in SEZs have worsened, despite the fact that SEZs have often been cited for their advanced environmental management. All four original SEZ cities and Haikou in Hainan have been named 'National Model Cities for Environmental Protection' by the Chinese government (Ministry of Environmental Protection, China, n.d.), and Shenzhen was named to the 'Global 500 Role of Honour' for its environmental protection efforts by the United Nations Environment Program (UNEP) (Luan et al. 2007: 99). Shenzhen, Zhuhai and Haikou have been cited by the Chinese government as having the most advanced environmental infrastructure of any cities in China, and Zhuhai and Haikou were cited as being among the five most 'environmentally friendly' Chinese cities (Qin 2004). Designations as green cities, however, have not prevented serious problems with air and water quality in SEZs.

Despite efforts to follow a sustainable development path, pollution control efforts within SEZs have often been overwhelmed by the scale of development and population growth that occurred, leading to deteriorating environmental conditions. After being named an SEZ, Shenzhen grew from fewer than 100,000 people to a city of more than 10 million, and has experienced an output growth rate of 25 per cent per year from 1979 to 2006 (Luan et al. 2007: 85). Xiamen saw the disposable income of its urban residents increase forty-seven-fold (Starmass Dream Co. 2009). Shenzhen has attracted over $40 billion in foreign investment (North America Representative Office of Shenzhen, PRC, n.d.), and is the leading export centre in the country, handling more than 14 per cent of the nation's trade (Luan et al. 2007: 98). Xiamen has recorded similar growth figures, attracting $20 billion in foreign investment in over 6,000 projects (Xiamen Investment Promotion Agency, n.d.), and Hainan Island has expanded its economy twenty-three-fold since becoming a special economic zone (Xu 2008).

Due to rapid population and economic growth, air quality in Shenzhen has deteriorated over time, with 218 days of severe smog in 2007, three times the number of hazy days recorded in the late 1990s (*Shenzhen Daily* 2007). Shenzhen now has more than 1.3 million vehicles registered, a number growing by 20 per cent per year (*Shenzhen Daily* 2009a). Acid rain caused by increasing nitrogen oxide emissions from power plants and vehicles is now a serious problem in Shenzhen and Zhuhai (Zhan 2008). Shenzhen has experienced 'black rain' events where the rainfall is so acidic it has severely damaged the paint on cars and exteriors of buildings (Shenzhen Information Network Center 2007). Xiamen has also reported worsening air quality due to a growing number of vehicles on the road (WOX News 2008).

In addition to air pollution, SEZs face problems with water pollution and solid waste management. Most sewage in SEZs flows untreated into local streams and rivers creating severe pollution problems. Reports indicate that 73 per cent of the streams in Shenzhen are now heavily polluted, and in 2007 the deputy director of the Shenzhen Municipal Bureau of Water Resources was forced to issue an apology to the citizens of Shenzhen for the city's lack of protection of water resources during the SEZ's rapid economic development (Nisbet 2008). Industry and housing continue to proliferate rapidly in water catchment areas of the city, leading to further degradation of water resources (Ng 2002: 27). Water pollution poses a serious long-term threat to the population, environment and economy in Shenzhen because the city must rely on local streams for drinking water. Solid waste problems also exist, with less than 10 per cent of Shenzhen's solid waste handled properly due to a severe shortage of properly run landfills or other disposal options (Ng 2002: 26). The Shantou region, one of the first SEZ areas, has become the world's largest centre of electronics waste recycling and disposal. Despite international scrutiny, electronics recycling in Shantou is largely unregulated, and has created severe heavy metal pollution of the soil and water and other environmental and health problems (Puckett et al. 2002: 15).

The water, air and land pollution in SEZs initially came from industry and growing populations within the SEZs themselves. In recent years, however, the sources of pollution have grown as the regions around SEZs develop. Shenzhen, for example, is in the midst of the rapidly developing Pearl River Delta, one of the most heavily industrialized and fastest growing areas of the country. The bulk of air and water emissions that impact Shenzhen now come from areas outside the control of the SEZ. In 2008, Shenzhen mayor Xu Zongcheng summed up the challenge by saying, 'Shenzhen has done a lot to improve air quality. But the problem needs more efforts by every [Pearl River] Delta city since we are mutually affected. When everybody adds fuel, the flames rise high.' (*Shenzhen Daily* 2008a). This situation points to the need for coordination between the SEZs and surrounding areas in pollution control efforts.

New efforts at cooperation among jurisdictions in areas such as transportation infrastructure, urban planning and environmental protection have been announced (Ji 2009). However, in the past, regional efforts to coordinate pollution control have foundered due to China's system of local government autonomy and control over the enforcement of pollution standards (Economy 2004: 109). Areas outside SEZs often encourage polluting industries to locate in their jurisdictions to promote local economic development (Yanfeng 2009). Many highly polluting firms now locate in areas outside the SEZs, creating a doughnut effect. Highly polluting industries locate in a ring around SEZs, avoiding the tighter SEZ restrictions, but remaining close enough to take advantage of the knowledge base and infrastructure in SEZs. This phenomena reduces the amount of pollution directly emitted within SEZ boundaries, but increases regional pollution output.

SEZs have directly and indirectly promoted this process by blocking the construction of new manufacturing facilities and encouraging the relocation of heavy polluters out of the SEZs and into nearby regions (Economy 2004: 120; *Shenzhen Daily* 2009b). SEZs have supported these policies to reduce pollution levels within the core urban area and to promote a shift up the production chain among firms in the SEZs. The goal is for firms remaining in the SEZs to focus on cleaner aspects of the production process, such as product design and marketing, while most raw material processing and manufacturing moves outside the central SEZ areas. Several high-profile examples of this process have been highlighted in the Chinese press, such as a proposal to construct a petrochemical plant producing paraxylene (PX) in Xiamen. Construction of the plant in Xiamen was blocked after widespread public protest. However, the site of the plant was then relocated to Zhangzhou, a city 100 kilometres from Xiamen, and construction of the plant has begun (Yanfeng 2009). The Xiamen protests have been heralded as the most successful example of public environmental action in China (Bristow 2008), but in the end only resulted in the relocation of the plant and not an overall reduction in the amount of pollution produced. A similar case occurred in Guangdong province, where public protests forced the relocation of a proposed petrochemical plant to be built by Sinopec and Kuwait Petroleum away from the city of Guangzhou to another part of the Pearl River Delta (ibid.).

A leadership role for SEZs

The regional nature of pollution problems highlights the need for SEZs to become not only models, but leaders in sustainable development. A leadership role will require SEZs to pioneer new environmental management policies and play an active role in ensuring that effective environmental programmes are adopted throughout the country. Environmental leadership will benefit SEZs by giving them a knowledge base and head start in developing and implementing emerging environmental technologies and policies, and allow SEZs to shape environmental policies for other jurisdictions and the nation.

A role model for the SEZs in this effort is California in the United States, which often adopts tighter environmental standards and new policies before the rest of the United States. David Vogel (1995) coined the term 'California effect' to describe how sub-national jurisdictions pioneering tighter environmental regulations can lead to a wider adoption of the policy. For example, California has been a national and international leader in setting automobile and other air emission standards, and has now created a low-carbon fuel standard that is being copied by other states (Kahn 2009).

SEZs have the opportunity in China to play a role similar to California by setting high environmental standards and serving as a testing ground for new environmental policies and technologies. Becoming a 'first adopter' of new anti-pollution measures will encourage local firms to develop innovative technologies and ideas, and allow firms to gain experience operating under higher pollution standards. SEZ firms and governments will be able to help shape the pollution policies adopted in other areas, offering SEZ firms an advantage in the marketplace. Several characteristics of the population of SEZs and firms operating there support this environmental leadership role for SEZs. For example, SEZs have relatively high income and education levels, their economies are open to foreign investment and trade, their pollution infrastructure is currently undergoing rapid development, and they are open to experimentation in regulations and policies. The sections below discuss these characteristics in more depth, and outline policy recommendations that SEZs can implement to support the development of an environmental industry.

High income and education levels support environmental policies

People living in SEZs are relatively affluent and well educated; thus they make higher demands for environmental quality and are willing and able to pay for environmental improvements. Studies have shown that the demand for environmental protection has high income elasticity, meaning that the demand for environmental protection rises rapidly as incomes rise (Copeland and Taylor 2004: 61). Elizabeth Economy found that the Chinese cities with the most advanced pollution control systems all have per capita GDP figures above national averages (Economy 2005: 111). Education opportunities and levels of educational attainment in China are closely linked to the income levels of residents (Qian and Smyth 2005: 4). Due to their open economic climate, rapid growth and concentration of foreign-invested enterprises, SEZs have attracted a large number of highly educated workers.

At low incomes, people are focused on providing for basic needs, such as housing and food, but as incomes rise, people begin to focus on improving their level of comfort, health and education. With increasing affluence, the public becomes more informed and concerned about water and air quality and other environmental conditions, and is willing to pay for pollution control measures to improve the environment. This effect is described and tested in the economics literature in the context of what are known as 'environmental Kuznet's curves' (EKCs). EKCs display an inverted U-shaped relationship between environmental degradation and income, where pollution levels fall as incomes rise beyond a certain level. In early stages of development, increased output leads to higher levels of pollution, but after a certain level of income is reached, pollution levels begin to fall even as output continues to rise, due to increased regulation and spending on pollution controls (Grossman and Krueger 1995: 370).

A number of studies have examined EKCs in countries around the world. Most studies find evidence that EKCs exist, with pollution levels rising for many air and water pollutants at income levels below \$5,000–8,000, and falling pollution concentrations at income levels above this threshold level (Dasgupta et al. 2002: 147; Grossman and Krueger 1995: 370). China as a whole in 2008 had a per capita income estimated at \$6,000 in purchasing power parity (PPP) terms (\$2,400 at official exchange rates) (Central Intelligence Agency 2009). SEZs have income levels substantially above this level, with Shenzhen reportedly recording per capita GDP of approximately PPP\$22,000 in 2007 (\$11,600 at official exchange rates), Xiamen at PPP\$15,600 and Zhuhai at PPP\$17,000 (Cox 2009). Haikou at PPP\$7400 and Shantou at PPP\$4700 are also reaching the stage where Kuznet's curves tend to bottom out and reductions in pollution begin to occur (Cox 2009). SEZs overall have some of the highest income levels of any cities in China, but income levels have been increasing across the country. As the economy grows, more and more Chinese cities, townships and rural areas will reach income levels that promote environmental protection efforts.

Empirical studies of EKCs have been conducted in China. Using data from 1989–2003, Liu et al. (2006: 566) showed that water pollution levels in all but one river in Shenzhen followed a classic EKC pattern for industrial sources, indicating falling concentrations of industrial pollutants. However, pollution from untreated residential sewage rose during this period, largely due to rapid population growth and a lag in the construction of sewage treatment facilities. Zheng et al. (2009: 20) found through a study of two key air pollution measures in thirty-five major Chinese cities, particulate and sulphur dioxide levels, that air pollution displayed classic EKC characteristics and began to fall once cities reached a per capita GDP of approximately \$2,300 at official exchange rates. All SEZs have now reached this level of per capita GDP and can be expected to experience falling levels of certain pollutants, as predicted by EKCs. EKCs, however, do not necessarily hold for all pollutants. Carbon dioxide and other greenhouse gases, for example, have continued to rise in most countries irrespective of the level of income.

Researchers cite several reasons for the EKC process, including growing environmental awareness among more affluent, better educated citizens, pressures placed on government to more tightly regulate pollution, a willingness by individuals to pay more for goods that have a lower environmental impact, and the availability of government and private funds to pay for pollution controls and environmental infrastructure (Kahn 2006: 31). Governments in SEZs have utilized their growing tax revenues to develop infrastructure such as subways, dedicated bus lines, water and sewage treatment facilities, recycling systems and waste disposal. Xiamen has pioneered an 'air corridor' of elevated bus lines throughout the city (*People's Daily Online*, 2009), Haikou has invested in projects such as waste-water treatment plants (Xu 2008), and Shenzhen has greatly expanded its subway system and bus systems (Luan et al. 2007: 105). Shenzhen was the first city in China to adopt comprehensive recycling legislation (HKTDC 2006), and Haikou plans to invest over $500 million to develop renewable energy sources (Xu 2008).

As incomes rise, the Chinese public is growing increasingly assertive with regard to environmental complaints. The Chinese and foreign press have noted a sharp rise in the number of complaints about pollution problems coming in to government hotlines, and a growing number of public protests related to pollution issues. In 2005, there were reportedly 50,000 environment-related riots, protests and disputes in China, an increase of 30 per cent from the year before (Magnier 2006). Chinese government officials receive hundreds of thousands of letters of complaint about environmental issues each year, and calls to telephone hotlines have been growing rapidly (Economy 2005: 116). Chinese cities with high income levels have much higher levels of public complaints about environmental issues due to higher levels of environmental education and awareness among the population (Economy 2004: 118). Public complaints play a key role in environmental enforcement in China, with most environmental enforcement actions coming as a result of public complaint (Economy 2005: 116).

The media in particular have played a key role in educating the public about environmental issues and putting pressure on companies and the government to address pollution problems (Economy 2005: 163). The media are increasingly willing to challenge government and corporate claims that environmental problems have been adequately addressed. While still small, the number and importance of environmental NGOs has also been increasing (Palmer 2007: 212). The Xiamen protests against the PX chemical plant were widely covered in the Chinese press, and were cited as one of the first environmental movements in China to use social media such as text messaging and the internet to rally the emerging Chinese middle class to oppose a major economic development project on environmental grounds. Many middle-class Xiamen residents cited fears about the property values of their homes among the reasons for opposing the plant (Bristow 2008). Similar protests occurred later in Guangzhou, where citizens rallied against a petrochemical complex, and in Shanghai, where residents opposed the construction of a high-speed magnetic rail line through a middle-class part of town (Yanfeng 2009).

The relative affluence and education level of people living in Chinese SEZs also provides an opportunity for improvements in environmental quality due to an increased demand for environmental products. An affluent and educated population is both willing and able to pay for goods that meet higher environmental standards in their production and use. People with more education are more likely to purchase products and services that have greater environmental benefits because they are more concerned about environmental conditions (Kahn 2006: 51). Studies have shown that Chinese consumers are becoming increasingly concerned about the characteristics of the products they buy, and are joining in the 'green' product revolution. The Boston Consulting Group found that Chinese consumers associated environmentally friendly products with high quality, and a majority were willing to pay a premium price for such products (Manget et al. 2009: 15, 17). The overall market for environmentally friendly products has been growing rapidly in China (Poon 2004). Due to their relatively affluent and well educated citizenry, SEZs can be expected to play a pioneer role in the development of green product markets in China. This offers an opportunity for firms in SEZ areas to become leaders in the production, marketing and sales of green products, a market that will expand rapidly as incomes increase across China.

The role of foreign investment and trade in fostering environmental management

A second characteristic of SEZs that supports their environmental leadership is their openness to foreign investment and deep involvement in international trade. For example, more than 75 per cent of the investment capital in Shenzhen comes from outside mainland China, and more than half of all goods manufactured in Shenzhen are exported (Ng 2003: 26). Researchers have found that foreign-invested firms in China have much lower pollution emission levels than domestic firms because they utilize advanced pollution control technology and techniques (Christmann and Taylor 2001; Zeng and Eastin 2007). Studies have also found spillover improvements in environmental conditions from foreign investment as advanced pollution control technologies and knowledge of environmental management systems diffuse from foreign firms to local firms and governments (Shin 2004; Zeng and Eastin 2007; Zhang et al. 2008). For a number of pollutants, emissions levels have actually fallen over time even as production has increased, due in part to the growing share of output from foreign-invested firms that utilize advanced environmental management techniques (Dean et al. 2009; He 2006; Liu, et al. 2007; Zheng et al. 2009).

These findings in China contradict the views of many globalization opponents, who fear that a primary motivating factor for investment abroad by firms from developed countries is a desire to avoid stringent pollution regulations in their home countries (Christmann and Taylor 2001: 439; Zeng and Eastin 2007: 971). Observers have been concerned that developing countries would lower environmental standards in an effort to attract foreign investment, an effect known as the 'race to the bottom' or 'pollution haven hypothesis' (Copeland and Taylor 2004: 67; Richardson 2004: 17). However, in China, studies have shown that the areas such as SEZs that are most open to trade and foreign investment have the most stringent pollution regulations and the most advanced environmental management systems and institutions (Shin 2004: 290; Zeng and Eastin 2007: 971). Rather than lowering environmental standards, multinational companies have played an important role in improving environmental management and technology in China (Christmann and Taylor 2001: 439).

Studies have highlighted a number of specific mechanisms through which trade and foreign investment raise local environmental standards in China and other countries (Angel and Rock 2005; Christmann and Taylor 2001; Shin 2004; Zeng and Eastin 2007). Multinational companies from developed countries face relatively strict environmental regulations and enforcement, and therefore have experience in utilizing advanced manufacturing technology and management techniques. To achieve managerial and operational efficiencies, they employ identical or similar technologies in all the facilities they operate no matter where they are located (Christmann and Taylor 2001: 446). An interesting example of these phenomena in China was found by Dean et al. (2009) in a study that examined foreign investment in China by firms in industries with high pollution potential. The study found that firms from Western countries were not deterred from investing in areas with high environmental standards because they had experience in utilizing advanced pollution controls in their home countries, and employed these technologies in China. However, firms from countries with lower environmental standards, such as Taiwan, tended to avoid investing in Chinese areas with high standards because they lacked experience with advanced pollution control technologies.

The standardization of environmental standards by firms across all their manufacturing facilities is encouraged because many firms now operate global production networks that allow them to produce products at any facility worldwide and ship these products to worldwide markets (Angel and Rock 2005: 1907). By setting firm-wide environmental standards equal to or greater than the most stringent standards in any of the firm's markets, a company can achieve efficient use of its resources through maximum flexibility in production and distribution. The firm also reduces operational costs through economies of scale by standardizing production processes and permitting the movement of personnel throughout the company. Firms have experienced 'dynamic learning economies' through standardization that permit faster innovation and improved efficiencies (Angel and Rock 2005: 1908). Overall, the benefits of flexibility and standardization are worth more to a firm than the additional costs they encounter by setting internal pollution standards above local standards.

Firms operating in global markets also face a number of external factors that encourage them to uphold high environmental standards, such as a desire to maintain their 'reputational capital' and regulatory standards in markets where products are sold (Angel and Rock 2005: 1908; Christmann and Taylor 2001: 446). Firms face regular scrutiny of their global operations by shareholders, NGOs, institutional investors, banks, insurance companies, ratings agencies, and other stakeholders. While such scrutiny in the past has been largely focused on labour conditions, the environmental impacts of company operations are now being more closely examined. In response, many large international firms have sought to improve their worldwide environmental performance by adopting corporate social responsibility guidelines and reporting that include environmental measures and by implementing certified environmental management systems (EMS) such as ISO standards. Many international firms, including General Motors, Ford, Motorola, and Hewlett Packard require both company-owned facilities and those run by their suppliers to adopt EMS systems and meet strict environmental standards, even when those standards exceed local requirements (Ariuma et al. 2008: 282; Christmann and Taylor 2001: 455). Retailers have adopted similar measures, including Walmart, the world's largest retailer, which has launched a 'Global Responsible Sourcing Initiative' that requires its suppliers to increase energy efficiency by 20 per cent and prove that they meet or exceed all required environmental standards (Walmart 2008). China was the first country where Walmart implemented this policy, reflecting the importance of Chinese manufacturers in Walmart's supply chain.

Several studies have found that corporate standards have played an important role in improving the environmental performance of firms in China (Christmann and Taylor 2001; Zhang et al. 2008). One visible sign of the role international corporations have played in improving production standards in China is the growing adoption by Chinese firms of voluntary international environmental standards, such as the ISO 14000 standards. Research has shown that international firms and Chinese firms that export to developed country markets were the primary early adopters of ISO 14001 in China (Christmann and Taylor 2001). Several international firms, such as Ford, have mandated ISO 14000 certifications for all company-owned manufacturing facilities worldwide (Angel and Rock 2005). Local suppliers of multinational firms and local firms that want to export products are encouraged to adopt international standards to qualify themselves for the international market (Angel and Rock 2005). As its international trade has grown, China has seen an exponential growth in the number of firms with ISO 14001 certification, from fewer than 100 in 1999 to more than 30,000 in 2007 (ACNielsen 2007: 27). China now has the largest number of facilities with ISO 14001 certification of any country in the world, more than five times the number in the United States (ibid.: 10).

Trade policies and a growing level of end-market product regulation have also played a role in pushing international firms in China to improve their environmental performance and in pushing the Chinese government to raise its environmental standards. Companies operating in developing countries fear the loss of international markets if production practices or local environmental standards are below global standards. Export-oriented companies in China were the earliest adopters of ISO standards, and environmental protection in China is strongest in cities and provinces with a strong focus on exports (Christmann and Taylor 2001: 439; Zeng and Eastin 2007: 971). Environmental issues have become an important part of international trade treaties and discussions, as evidenced by a focus on the environment by the World Trade Organization (WTO, n.d.), measures such as the North American Agreement on Environmental Cooperation – a side agreement that was negotiated between the US, Mexico and Canada in conjunction with the creation of the North American Free Trade Area (NAFTA) (Foreign Affairs and International Trade Canada, n.d.) – and a strong emphasis on environmental issues by the US Trade Representative's Office within the Obama administration (USTR, n.d.). Trade regulations related to environmental standards can be expected to become more prevalent in the future as countries seek to ensure that domestic firms are not disadvantaged when they adopt new environmental rules. For example, China has been highlighted as a potential target for trade sanctions by the USA due to its growing greenhouse gas emissions (Hitt and Power 2009). Legislation that has passed the US House of Representatives and is now being considered by the US Senate permits the USA to restrict imports from countries, such as China, that do not have greenhouse gas emissions reduction policies in place that are as strict as the proposed US programme (Hitt and Power 2009).

Restrictions on the sales of products that contain hazardous or environmentally damaging materials are also influencing the environmental practices of global firms operating in China. For example, the European Union has adopted requirements restricting the amounts of certain hazardous substances in electronics equipment and requiring that such equipment be recyclable (Angel and Rock 2005: 1908). These measures restrict the import of products that are produced through environmentally harmful processes, and therefore require export oriented firms in China to reduce the environmental impact of their production practices. These efforts are also encouraged by international environmental treaties and agreements, such as the Basel Convention on the Trans-boundary Movements of Hazardous Wastes and their Disposal and the Stockholm Convention on Persistent Organic Pollutants, which establish global environmental standards for international companies that operate in countries, such as China, that have signed the agreements (Basel Convention, n.d.; Stockholm Convention, n.d.).

Chinese SEZs are well positioned to become the centers of environmental management within China due to their strong international links through investment and trade. SEZ firms and governments have a good understanding of the techniques and technologies necessary to meet the strict environmental standards found in Europe, North America and other advanced markets. As pollution regulations across China tighten and the demand for pollution control technologies and products grows, SEZ firms are well positioned to play a leading role in the Chinese market for environmental services and products, which is estimated to be worth \$112 billion in 2010, with a growth rate of over 15 percent per year (Xinhua 2006). The following section outlines several recommendations for policies and actions SEZs might take to address the environmental problems they face, while also promoting their continued economic development.

Recommendations

The growing Chinese and international market for environmental services and products offers SEZs an opportunity to achieve the double benefit of improved environmental conditions together with expanded economic opportunities. SEZs in China have been seeking to move up the production chain by emphasizing the development of knowledge industries over commodity production. In the environmental field, SEZs can achieve this goal by focusing on the technology and service side of environmental management, rather than on the mass manufacturing of environmental products such as solar panels. SEZs are well positioned to become leaders in environmental-related fields such as research on environmental products, product design, environmental finance and environmental services such as energy management. The development and enforcement of innovative, strong environmental standards in SEZs can help create a market and training ground for entrepreneurs and firms in environmental management, while also creating better living conditions that will help attract a well educated, affluent workforce. This chapter offers five recommendations that will support efforts by SEZs to become leaders in the knowledge side of the environmental management field.

First, SEZs can raise and strictly enforce local environmental standards and technology requirements to encourage the development of an environmental industry. Setting high environmental standards will force local firms to develop and adopt advanced pollution control technology and will support other environmental initiatives. While high standards will impose a cost on local firms, it will also allow local firms to develop expertise that may result in new market opportunities domestically and abroad. Goods coming from firms in the SEZs would meet global standards opening new markets, and SEZ firms might be able to sell the pollution control technologies they develop to other firms both domestically and internationally. Experience in other East Asian countries has shown that these efforts can be enhanced by integrating environmental policies together with industrial development and foreign investment policies (Rock and Angel 2007: 19). For example, SEZs could encourage the import and utilization of advanced technologies by requiring that firms wishing to build facilities in the zones utilize the most advanced pollution control technology available. The new technologies would be expected to influence national standards and have a significant spillover effect by demonstrating best practices and encouraging domestic innovation (Cheung and Lin 2004). Firms operating in the SEZs would benefit by being early adopters and gaining experience with new technologies ahead of firms in other parts of the country, creating opportunities for SEZ firms to market their expertise and equipment.

SEZs can support the development of new pollution control technologies through support for research and development efforts. Shenzhen is a recognized leader in research and development in China, in particular applied commercial research. Shenzhen spends 3.4 per cent of its GDP on research and development activities, much higher than the national average of 1.4 per cent (*Nature* 2007: 3). Corporations lead research and development in Shenzhen in contrast with research efforts in other Chinese cities that are led by government organizations and universities (Chen and Kenney 2007: 1069). Shenzhen-based corporations lead the country in research activities, with six of the top ten domestic enterprises applying for patents based in the city (State Intellectual Property Office of the PRC 2009: 41). The direct sponsorship of research by corporations will help companies develop technologies that reduce environmental impacts. Shenzhen has supported the research efforts of local corporations by building a university town that combines corporate research and a university area where top national universities, such as Peking University and Tsinghua University, offer postgraduate degrees in science and technology fields through satellite campuses in Shenzhen (Cyranoski 2007: 503). Shenzhen has also created a 'virtual university park' that houses a business incubator and where domestic and international schools offer a variety of continuing education and degree programmes (Cyranoski 2007: 503). SEZs can support the development of environmental technologies and expertise by helping to fund research efforts by universities and companies located in SEZ areas, and by encouraging the use of these technologies by local businesses through subsidies and the design of pollution control policies.

Second, SEZ governments can encourage companies to adopt EMS and other internal policies to reduce environmental impacts. Adoption of EMS, such as ISO 14001, has been shown to improve the environmental performance of companies in China because these systems encourage continuous efforts by companies to reduce the amount of hazardous inputs used and the amount of waste produced (Christmann and Taylor 2001; Zhang et al. 2008). Studies have shown that governments can speed up the adoption of EMS by adopting and enforcing high environmental standards, supporting education and training efforts for company management and personnel so they become familiar with the operation and advantages of EMS, offering tax advantages or subsidies to firms that adopt EMS, or by reducing the frequency of regulatory visits and requirements for companies with effective EMS (Ariuma et al. 2008: 287). SEZs have high adoption rates for EMS because of the international focus of many firms located there, providing a strong base of expertise. A number of firms based in SEZs offer EMS consulting services, and SEZs can encourage the further development of this field by supporting the development of EMS education programmes at local technical schools and universities, and actively working with the central government and other jurisdictions to expand the adoption of EMS in China.

Third, SEZs can become leaders in the design and production of 'green' goods for the Chinese domestic market and for export. Demand for environmentally friendly products is growing in China and around the world, creating market opportunities for products produced in environmentally friendly ways. International markets for environmental goods produced in SEZs may also be given a boost through talks on the elimination of tariffs and other barriers to trade in environmental goods that have been held between China, the EU and the United States in conjunction with the Copenhagen Climate Conference (International Center for Trade and Sustainable Development 2009). SEZs are well positioned to play a key role in the development, production and marketing of green goods. Shenzhen was the first Chinese city to adopt laws requiring companies to take back products at the end of their life cycle, forcing local firms to redesign and rethink their products (HKTDC 2006). Efforts at improving product design in Shenzhen have been supported by the city's growing design industry. Shenzhen is home to more than 6,000 design companies with 60,000 designers, and has been named a UNESCO 'City of Design' (Shenzhen Daily 2008b). This large base of designers can assist local manufacturing firms wanting to design and market green products for markets in China and abroad. China recently adopted a recycling law similar to the one that has been in place in Shenzhen, opening additional opportunities for green product design and sales across China (Xinhua 2008).

Fourth, SEZs can play a leading role in the development of environmental infrastructure in China. China has a poorly developed, but rapidly expanding, environmental infrastructure for drinking water supply, sewage treatment, solid waste disposal and public transportation. More than 400 cities in China face severe water shortages, a problem exacerbated by the low level of sewage treatment, which leads to severe pollution of streams and lakes (Zhang et al. 2007: 284). The water treatment rate in Chinese cities is estimated to be below 60 per cent, and China is expected to spend well over $100 billion on water and wastewater projects in the next five years, on top of the more than $75 billion spent in the past five years (Dasgupta 2009). The public transportation infrastructure in China is also undergoing rapid expansion, creating a market worth several hundred billion dollars. For example, $248 billion is expected to be spent on railroad expansion through the economic stimulus package announced by the Chinese government in 2008, and numerous Chinese cities are building or planning new subway systems (Bradsher 2009; Tschang 2008). China's growing economy has created a solid waste crisis as the volume of waste grows but fewer sites are available for landfills (Huang et al. 2006).

SEZs in China have a relatively well developed environmental infrastructure, which has given SEZ firms and governments experience planning, building and financing environmental infrastructure projects. One growing field in which SEZs have taken the lead is in private financing initiatives for environmental infrastructure, including build operate and transfer projects (BOT) and build operate and own projects (BOO). Because China's environmental infrastructure needs are so great, a large amount of private financing will be necessary to finance the construction of water projects, transportation projects and solid waste management facilities. Shenzhen was the first Chinese city to combine its water and sewage services into one entity and turn these services over to a private company, the Shenzhen Water Group (Zhong et al. 2008). The Shenzhen government helped create and support the firm by passing the necessary supporting regulation, allowing water and sewage rates paid by customers to rise, and offering tax and other incentives (Kitakyushu Initiative for a Clean Environment: Successful and Transferrable Practices, n.d.). The Shenzhen Water Group is partly owned by the French firm Veolia, and is the largest water and wastewater operator in China, with over forty-nine water plants in seventeen cities across seven provinces (Globalization Monitor, n.d.). Shenzhen is now extending the privatization concept to other fields, such as solid waste management, with Shenzhen-based firms now operating waste-to-energy plants and handling solid waste incineration and disposal in Shenzhen and other Chinese cities (Kitakyushu Initiative for a Clean Environment: Successful and Transferrable Practices, n.d.).

SEZ governments can support the development of environmental infrastructure firms by creating opportunities for privatization or public-private partnerships in the development of their own environmental infrastructure, by offering incentives to domestic and international firms to set up headquarters or operational centres in SEZs, and by supporting education programmes. SEZs can also help support the development of innovative infrastructure projects. For example, because of its extreme shortage of water, Shenzhen has developed a plan for a sustainable urban sewerage system (SUSS) that treats sewage as a potential source of resources to be recovered, including water for reuse in industrial and agricultural applications, heat and bio-solids that can be used to produce energy or fertilizer, and other resources (Zhang et al. 2007: 286). Shenzhen has also explored opportunities for bio-remediation of sewage, a growing field worldwide (Yang, 2008). The development of these projects in SEZs provides companies operating there a testing ground for new ideas, and the experience necessary to develop similar projects in other cities.

Finally, SEZs can become the knowledge and finance centres for emerging environmental priorities in China, such as energy efficiency, alternative energy production and carbon credits. The Chinese government has pledged to reduce the greenhouse gas intensity of production by 40–45 per cent by 2020 from 2005 levels, a goal that will require the widespread adoption of energy efficiency improvements, alternative energy sources and policies such as cap-and-trade markets for carbon emissions to meet that goal (Jing 2009). SEZs can play an important role as centres of knowledge and finance to support these environmental goals.

Chinese industry and housing are relatively energy-inefficient, and the potential for clean energy development is high. Rates of returns on investment in energy efficiency projects in China often exceed 50 per cent per year; however, several bottlenecks, such as financing constraints, regulatory restrictions and a lack of technical expertise, have hindered the development of energy efficiency and alternative power projects in China (Chandler and Gwin 2008: 9). SEZs can utilize their international links and strengths in fostering the development of new enterprises to become centres of these emerging industries. Two areas of particular focus include fostering the development of energy service companies (ESCOs) and the related development of financial expertise in alternative energy and energy efficiency.

ESCOs are companies that help to identify opportunities for energy efficiency in companies or buildings, and then often finance and implement energy saving projects. A typical model for ESCO operation is for an ESCO to reach an agreement with a company or government to reduce energy costs organization-wide or in a particular facility, in exchange for a share of the savings generated. ESCO operations in the United States have grown rapidly in recent years, producing $5.6 billion in revenue in 2009, a figure expected to grow by 25 per cent per year over the next decade (Pike Research 2010). ESCO operations in China have been modest, less than $50 million in 2001 (Vine 2005). Similar problems have faced alternative energy companies, who have difficulties acquiring finance to put projects into operation and face regulatory burdens, such as high tax rates and difficulties qualifying projects for eligibility for potential revenue from carbon credit schemes such as the Kyoto Protocol's Clean Development Mechanism (CDM) (Chandler and Gwin 2008: 15).

SEZs can support energy efficiency goals through the development of ESCOs and environmental finance. SEZs can serve as testing grounds for energy efficiency and alternative power by raising energy prices locally through a carbon tax or other means, through regulations that require new buildings in SEZs to meet high energy efficiency standards, and by providing subsidies, tax breaks and other incentives to promote energy efficiency improvements and alternative power use in existing offices, housing and manufacturing facilities. SEZ governments can support education and research efforts in local technical schools and universities to create the personnel and ideas necessary to improve energy efficiency and develop alternative clean energy sources. These policies would create a local market for energy efficiency expertise, and generate knowledge that can be transferred to other jurisdictions.

SEZs can also play a very important role in developing the financial infrastructure necessary to support energy efficiency and alternative efforts. SEZs have a great deal of experience in supporting new, innovative firms by offering a dynamic business environment and access to capital and services not available in other Chinese cities. For example, it is estimated that over one third of all venture capital in China is concentrated in Shenzhen, and the Shenzhen Stock Exchange is focused on small and medium-sized enterprises (Guo and Feng 2007: 9). Two recent funds in China have helped highlight opportunities in this field, one a loan guarantee programme for energy efficiency projects run by the IFC, and a broader Environment Industry Fund established by the China General Technology Investment Fund Management Corp. (Chandler and Gwin 2008: 11; Xinhua 2009b). SEZs can build on these successful models and tap into foreign pools of capital and expertise that can support energy efficiency efforts. SEZ governments can assist the development of financing for energy efficiency by working with private firms to educate bankers and other financial professionals to gain a better understanding of environmental finance opportunities and innovative ways to structure projects.

SEZs also have an opportunity to play a leading role in the creation of carbon markets in China. China has committed to an ambitious goal of reducing carbon emissions intensity by over 40 per cent by 2020, and is under pressure from the United States and other countries to develop firm targets and programmes to reduce carbon emissions. One policy that has gained prominence worldwide for addressing carbon emissions is a system of pollution permits known as a 'cap-and-trade' emissions system. Under this system, large carbon emitters are issued permits that allow a certain amount of carbon emissions. If firm emissions are higher than the number of emissions permits held, the firms must purchase emissions credits from other firms. The European Union has adopted a cap-and-trade system for major carbon emitters, and the USA is considering adopting a similar system. Cap-and-trade emissions systems have been explored in China, but have yet to be adopted (Morgenstern et al. 2005). China has played an important role in international climate markets firms through the Clean Development Mechanism (CDM) of the Kyoto Protocol, and it is expected that China will play an important role in worldwide systems of carbon credits and carbon markets in the future.

Implementing a cap-and-trade system requires an infrastructure of professionals who can measure and verify the carbon emissions of firms, estimate reductions of emissions based on actions taken by firms, certify emissions reductions, develop contracts for emission credit transactions, and help finance arrangements. SEZs have the opportunity to become the centres of carbon finance in China by supporting the development of carbon markets and the personnel necessary for market operation. This can be done through the development of local, trial carbon markets in SEZ areas, and support for education programmes at universities and technical schools. By creating smaller markets at a local level, and encouraging local firms to participate in Clean Development Mechanism trades, SEZs can position themselves to play a central role in future carbon markets in China.

Conclusion

SEZs have an opportunity to replicate the role they played in the development of foreign investment and trade in China in the field of environmental management. A focus on the technology and service side of environmental management will support the economic transition of SEZs from manufacturing centres to centres of knowledge and finance. The experience and culture in SEZs that promotes entrepreneurship and innovation positions them well to lead efforts to research and develop environmental products, find new and innovative ways to design and market environmentally friendly products, and finance environmental infrastructure in areas such as water and wastewater treatment, transportation, and energy efficiency. China faces severe pollution problems, and both the Chinese government and Chinese public support the development of policies and technologies that can help improve environmental conditions. SEZs can utilize their international ties and the increasing capabilities of domestic firms and researchers to develop innovative policies and technologies that will allow China to achieve both improvements in environmental conditions and continued economic growth and development.

Bibliography

ACNielsen (2007) *The ISO Survey – 2007*, Retrieved 1 September 2009, from www.iso.org: www.iso.org/iso/survey2007.pdf

Angel, D and Rock, M (2005) 'Global standards and the environmental performance of industry', *Environment and Planning* A37: 1903–18.

Arimura, T, Hibiki, A and Katayama, H (2008) 'Is a voluntary approach an effective environmental policy instrument? A case for environmental management systems', *Journal of Environmental Economics and Management* 55(3): 281–95.

Basel Convention. (n.d.). *Basel Convention on the Transboundary Movements of Hazardous Wastes and their Disposal*, retrieved 14 January 2009, from www.basel.int/index.html

Bradsher, K (2009, March 26) 'Clash of subways and car culture in Chinese cities', *New York Times*, retrieved 14 January 2010, from: www.nytimes.com/2009/03/27/business/worldbusiness/27transit.html

Bristow, M (2008, January 22) 'China's rising people power', *BBC News*, retrieved 15 December 2009 from: http://news.bbc.co.uk/2/hi/asia-pacific/7195434.stm

Central Intelligence Agency (2009) *World Factbook: China*, retrieved 14 September, 2009, from: https://www.cia.gov/library/publications/the-world-factbook/geos/ch.html

Chandler, W and Gwin, H (2008) *Financing energy efficiency in China*, Washington, DC: Carnegie Endowment for International Peace.

Chen, K and Kenney, M (2007) 'Universities/research institutes and regional innovation systems: The cases of Beijing and Shenzhen', *World Development* 35(6): 1056–74.

Cheung, KY and Lin, P (2004) 'Spillover effects of FDI on innovation in China: Evidence from the provincial data', *China Economic Review* 15(1): 25–44.

China Digital Times. (n.d.). *Xiamen PX*. Retrieved 26 August 2009 from: www.chinadigitaltimes.net/china/xiamen-px/

Christmann, P and Taylor, M (2001) 'Globalization and the environment: Determinants of firm self-regulation in China', *Journal of International Business Studies* 32(3): 439–58.

Copeland, B, and Scott Taylor, M (2004) 'Trade, growth and the environment', *Journal of Economic Literature* 42(1): 7–71.

Cox, W (2009, September 3) *China's metropolitan regions: Moving toward high income status.* Retrieved 14 September, 2009 from: www.newgeography.com/content/001007-china%E2%80%99s-metropolitan-regions-moving-toward-high-income-status

Cyranoski, R (2007, September 27) 'Enter the dragon', *Nature* 449(7161): 502–4.

Dasgupta, R (2009, December 21) 'Rising water shortage stimulates growth for water recycling and desalinization in China', Retrieved 15 January 2010, from: www.frost.com/prod/servlet/market-insight-top.pag?Src=RSS&docid=188065151

Dasgupta, S, Laplante, B, Wang, H and Wheeler, D (2002) 'Confronting the environmental Kuznets curve', *Journal of Economic Perspectives* 16(1): 147–68.

Dean, J, Lovely, M and Wang, H (2009) 'Are foreign investors attracted to weak environmental regulations? Evaluating the evidence from China', *Journal of Development Economics* 90: 1–13.

Economy, EC (2005) 'Environmental enforcement in China', in KA Day, *China's environment*, 128–46. Armonk, NY: ME Sharpe.

—— (2004) *The river runs black: The environmental challenge to China's future.* Ithaca, NY: Cornell University Press.

Eskeland, G and Harrison, A (2003) 'Moving to greener pastures? Multinationals and the pollution haven hypothesis', *Journal of Development Economics* 70(1): 1–23.

Foreign Affairs and International Trade Canada (n.d.). *Side Agreements.* Retrieved 14 January 2010 from: www.international.gc.ca/trade-agreements-accords-commerciaux/agr-acc/nafta-alena/side.aspx?lang=eng

Globalization Monitor (n.d.) *Privatization of water utilities in China:The Shenzhen case,* retrieved 6 January 2010 from: www.rightsresearch.org/site/page10/page17/files/China-WaterPrivatization.ppt

Grossman, G and Krueger, A (1995) 'Economic growth and the environment', *The Quarterly Journal of Economics* 110(2): 353–77.

Guo, W and Feng, Y (2007) *Special economic zones and competitiveness: A case study of Shenzhen, the People's Republic of China.* Islamabad: Asian Development Bank PRM Policy Note.

Hanson, A and Martin, C (2006) *One lifeboat: China and the world's environment and development.* Winnipeg, Manitoba: International Institute for Sustainable Development.

He, J (2006) 'Pollution haven hypothesis and environmental impacts of foreign direct investment: The case of industrial emissions of sulfer dioxide (SO_2) in Chinese provinces' *Ecological Economics* 60(1): 228–45.

Hitt, G and Power, S (2009, June 28). 'House passes climate legislation', *Wall Street Journal,* retrieved 20 January 2010 from: http://online.wsj.com/article/SB124610499176664899.html

HKTDC (2006, May 1). 'Shenzhen becomes first mainland city to enact recycle economy legislation', retrieved 15 January 2010 from: www.hktdc.com/info/mi/a/bacn/en/1X0083P2/1/Business-Alert-%E2%80%93-China/Shenzhen-Becomes-First-Mainland-City-to-Enact-Recycle-Economy-Legislation.htm

Hon, C (2007, December 18). 'China's new Special Environmental Zones: Beijing picks two clusters of cities to push new green policy aimed at sustainable development', *Straits Times.* Retrieved 20 January 2010 from: http://app.mfa.gov.sg/pr/read_content.asp?View,9093

Huang, Q, Wang, Q, Dong, L and Xi, B (2006) 'The current situation of solid waste management in China', *Journal of Material Cycles and Waste Management* 8: 63–69.

International Center for Trade and Sustainable Development. (2009) *New deal could slash tariffs on green goods in OECD,* China, Geneva: International Center for Trade and Sustainable Development.

Invest Shenzhen (n.d.) *Why do business in Shenzhen?* Retrieved 9 September 2009, from: www.investshenzhen.gov.cn/why/sector/index.htm

Ji, Z (2009, December 3) 'Guangdong Special: Formation of three economic circles boosts Delta integration', *China Daily*, retrieved 10 January 2010 from: www.chinadaily.com.cn/cndy/2009-12/03/content_9105927.htm

Jing, F (2009, December 18) 'Wen says China will strive for climate goals', *China Daily*, retrieved 10 January 2010 from: www.chinadaily.com.cn/china/2009copenhagenclimate/2009-12/18/content_9197533.htm

Kahn, D (2009, April 24) 'California adopts low-carbon fuel standard', *Scientific American*, retrieved 12 January 2010, from: www.scientificamerican.com/article.cfm?id=california-adopts-low-car

Kahn, M (2006) *Green cities: Urban growth and the environment*, Washington, DC: Brookings Institution Press.

Kitakyushu Initiative for a Clean Environment: Successful and Transferrable Practices (n.d.) *Shenzhen (China): Market model for construction and operation of environmental infrastructure*, Beijing: Policy Research Center for the Environment and Economy of the State Environmental Protection Agency, People's Republic of China.

Lai, H (2006) 'SEZs and foreign investment in China: Experiences and lessons for North Korean Development', *Asian Perspectives* 30(3): 69–97.

Lee, Y (2005) 'Public environmental consciousness in China: Early empirical evidence', in K Day, *China's environment*, 61–91. Armonk, NY: ME Sharpe.

Liu, X, Heilig, GK, Chen, J and Heino, M (2006) 'Interactions between economic growth and environmental quality in Shenzhen, China's first special economic zone', *Ecological Economics* 56(4): 559–70.

Liu, Y, Mol, P and Chen, J (2007) 'The Development of environmental industry in China', in P Ho, *Greening industries in newly industiralized economies: Asian-style leapfrogging*, 79–105. London: Kegan Paul.

Luan, S, Huang, Y and Zhang, J (2007) *Shenzhen environment* outlook, Bangkok: United Nations Environment Programme.

Magnier, M (2006, September 3). 'As China spews pollution, villagers rise up', *Los Angeles Times*, retrieved 20 January 2010, from: http://articles.latimes.com/2006/sep/03/world/fg-enviro3

Manget, J, Roche, C and Munnich, F (2009) *Capturing the green advantage for consumer* companies, Boston, MA: Boston Consulting Group.

Ministry of Environmental Protection, China (n.d.) *National model cities for environmental protection*, retrieved 1 September 2009, from http://english.mep.gov.cn/inventory/Model_cities/

Morgenstern, R, Abeygunawardena, P, Anderson, R, Greenspan Bell, R, Krupnick, A and Schreifels, J (2005) 'Emissions trading to improve air quality in an industrial city in the People's Republic of China', in K. Day (ed.) *China's environment*, 176–205. Armonk, NY: ME Sharpe.

Nature (2007) *Spotlight on Shenzhen*. Nature.com. Retrieved 8 January 2010 from: www.nature.com/naturejobs/2007/070927/full/nj0181.html

Ng, M (2002) 'Sustainable urban development issues in Chinese transitional cities: Hong Kong and Shezhen', *International Planning Studies* 7(1): 7–36.

—— (2003) 'Shenzhen: City profile', *Cities* 20(6): 429–41.

Nisbet, P (2008) 'A Shenzhen lesson for sustainable water use', retrieved 20 January 2010 from the website of the Sichuan Provincial People's Government: http://english.sc.gov.cn/news//bignews/200804/t20080418_269650.shtml

North America Representative Office of Shenzhen, PRC (n.d.) *About Shenzhen*. Retrieved 9 September 2009 from: www.shenzhenoffice.org/about_shenzhen.htm

Palmer, M (2007) 'Towards a greener China? Accessing environmental justice in the People's Republic of China', in A Harding, *Access to environmental justice: A comparative study*, 205–35. Leiden: Brill.

People's Daily Online (2009, March 25) 'Xiamen's "air corridor" allows public buses to run at high speeds', Retrieved 5 January 2010, from: http://english.people.com.cn/90001/90776/90882/6622299.html

Pike Research (2010) *U.S. energy service company market to increase 250% by 2020*, Boulder, CO: Pike Research.

Pocha, J (2005, December 4). 'Environmental awareness and anger grow in China', *Boston Globe*. Retrieved 15 December 2009 from: www.boston.com/news/world/asia/articles/2005/12/04/environmental_awareness_and_anger_grow_in_china/

Poon, D (2004) *Growing demand for 'green' products in China*. Hong Kong: Hong Kong Trade and Development Council.

Puckett, J, Byster, L, Westervelt, S, Guttierez, R, Hussain, A, Dutta, M, Smith, T and Davis, S (2002) *Exporting harm: The high-tech trashing of* Asia, Seattle, WA: Basel Action Network.

Qian, X and Smyth, R (2005) *Measuring regional inequality of education in China: Widening coast-inland gap or widening rural-urban gap?* Monash, Australia: ABERU Discussion Paper.

Qin, J (2004, July 15) 'Most polluted cities in China blacklisted', *China Daily*. retrieved 20 January 2010, from: www.chinadaily.com.cn/english/doc/2004-7/15/content_348397.htm

Richardson, B (2004) 'Is East Asia industrializing too quickly? Environmental regulation in its special economic zones', *UCLA Pacific Basin Law Journal* 22(1): 150–244.

RightSite Team (2009, December 21). 'Green development zones take root', *RightSite.Asia.com*. Retrieved 28 January 2010 from: http://rightsite.asia/en/article/green-development-zones-take-root

Rock, M and Angel, D (2007) 'Grow up first, clean up later? Industrial transformation in East Asia', *Environment* 49(4): 8–19.

Shenzhen Daily (2007, December 20) '218 hazy days recorded', *Shenzhen Daily*, retrieved 20 January 2010 from Shenzhen Government Online: http://english.sz.gov.cn/ln/200712/t20071220_1105529.htm

—— (2008a, January 21) 'Cities urged to tackle smog', *Shenzhen Daily*, retrieved 20 January 2010 from Shenzhen Government Online: http://english.sz.gov.cn/ln/200801/t20080121_1105646.htm

—— (2008b, June 10) 'Shenzhen, A booming city of design', *Shenzhen Daily*, retrieved 15 December 2009 from: http://paper.sznews.com/szdaily/20080610/ca2898520.htm

—— (2009a, January 20) 'Curbs ahead as SZ vehicles surpass 1.3 million', *Shenzhen Daily*, retrieved 20 January 2010, from Shenzhen Government Online: http://english.sz.gov.cn/ln/200901/t20090120_1106345.htm.

—— (2009b, August 26) 'Heavy polluters likely to be moved out of Qianhai', *Shenzhen Daily*, retrieved 20 January 2010 from Shenzhen Government Online: http://english.sz.gov.cn/ln/200908/t20090826_1162215.htm

Shenzhen Government Online (2009) 'Opening up to the outside world', retrieved 20 September 2009, from: http://english.sz.gov.cn/economy/200708/t20070824_1100395.htm

Shenzhen Information Network Center (2007, August 17). *Nanshan powerplants blamed for acid rain*. Retrieved 11 September 2009 from Shenzhen Government Online: http://english.sz.gov.cn/ln/200708/t20070817_1105202.htm

Shin, S (2004) 'Economic globalization and the environment in China: A comparative study of Shenyang and Dalian', *The Journal of Environment and Development* 13(3): 263–94.

Starmass Dream Co. (2009) *Xiamen Demographic Information*, retrieved 26 August 2009 from: www.starmass.com/china_review/city_overview/xiamen.htm

State Council of China (2006, June) *Environmental protection in China (1996–2005)*, retrieved 1 September 2009 from: www.china.org.cn/english/2006/Jun/170355.htm

State Intellectual Property Office of the PRC (2009) *Annual report 2008*. Beijing: State Intellectual Property Office.

Stockholm Convention (n.d.) Accessed 14 January 2010 from Stockholm Convention on Persistent Organic Pollutants: http://chm.pops.int/

Tschang, C (2008, October 23) 'China's great railway expansion', *Business Week*, retrieved 20 January 2010 from: www.businessweek.com/magazine/content/08_44/b4106067132043.htm

USTR (n.d.) *Environment*. Retrieved 14 January 2010 from United States Trade Representative's Office: www.ustr.gov/trade-topics/environment

Vennemo, H, Aunan, K, He, J, Hu, T, Li, S and Rypdal, K (2008) 'Environmental impacts of China's WTO-accession', *Ecological Economics* 64: 893–911.

Vine, E (2005) 'An international survey of the energy service company (ESCO) industry', *Energy Policy* 33(5): 691–704.

Vogel, D (1995) *Trading up: Consumer and environmental regulation in a global* economy, Cambridge, MA: Harvard University Press.

Walmart (2008, October 22). 'Walmart announces global responsible sourcing initiative at China summit', retrieved 12 January 2010, from: http://walmartstores.com/factsnews/newsroom/8696.aspx

WOX News (2008, December 13) 'Measures to keep Xiamen from becoming overly polluted', *WOX News*, retrieved 27 January 2010 from: www.whatsonxiamen.com/news4376.html

WTO (n.d.) *An introduction to trade and the environment in the WTO*, retrieved 14 January 2010 from www.wto.org/english/tratop_E/envir_e/envt_intro_e.htm

Xiamen Investment Promotion Agency (n.d.) *Facts of foreign investment*, retrieved 9 September 2009 from www.xipa.com.cn/en/xiamen3.php

Xinhua (2006, December 10) 'Output in environmental protection industry to hit US$112b in 2010', *China Daily*, retrieved 27 January 2010 from: www.chinadaily.com.cn/bizchina/2006-12/10/content_754883.htm

—— (2008, August 29) 'China adopts recycling law', *China View*, retrieved 27 January 2010 from: http://news.xinhuanet.com/english/2008-08/29/content_9736158.htm

—— (2009a, May 22) 'China's first special economic zone aims to be 5 times bigger', *China Daily*, retrieved 15 January 2010 from: http://english.peopledaily.com.cn/90001/90778/90857/90862/6663631.html

—— (2009b, December 29) 'China's first environmental industry fund established', retrieved 15 January 2010 from: http://english.peopledaily.com.cn/90001/90778/90860/6854346.html

Xu, S (2008, December 10). 'Growing both the economy and environment', *China Daily*, retrieved 20 Janauary 2010 from: www.chinadaily.com.cn/world/2009green/2008-12/10/content_8249262.htm

Yanfeng, Q (2009, August 4) 'Protests help clear the air', *China Daily*, retrieved 20 January 2010 from: www.chinadaily.com.cn/china/2009-08/04/content_8514601.htm

Yang, Q (2008) 'Potential use of mangroves as constructed wetland for municipal sewage treatment in Futian, Shenzhen, China', *Marine Pollution Bulletin* 57(6–12): 735–43.

Zeng, K, and Eastin, J (2007) 'International economic integration and environmental protection: The case of China', *International Studies Quarterly* 51(4): 971–95.

Zhan, L (2008, September 9) 'Guangdong Province faces acid rain', *China Daily*, retrieved 20 January 2010 from: www.chinadaily.com.cn/cndy/2008-9/06/content_7004197.htm

Zhang, B, Bi, J, Yuan, Z, Ge, J, Liu, B and Bu, M (2008) 'Why do firms engage in environmental management? An empirical study in China', *Journal of Cleaner Production* 16(10): 1036–45.

Zhang, J, Cao, X and Meng, X (2007) 'Sustainable urban sewerage system and its application in China', *Resources Conservation and Recycling* 51(2): 284–93.

Zheng, S, Kahn, M and Liu, H (2009) 'Towards a system of open cities in China: Home prices, FDI flows and air quality in 35 major cities', National Bureau of Economic Research Working Paper 14751.

Zhong, L, Mol, A and Fu, T (2008) 'Public-Private partnerships in China's urban waste sector', *Environmental Mangement* 41: 863–77.

6 Special economic zones and freeports

Challenges and opportunities in the bases conversion and development experience in the Philippines

Arnel Paciano D. Casanova[1]

Introduction

The last decade of the twentieth century ushered in major international and domestic upheavals in the Philippines, both politically and economically. The fall of the Marcos dictatorship gave birth to a new democracy and new Philippine Constitution. This event helped ignite a spark of dissent against dictators and oppressive regimes around the world that inflamed the global uprisings against oppressive regimes.

With glory comes burden. In the succeeding years, the Philippines suffered the pains of nurturing a democracy. The series of bloody coup attempts by rightist military rebels threatened the gains of the people. With the rise in nationalistic fervour, the Philippine government terminated its military bases agreement with the United States (USA). This compelled the US military to withdraw from the Subic Naval Base, the Clark Air Base and other smaller US military camps in the Philippines. The economic impact of such withdrawal was feared because of the inevitable dislocation of thousands of Filipino workers in those major US bases. Such fear was compounded by two major natural disasters. First came the 1990 earthquake which devastated Northern Luzon. Second, in 1991 the wrath of the Mount Pinatubo eruption buried thousands of hectares of agricultural, commercial and residential land under millions of tons of ash and murderous lahar. The Philippines, in the midst of a fast-changing globalized world, was hit by major natural and man-made disasters that brought it to the brink of economic collapse.

Globally, a new economic order was taking shape with the fall of protectionist barriers to trade and the opening of global markets. The privatization of government assets and the liberalization and deregulation of industries that used to be monopolies happened at a fast pace as the private sector assumed roles that governments used to perform. Competition for foreign direct investment (FDI) ensued among developing countries such as the Philippines, Malaysia, Thailand, Vietnam, China and others.

In the face of these challenges, the Aquino presidency in its last year (1992) looked at the opportunities that the former bases could offer. At the same time, businesses were going around the world looking for countries that could provide the best environment for investment. The bases conversion and development programme was therefore drafted by the Philippine legislative and executive offices to meet the challenges of a globalized world and put the former military camps to their best use.

This chapter explains the rationale behind the creation of the SEZs and freeports under the bases conversion programme embodied in Republic Act no. 7227 as amended, and evaluates the roles that they played in the national economic development and security of the Philippines. A further aim of this chapter is to identify challenges that have been faced by the government in these zones which have led to economic losses. In particular these challenges have included the effects of the abuse of incentives and privileges; corruption and smuggling; ambiguity in the legal framework governing the zones; and other factors that have hindered their full potential as catalysts for national development.

While the chapter also discusses policy issues, the perspective of discussion is primarily from an operational and management perspective.

The loss of the economic contribution of the US military bases

Financially, the benefits derived by the Philippines from the US bases constituted a significant percentage of its gross domestic product. In 1990, it was estimated to be 1.9 per cent of the Philippine GDP. It was likewise substantial in terms of employment. In 1990, an estimated 120,000 Filipinos relied on these bases as their source of employment and livelihood. Among the specific economic benefits that these bases contributed to the Philippine economy were: bases expenditures; employment; housing and service contracts; the Economic Support Fund; the Military Assistance Program (Legislative-Executive Bases Council 1990: 5). The loss of these economic benefits derived from the presence of the US military bases was staggering. It was certain that a drastic rise in unemployment in the midst of the natural disasters which struck the country would have disastrous results that would further hit the already badly shaken Philippine economy.

The responsibility for coming up with alternatives fell on the shoulders of the members of the Bases Council. Upon them fell the expectations of the entire country. These expectations were high, for they were then given the responsibility of weighing how the economic price of sovereignty would impact on all Filipinos and their future.

The bases conversion programme and the mandate of the Bases Conversion and Development Authority

The bases conversion programme came into legal existence through the creation of the Legislative-Executive Bases Council which had the task of drawing up the master plan for the comprehensive conversion programme of the US military bases and other camps in Metro Manila (Legislative-Executive Bases

Council 1990: 5). The military camps located in Metro Manila were occupied by the Armed Forces of the Philippines, not by US military forces. However, the series of coup attempts against the Aquino regime convinced the public and the policy-makers and security analysts that the presence of major military camps and their operating units in Metro Manila served as national security threat. Likewise, these camps were considered prime real estate as they were located in business and commercial districts. Coupled with the need to generate funds for the conversion of the US military bases, the Aquino administration saw the sale and privatization of these camps, and moving the major operating units of the military outside Metro Manila, away from the seat of political power and business districts, as a viable source of development funds. It was an undertaking of the two major branches of government. The result of the study of the Bases Council formed the foundation for a policy direction implemented through the enactment of Republic Act no. 7227 by the Philippine legislature in March 1992.

This law created two legal entities to implement it. As it was originally proposed and planned, the Bases Conversion and Development Authority (BCDA) should have been the only authority to put this law into reality. However, upon vigorous lobbying of then Mayor Richard Gordon of Olongapo City where the Subic Naval Base was located, the Subic Bay Metropolitan Authority (SBMA) became the government corporation to administer the conversion of the Subic Naval Base with the BCDA exercising an oversight function over it. The distinction between the two authorities would later on be of material significance, particularly regarding the power to grant tax incentives under the Constitution and Philippine tax laws when the Philippine Supreme Court decided on the case of *John Hay Peoples Alternative Coalition et al. vs Lim et al.*[2]

The master plan for the bases conversion programme envisioned the transfer of the properties of the former US bases to the BCDA to be developed as SEZs and freeports. In turn, the BCDA was expected to be revenue-generating and self-sustaining without depending on funding from the national government. To achieve this, it was given the former military camps as its land assets to be sold, leased, or dealt with in any other form of privatization such as securitization in a joint venture with the private sector. The proceeds generated from the sale or privatization of these government lands would serve as BCDA's initial operating capital with the long-term objective of sustaining it for the rest of its corporate life.[3] The newest and premier central business district in the Philippines, the Bonifacio Global City, is the product of this privatization through joint-venture agreement with the private sector. It was considered the biggest real estate deal in Asia in 1995. The proceeds of this sale energized the infrastructure development of the SEZs.

The Bases Council proposed the development and operation of global and world-class infrastructure in these areas, namely: development of the Clark Air Base as a civil aviation complex; development of a maritime industrial complex in Subic Naval Base; and creation of industrial estates and other developments.

The projects were expected to 'reduce the country's need to export its skilled manpower resources' as it would be 'replaced by the inward movement of trade and commerce into the new Clark and Subic' as the Philippines transforms itself to a 'new agro-industrialized' economy (Legislative-Executive Bases Council 1990: 2–3).

The Bases Council also, in its pragmatic and realistic recognition of the essential requisites of the conversion programme, set out the conditions that had to occur to ensure its success. Thus it stated that laying out and upgrading of infrastructure must be undertaken to support the development of these converted bases. As its aim was to encourage investment, preferably FDI, the conversion programme had to be nurtured by an improved investment climate that came with political stability, the absence of graft and corruption in both the public and private sectors, reduced red tape, and improved telecommunication facilities. An essential component of this was the 'imperative' need for BCDA to be 'thoroughly professional and beyond reproach', competent, insulated from and capable of resisting political pressures (ibid.). As the discussion proceeds, these essential requisites will serve as criteria in measuring how the bases conversion programme has performed since its inception in a comparison of the plan and the actual reality that transpired.

Distinction of BCDA SEZs from PEZA and other eco-zones

The Philippines, as of 2007, had four public economic zones with 423 operating firms; 45 private economic zones with 528 firms; 70 IT parks/centres/buildings (mostly in Metro Manila), with 265 operating firms; and 5 tourism zones with 5 operating firms. It has two major zones located in the Subic Bay Special Economic and Freeport Zone and the Clark Special Economic and Freeport Zone, created under the bases conversion programme (Senate Economic Planning Office 2008: 2).

The SEZs in the Philippines are created under different regulatory and administering bodies. First, there are SEZs that are generally regulated and governed by the Philippine Economic Zone Authority (PEZA), whose mandate covers most of the SEZs in the Philippines. These PEZA SEZs are mostly owned and operated by the private sector. Aside from the PEZA SEZs, there are, second, those that are created and governed by their special charters. These are the SEZs, EPZs or freeports that were created directly by the legislature through a special law or charter. The third kind are the SEZs and freeports created and administered under the BCDA law, Republic Act no. 7227, and other relevant executive orders and proclamations. Currently, there are calls to rationalize these incentives under one governing legal structure.

While BCDA SEZs are similar to other SEZs in the Philippines in aiming to encourage the inward flow of FDI, they differ in the very rationale upon which the conversion programme was conceived. BCDA SEZs aim not solely to attract FDI but also to address the impending dislocation of workers; the loss of revenue generated from the US military bases; the national security threat posed by restless soldiers in the major military camps in the capital and seat of political power; and the need to spur economic activity in the regions devastated by the earthquake and volcanic eruption. It was imperative for the BCDA to find alternative uses for the military camps to serve as a catalyst for development within the region and to help in the modernization of the armed forces which were experiencing internal restlessness.

The locators in the BCDA zones are mixed. While it was encouraged to have multinational corporations and foreign investors in those zones, domestic enterprises and businesses are likewise given the privileges and incentives for establishing their operations and offices there.

Moreover, to further encourage FDI, Congress, in enacting the Foreign Investors Lease Act (Republic Act no. 7652 of 1993) liberalized the lease of lands by foreign nationals and corporations by allowing direct contract negotiations instead of competitive bidding, which is the general rule in government privatization. To grant them better certainty of tenure on the leased land, which is mostly a requirement for capital-intensive manufacturing industries, the length of the lease period was allowed to be extended up to seventy-five years, which is substantially longer than the usual twenty-five-year lease renewable for another twenty-five years. The executive, through Executive Order no. 429 (1997), further expanded the coverage of this law by allowing Filipino nationals also to avail themselves of these terms.

Other SEZs which are not governed by the PEZA law or the BCDA law fall within the terms of the law for which they were specifically created. These SEZs are marked by their location and were usually the result of a local government or a congressman who lobbied for the creation of such an SEZ in their territorial jurisdiction. Because of this, the creation of these SEZs became more of a political decision to serve as the accomplishment of a politician who needed to showcase such an SEZ to his constituency come election time. Hence, most of these SEZs were known for their non-performance as their creation had not been fully thought out in terms of sound economic policy-making.

Special economic zones and freeports under the bases conversion programme

The Philippine Congress decided to create SEZs and freeports on all former US military bases. Among these, the Subic Naval Base and the Clark Air Base were the major ones. Republic Act no. 7227 created two major authorities, the BCDA and the Subic Bay Metropolitan Authority. The BCDA serves as the overall implementing authority of the bases conversion programme in all former US bases except the Subic Naval Base, which was established as the Subic Bay Freeport and Special Economic Zone administered by the SBMA.[4]

The following are the SEZs and freeports created directly under the BCDA:

Clark Freeport and Special Economic Zone (CSEZ). It is envisioned that the Clark Air Base will be converted into an international civil aviation complex, a modern industrial estate and tourism, trade and business centre for Luzon and Asia.[5] To implement this plan, the BCDA was tasked with the creation of two subsidiaries – the Clark Development Corporation (CDC) and the Clark International Airport Corporation (CIAC). The CDC administers the regulation of incentives within the CSEZ while the CIAC's main mandate is to develop the Clark Aviation Complex into the premier international airport of the Philippines and an aviation-logistics hub in Asia.[6] One of its major locators, the United Parcel Service (UPS), uses it as its regional distribution hub.

Poro Point Freeport and Special Economic Zone (PPFSEZ). The former Wallace Air Station in Poro Point, San Fernando, La Union, in the north of the Philippines, was converted into a freeport and SEZ. To complement the development of this minor US military base with the necessary infrastructure, the San Fernando Airport and the Poro Point Seaport were transferred to the BCDA.[7] The SEZ is managed by its subsidiary, the Poro Point Management Corporation (PPMC). The two major investors in this zone are the Bulk Handler's Inc., a Filipino corporation engaged in the operation of the seaport, and the Thunderbird Hotel and Resorts, an international group of hotel resorts and gaming corporation.

John Hay Special Economic Zone (JHSEZ). This tourism area, which was once called the John Hay Air Station, is located in Baguio City, north of Manila. A BCDA subsidiary, the John Hay Management Corporation, manages this SEZ. Its major locator is the Camp John Hay Development Corporation which built hotels, a golf course and a convention centre.

Morong Special Economic Zone (MSEZ). Located in Morong, Bataan, adjoining the Subic Bay Freeport and SEZ, this was not originally part of the bases conversion programme but used to be the site of the processing centre for refugees from Vietnam, Cambodia and Laos. BCDA created a subsidiary, the Bataan Technology Park Inc., to develop it into a technology park. Currently, it is generally undeveloped.

Investment climate and tax incentives

Republic Act no. 7227 created a special investment climate in the form of special privileges, such as a separate customs territory outside the jurisdiction of Philippine customs and tariff laws, to the locators of the Subic Freeport and SEZ. In lieu of all national and local taxes, the businesses registered there are made to pay only 5 per cent tax based on the gross income earned (GIE).[8]

While Republic Act no. 7227 provided for the creation of SEZs in the former bases, it did not grant a clear mandate to extend the same privileges and investment regime to the other BCDA SEZs. The view was that the lack of tax incentives in these SEZs would not make the conversion to alternative uses of these former bases into economic catalysts in the region because they could not attract FDI without incentives for businesses to relocate. In the face of stiff competition with other newly industrialized countries in Southeast Asia, Philippine policy-makers believed that the tax incentives were necessary components for the country's competitiveness in a globalized world. Thus, aside from the Subic SEZ and freeport, all the other SEZs under the bases conversion programme were given the same investment and tax regime. All presidential issuances, executive orders and proclamations earlier cited creating the SEZs and freeports, other than the Subic SEZ and freeport, contained an executive order provision applying all the incentives under Republic Act no. 7227, the Omnibus Investments Code 1987, the Foreign Investments Act 1991, and any new investment laws subsequently enacted. These provisions extended the 5 per cent tax based on GIE to all locators in John Hay SEZ, Poro Point SEZ and freeport, and the Morong SEZ. These provisions applying the same incentives to the SEZs other than Subic were nullified by the court for violating the constitutional principle that tax incentives must be legislated and are not a function of the president or of the executive branch.[9]

The nullification of the tax incentives resulted in the instability of the legal framework within which the incentives were granted, thereby radically affecting the operations of the businesses located therein. This likewise worked to the disadvantage of the BCDA and its subsidiaries in light of locators who defaulted on their obligations regardless of the ruling because it provided these locators with an excuse to do so. In the case of John Hay SEZ, this became the excuse of a company which went to court to compel the BCDA to restructure its 2.5 billion peso arrears, thereby resulting in a loss of opportunity for the BCDA to collect that amount.

All locators in all of the BCDA SEZs raised grave concerns. The court took away the reason for the attractiveness of these SEZs for investment. Hence, the BCDA and the Office of the President of the Philippines lobbied for the enactment of a law that would cure this deficiency in the law and the executive orders that mandated the creation of these SEZs and the incentives given to them.

Governance challenges

The planners of the bases conversion programme laid out a number of requisites for its success – improved and sufficient infrastructure, an improved investment climate, political stability, the absence of graft and corruption in both the public and private sectors, reduced red tape, and improved telecommunication facilities. The Senate Economic Policy Office (SEPO) further expounded that it was necessary to have a supportive and conducive policy environment in areas where the SEZs were situated for their growth and effectiveness (Senate Economic Planning Office 2008: 3–5). In a Bearing Point study presented to the Philippine Senate, the development of a robust legal and regulatory framework as well as the build-up of regulatory authorities' capabilities were identified as factors that could make SEZs and freeports 'highly-effective'.[10]

Fulfilling these conditions presented major challenges. Creating a supportive and conducive policy environment proved elusive at some points, which resulted in revenues foregone and economic opportunities lost. The path to good governance was a difficult one. The pervasive and perceived corruption continued to erode investor confidence and deprive the government of revenues that could have been invested in infrastructure development and the delivery of services, such as healthcare and education – factors necessary for competitiveness.[11]

Relationship with national and local government

The quality of the relationship between local government units (LGUs) and the SEZs located within their political jurisdiction is mixed. While most LGUs compete to have SEZs in their areas in recognition of the potential economic benefits that these SEZs would bring, those who have existing SEZs in their areas, particularly those cities and municipalities that the SEZs straddle, complain about the lack of revenues to deal with the social and environmental costs attendant to them. While there is an allotment of a 1 per cent tax on the GIE for the affected LGUs, it takes a lot of time in the bureaucracy before the national government releases the amount to them, thereby delaying the development of the necessary services and infrastructure. Because of this, the LGUs are demanding the remittance of the 1 per cent tax on GIE directly to the LGU. However, the businesses located in the SEZ do not welcome this because of the additional bureaucracy in examining their books this would entail. Aggravated by their vulnerability to corrupt officials, the investors do not want to deal with different offices in the bureaucracy as it increases the cost of doing business.

Prior to the enactment of Republic Act no. 9400 in 2007, the tax incentives likewise exempted the SEZ businesses from paying local taxes, particularly real estate taxes. This runs counter to the principle of enhancing local fiscal autonomy. Thus section 234 of the Local Government Code (Republic Act no. 7160 of 1992) withdrew most of the exemption from real estate tax to make LGUs more self-reliant and capable of financing their own development projects and initiatives. LGUs depend on real estate tax as one of their biggest source of revenue (Senate Economic Planning Office 2008: 8).

With the strong lobbying from LGUs, Congress provided for the direct remittance of 2 per cent of GIE to the treasurer's office of the city or municipality where the SEZs were located, except for Subic where 2 per cent of GIE is directly remitted to the SBMA, which is responsible for its distribution to the LGUs. It also specifically denied the Morong SEZ any real estate exemption in recognition of the need for the Municipality of Morong to generate more revenues, it being one of the poorest municipalities hosting an SEZ.[12]

Corruption

One of the major factors that the planners of the bases conversion programme identified as a key to success was the eradication of graft and corruption. Reside (2006) proposed that the necessary rationalizing of incentives had to go hand-in-hand with the reduction of corruption in the government.

Over the years since the inception of this programme, the Philippines has suffered in international perception as a country afflicted by graft and corruption. Transparency International (TI), which ranks countries on the basis of a corruption index, ranked the Philippines quite consistently below three out of ten[13] from 1995 to 2008 except in the last two years of the Ramos presidency in 1997 and 1998. What is more alarming is the continued decline of the Philippines in its corruption index ranking, giving the impression that corruption is worsening instead of being abated. Such perceptions will prevail even if the government consistently denies its corrupt image.

The lack of closure and accountability in the string of corruption scandals faced by the present administration further caused the public's confidence to erode. As a consequence foreign investors are ambivalent about bringing their investments into the country as they consider the increasing political risk that their businesses may face in the Philippines. While there have been a number of major investments that have come in, the volume has fallen below expectations. Businesses always complain of the rising cost of doing business and inefficiency in the bureaucracy.

Smuggling

Claims abound that whatever the gains received in the SEZs and freeports, these were eventually lost to unabated corruption and rampant smuggling. According to data provided by Senator Gordon, of the 90,000 smuggled cars that passed through Subic SEZ and freeport in 2000–2003, only 128 were re-exported abroad. This amounted to an approximate loss to the government of 45 billion pesos based on computations made by the Bureau of Customs (Senate Committee on Government Corporations and Public Enterprises 2005). Most of these cars were re-used right-hand-drive vehicles that were eventually converted into left-hand drive. The dubious roadworthiness and inefficiencies of these vehicles contributed to a number of vehicular accidents and environmental problems.

The smuggling of goods is a product of the collusion of corrupt officials tasked with enforcing the law. In some instances, the Anti-Smuggling Task Force apprehended smuggled cars that were 'already registered with the Land Transportation Office (LTO) while still loaded in vessels'. The importation of these used cars likewise had an adverse effect on the local automotive manufacturing industry that resulted in the displacement of more workers in the industry (Senate Committee on Government Corporations and Public Enterprises 2005).

The loss in revenues incurred by the government has yet to be explained because of the difficulty in managing and securing the SEZs. Revenue leaks and abuses of incentives occur within them. Reports are many of the rampant smuggling of used cars and petroleum in the Subic SEZ and freeport (Senate Economic Planning Office 2008: 7).

Ambiguity in the legal framework

One of the biggest challenges facing the BCDA SEZs is the confusion in the legal environment governing these SEZs. The nullification of incentives by the Supreme Court in the *John Hay Peoples Alternative Coalition* case affecting the John Hay SEZ and even the Clark SEZ, emphasized that glaring flaw in their administrations. It has cost the BCDA the loss of the opportunity to collect for the government a 2.5 billion peso receivable on time and made it accept the bitterness of restructuring an obligation which otherwise would have either been promptly received or the government would have brought measures for the take-over of the asset.

This flaw was caused by the inability of Congress to clearly indicate the need for tax incentives for these SEZs. Because of that failure, the executive branch took it upon itself to provide the tax regime in order to address the economic needs of that time. This came, however, at the high price of violating the Constitution. It was clearly a failure to set a clear path for the SEZs and give flesh to it in the form of unequivocal provisions in law. Recognizing such a flaw in law-making, the court said:

> It is the legislature, unless limited by a provision of the state Constitution, that has full power to exempt any person or corporation or class of property from taxation, its power to exempt being as broad as its power to tax. Other than Congress, the Constitution may itself provide for specific tax exemptions, or local governments may pass ordinances on exemption only from local taxes. The challenged grant of tax exemption would circumvent the Constitution's imposition that a law granting any tax exemption must have the concurrence of a majority of all the members of Congress ... *The claimed statutory exemption of the John Hay SEZ from taxation should be manifest and unmistakable from the language of the law on which it is based; it must be expressly granted in a statute stated in a language too clear to be mistaken. Tax exemption cannot be implied as it must be categorically and unmistakably expressed.*
>
> (Emphasis supplied)

This same confusing legal environment led to revenue leakages and even corruption because the ambiguity was exploited to expand the incentives and the nature of businesses allowed within these SEZs which could have been otherwise illegal outside them. Take for example the case of the importation of vehicles. The nature of a freeport as a separate customs territory allowed for the importation of used right-hand-drive vehicles by the thousand under the pretext of transhipment. It is claimed that these vehicles were imported to be reconditioned and converted to left-hand-drive for the purpose of being re-exported to another country. But the reality is to the contrary. Thousands of used and converted vehicles proliferated on the streets of the Philippines outside the SEZs instead of being re-exported to another country. The effect of such a huge volume of vehicles entering the Philippine domestic market adversely affected the local automotive industry. Worse, the smuggling of luxury cars such as Porsche, BMW, Ferrari and Mercedes Benz increased when they were improperly declared as used instead of new.

When the president tried to clamp down on this business by invoking Executive Order no. 156 prohibiting the importation of used motor vehicles into the Philippines, the importers of used vehicles filed a case for declaratory relief to have the Executive Order declared unconstitutional. In the case of *Executive Secretary et al. vs South Wing Heavy Industries*[14] the executive secretary, representing the Office of the President and other executive departments, petitioned the Supreme Court to overturn the rulings of the lower courts declaring the prohibition unconstitutional. They argued that the prohibition applies to the entire country, including all freeports. The Court in resolving the issue modified the ruling of the lower courts by stating that there is a valid prohibition insofar as the used vehicles should not enter the domestic market, but it is unconstitutional insofar as it is made applicable to the Subic freeport. In making the distinction, it stated:

> The problem, however, lies with respect to the application of the importation ban to the Freeport. The Court finds no logic in the all encompassing application of the assailed provision to the *Freeport which is outside the customs territory. As long as the used motor vehicles do not enter the customs territory, the injury or harm sought to be prevented or remedied will not arise* … To apply the proscription to the Freeport would not serve the purpose of the EO. Instead of improving the general economy of the country, the application of the importation ban in the Freeport would subvert the avowed *purpose of RA 7227 which is to create a market that would draw investors and ultimately boost the national economy.*
>
> (Emphasis supplied)

While the arguments presented in the decision seem to be plausible, the court failed to elucidate on the definition of what constitutes real economic value of such business in 'creating a market that would draw investors to boost the national economy'. It failed to state that the kind of investment contemplated in the creation of these SEZs is FDI and not domestic investment – which all of these imported used motor vehicles are. As these domestic businesses are mostly involved in importation, they actually do not contribute to the national economy. On the contrary, they drain further the country's foreign reserves and directly hurt the foreign investments of multinationals involved in the local automotive manufacturing industry that creates thousands of jobs and helps in innovation in technology. The importation and conversion of used right-hand-drive motor vehicles clearly does not bring in new investment that would spur economic growth. In fact it damages the economy and increases the environmental cost of such businesses. Because of this confusion in the law, the importation of used motor vehicles, an activity clearly prohibited by national policy, found legal justification in jurisprudence that forms part of the law of the land. Further, with the collusion of corrupt customs officials, the vehicles continue to enter the domestic market, defeating the very reason why an SEZ and freeport was created.

Thus, the ambiguity in the law and its arbitrary interpretation and implementation led to the broad coverage of exemption from all taxes, fees, licenses, duties, imposts and other charges which created opportunities for abuse and revenue leakages (Senate Economic Planning Office 2008: 4).

Other challenges

Aside from those problems mentioned above, there are other challenges that plague the SEZs. These issues cover problems related to the environment, labour rights and welfare and gender sensitivity, amongst others. According to a 2004 UN report, most of those working in SEZs are women, comprising approximately 80 per cent of the workforce. Among their serious problems are low pay, excessive salary deductions, forced overtime, high production, quotas, and a lack of incentives. The violation of labour laws involves 'no union policy, unpaid overtime work, non-remittance of social security payments, non-regularization (contractualization), as well as sexual harassment, and gender bias in promotion' (Senate Economic Planning Office 2008: 2). The Clark SEZ, through its international airport, is also identified as a port where human trafficking has occurred, prompting the Clark International Airport Authority (CIAC), together with the national police force and other agencies and civil society groups, to implement strict measures to curb criminal activities (*Business Mirror* 2008).

In the Subic SEZ, an ongoing controversy at the time of writing is brewing involving its power to issue environmental clearance certificates (ECC) to developers within the SEZ. However, upon the protest of some individuals and sectors against the planned felling of 300 trees, such power was revoked by the Department of Environment and Natural Resources (DENR) (De Vera 2009: A-8).

Opportunities

While there are major challenges, there are gains and opportunities as well. One of the bright notes on the horizon for the BCDA SEZs is the development of infrastructure by the BCDA and the SBMA. Based on SBMA data, an additional US$1.5 billion infrastructure development budget has been allocated to enhance the competitiveness of the Subic-Clark area (SBMA 2008).

Subic Bay port development

As envisioned in the bases conversion programme, the Subic SEZ and freeport is at the time of writing on the path to full development of its maritime industrial complex. The Subic seaport has been upgraded and modernized to the amount of 6.91 billion pesos, enticing Hanjin, the Korean global company, to set up one of the biggest shipyards and facilities in the freeport. The entry of Hanjin[15] to the Philippines blazed the trail for increased Korean investment, not only in the industrial and manufacturing industry but in real estate and other projects as well. As of January 2007, Korean investments amounted to US$1.05 billion with thirty-three companies located in the Subic SEZ, followed by Filipino (US$632 million), American (US$454 million), Japanese (US$225 million) and other nationalities. The cumulative committed investments in Subic increased from US$2.1 billion in 2001 to US$5.708 billion as of May 2008 (SBMA 2008).

Sub-Clark-Tarlac Expressway Project (SCTEX)

To serve as a backbone for an Asian regional logistics hub that would form a new economic corridor outside Metro Manila, the BCDA constructed a 94.5 kilometre toll road connecting the Subic SEZ, the Clark SEZ and up to the end of La Paz, Tarlac with access to the Luisita SEZ. Funded by the Japan Bank for International Cooperation (JBIC), it has cost approximately US$ 640 million.[16] It is the longest and most modern expressway in the Philippines. The completion of this important piece of infrastructure has allowed for the faster movement of people, goods, and services among the three major SEZs and freeports in Central Luzon. It has reduced travel time from Subic to Clark to about 45 minutes, a trip that used to take almost two hours.

Development of the Clark International Airport

With the interconnectivity via the SCTEX of the Subic International Seaport and the Clark International Airport, these three important major pieces of infrastructure will spur development. The seaport and the tollway are completed and what remains is the upgrading of the Clark International Airport (also known as the Diosdado Macapagal International Airport). It is therefore now considered to be one of the priority infrastructure projects of the country. With congestion being experienced in the Manila International Airport (also known as the Ninoy Aquino International Airport), the Clark International Airport provides the only available facility with the space and the support infrastructure to be developed as the next premier gateway to the Philippines.

In the last quarter of 2008, the Clark International Airport Corporation (CIAC), the BCDA implementing arm tasked to develop the airport, tendered the financing, construction, operation and maintenance of Terminal 2 of the airport to the public. With the required minimum investment of US$142 million for a passenger terminal with a capacity of 7 million passengers, several bidders expressed and participated in the tendering. However, all of the bidders were eventually declared to be ineligible, thereby scuttling plans for developing the airport by the end of 2008. CIAC is now, at the time of writing, mulling over other options available for faster implementation of the project. On a positive note, they continue to gain favourable agreements and terms in the talks between the Philippines and other countries that will increase the airport's passenger and cargo traffic.

Conclusions

Assessments of how the bases conversion programme performed fifteen years after its inception can be made from different perspectives. Viewed by the manner it responded to the challenges of the times within which it was created, it is a success. The conversion of Subic Naval Base and Clark Air Base clearly prevented the economic disaster that might have transpired if the US bases had closed without any alternative use. In the short term, the location of multinational manufacturing firms to these SEZs provided a safety net and opportunities for employment to those adversely affected. In 1993, a year after the last US troops left, Subic garnered a total committed investment amounting to US$33 million. And in 1994, US$314 million in foreign investment came in, led by Federal Express (Fedex) which started operations in 1995.

In 1996, the Philippines hosted the summit meeting of the Asia-Pacific Economic Cooperation and welcomed the gathering of eighteen world leaders including US president Bill Clinton.[17] This boosted international confidence in the Philippines as a business haven.

Credit must also be given to the people in that region for their resilience and industry. The positive spirit of volunteers in the transformation of Subic freeport and SEZ laid the foundation for a hopeful rebuilding of necessary infrastructure therein and created an environment suitable for investment and trade.

The Clark and Subic SEZs continue to provide much needed FDI to help the economy. The other BCDA SEZs continue to be hounded by lack of investment and recurring expenses for their operations and capital expenditures.

Viewed from the perspective of how the SEZs and freeports contributed to the advancement of the Philippine economy in their role in attracting FDI, success here is debatable. The continued and increasing dependence of the Philippine economy on remittances[18] from overseas Filipino workers who unabatedly leave their homes for jobs abroad is a conclusive testament to the failure to realize the vision of inward movement of trade and commerce into the new SEZs and freeports and thus help provide jobs domestically and reduce the necessity of finding them elsewhere in the world. In a culture centred on family, the separation of family members has had tremendous social costs as well.

The Philippine government gained a measured success in transforming the former bases into SEZs and freeports in order to generate the needed investment and employment in the first years of the programme. They serve as anchors of economic activity in the areas they are located, but their success is dependent on both domestic and global circumstances.

As proven by the other non-performing SEZs, incentives alone do not guarantee that investments will come in. Moreover, the government always bears the cost of creating and sustaining the SEZs in terms of infrastructure, administrative and regulatory cost. There are also global factors that directly affect their viability. The entry of China into the WTO and its increasing influence in global trade made the BCDA SEZs unable to compete. An example of this is the decision of Fedex to transfer its Asia-Pacific operations from Subic to China. Other investors too decided to transfer their businesses to other developing countries that could provide either cheaper labour costs or better incentives. This has somehow engaged the Philippines and other developing countries in a drive to the bottom, further lowering labour costs to the prejudice of the workers and granting increasingly liberal incentives that have drained countries of revenue that could have funded the development of necessary infrastructure and the delivery of basic services. Ironically, Reside's study shows that these incentives are mostly redundant; that is even without the incentives, they would have invested anyway as they have been proven profitable from the start. The cost of redundant fiscal incentives for the Philippines in 2004 was estimated at 43.2 billion pesos, close to 1 per cent of GDP, for the BOI alone (Reside 2006). Reside argues that the 'continued emphasis on incentives as an investment inducement is an illusion', and that these agencies, including the BCDA SEZs, are undermining their own efforts at promoting the country as an investment destination (ibid.).

Therefore, while the BCDA SEZs and freeports enjoyed success in lifting the country from possible economic collapse with the pull-out of the bases and the string of natural disasters, the viability of its SEZs must be reviewed to adjust to the needs and challenges of the times and the evolving global economic conditions.

Notes

1 The points raised in this chapter are solely within the individual perspective of the author in his personal knowledge and experiences derived as an executive of the Bases Conversion and Development Authority, and are not those of the BCDA, of its leadership or any other individual.
2 GR no. 119775, 24 October 2003.
3 BCDA retains only a portion of the net proceeds of the sale or disposition. The rest is to be used, according to Republic Act no. 7917, amending Republic Act no. 7227, for social and infrastructural purposes.

4 Section 12, Republic Act no. 7227.
5 Executive Order no. 80, Series of 1993.
6 Executive Order no. 192, Series of 1994 and Executive Order no. 174, Series of 1994.
7 Proclamation 216, Series of 1993.
8 Section 12, Republic Act no. 7227.
9 See *John Hay People's Coalition et al. vs Lim* in relation to Sec. 28(4), Article VI of the Philippine Constitution; note 2 above.
10 Power point presentation prepared by the consulting firm Bearing Point in 2004, presented to the Philippine Senate in the deliberations of the tax incentives in SEZs and freeports.
11 The Philippine Senate Economic Planning Office (SEPO) stated that infrastructure supporting industrial agglomeration must be present for the SEZs to be viable. Most of the SEZs in the Philippines failed because of (1) low road density ratio; (2) low telephone densities; (3) and power. It further stated that creation of such zones does not guarantee a surge in investment, and infrastructure spending is key to improvement of investment climate in remote areas.
12 See Republic Act no. 9400, amending certain provisions of Republic Act no. 7227. The Bureau of Internal Revenue issued Revenue Memorandum Circular no. 27–2007 containing such amendments for all internal revenue officials to implement.
13 The 2009 ranking is 2.4, i.e. 139th in the world.
14 GR no. 164171, 20 February 2006.
15 As of 2007, Hanjin committed to invest an additional US$684 million on top of its US$1 billion initial investment.
16 Data sourced from the BCDA Finance Department and computed at approximately US$1:Php45.
17 Sourced from BCDA documents and brochures.
18 The OFW remittances are a major contributor to the economy. In the first eleven months of 2008, remittances from overseas Filipino workers reached US$15 billion.

Bibliography

Business Mirror (2008) *Human trafficking syndicate uses Clark as exit point-center* (24 June).

De Vera, E (2009) 'DENR revokes SBMA power to issue environmental permits', *Manila Bulletin*, 8 January, A-8.

Legislative-Executive Bases Council, Republic of the Philippines (1990) *'Kumbersyon', Comprehensive conversion program, alternative uses of the military baselands and the military camps in Metro Manila.* A summary of the program submitted to Her Excellency Corazon C. Aquino, President of the Philippines, Hon. Jovito Salonga, President of the Senate and Hon. Ramon V. Mitra, Speaker of the House of Representatives (24 August).

Reside, Renato E Jr (2006) *Towards rational fiscal incentives: Good or wasted gifts?* EPRA Sector: Fiscal Report no. 1, Final Report, 7 June.

SBMA (Subic Bay Metropolitan Authority) (2008) Presentation for the Committee on Oversight, House of Representatives (14 July).

Senate Committee on Government Corporations and Public Enterprises (2005) *Highlights of Hearing*, 30 September.

Senate Economic Planning Office, Senate of the Philippines (2008) *Creation of economic zones: A need for review* (Policy Brief).

7 Iskandar Malaysia and Malaysia's dualistic political economy

Tey Tsun Hang[1]

The background of the bumiputera policy in Malaysia

Malaysia is a predominantly Muslim country situated in Southeast Asia. It gained independence from British colonial rule in 1957[2] and was subsequently joined by Singapore (which later separated from the Federation in 1965) and the states of Sabah and Sarawak in Borneo, to form a new Federation in 1963. Today, Malaysia is a constitutional monarchy and consists of thirteen states and carries a population of about 27.73 million comprising 53.3 per cent Malays, 26.0 per cent Chinese, 11.8 per cent other indigenous races, 7.7 per cent Indians and 1.2 per cent others.[3] Its government closely follows the British Westminster model and essentially adopts a parliamentary system of government which is bicameral in character – the two chambers of Parliament are the Senate (*Dewan Negara*) and the House of Representatives (*Dewan Rakyat*). Political power in the government has been dominated – without interruption – by the Barisan Nasional (BN) coalition[4] led by the United Malays National Organisation (UMNO) – a Malay political party.

There is no constitutional definition of 'bumiputera'. The word literally means 'son of the soil' and is usually co-relational to the usage of words such as 'native', 'aboriginal', 'indigene' and – most conveniently – 'Malay' (King 1995: 290, 435).[5] Article 160(2) of the Federal Constitution states that a Malay is 'a person who professes the Muslim religion, habitually speaks the Malay language [and] conforms to Malays custom'. Thus the definition does not technically demand that an individual be of Malay ethnicity before he is considered to be Malay (ibid.: 292). The special position of the bumiputera in Malaysia is constitutionally enshrined in Article 153 of the Federal Constitution and the respective state constitutions.[6] This special position has been reflected in Malaysia's government policies in the form of the New Economic Policy (NEP) – first established in 1970 – which provides preferential treatment to bumipiutera in areas such as scholarships, exhibitions, public services, and other educational or training privileges or facilities, and trade and business licences or permits. To date, there has been a total of nine Malaysia Plans promulgated by the federal government to tackle national objectives and issues such as the economy, growth and nation-building.

The latest plan, the Ninth Malaysia Plan, envisages and lays down the future direction of Malaysia's progress for the period of 2006–10.[7]

The historical development of the NEP can be traced to the simmering discontent among the Malays predating the infamous 1969 racial riot. Notwithstanding the confluence of factors that led to the racial riots in 1969, the economic inequality between the Malays and other minority races around that time formed a significant reason for the resentment that was brewing among the Malays in the run-up to the 1969 riots (Idriss 1990: 34–35; Jomo 1990: 2–5). By the 1960s the Malaysian economy was dominated by the Chinese community which formed a significant minority of Malaysia's population. This meant that while numerically speaking the Malays formed the majority population in Malaysia (and they enjoyed political dominance as well), the bulk of the country's wealth and assets were in the hands of the Chinese community (Idriss 1990: 33). This gave rise to a sharp disparity in wealth between the Malays and the Chinese;[8] the Malays were largely less prosperous than their Chinese counterparts because the Malays of that time were relatively inactive both industrially and commercially, but were instead predominantly occupied with agricultural activities that were not as lucrative (ibid.). Another significant factor was that the Malays largely resided in the rural areas, resulting in uneven population distribution across the country.

Such factors eventually led to the formulation of the NEP which aimed to promote 'national unity' under a two-pronged strategy: first, by eradicating poverty in Malaysia regardless of race; and second, by restructuring Malaysian society to correct the economic imbalance that had been plaguing the Malays and other natives of Malaysia for years (ibid.: 39).[9] It was envisaged that pursuing the latter goal would eventually lead to the elimination of the identification of race with economic function in Malaysia, the means to this end being 'the modernisation of rural life, the rapid and balanced development of urban activities, the establishment of new growth centres and the creation of a Malay commercial and industrial community in all categories and at all levels of operation' (ibid.).[10]

One of the major programmes consequently implemented was the creation of the Bumiputera Commercial and Industrial Community (BCIC) which

> has since become the focal point of the subsequent national development plans including the Five-Year Plans, the First Outline Perspective Plan 1971–90 (OPP1), the Second Outline Perspective Plan 1991–2000 (OPP2) and the National Development Policy (NDP) … [as well as the] Vision 2020 … and the Industrial Master Plan (IMP).
>
> (Abdul Rahman 1994: 19–20)

Simply put, the bumiputera policy during the NEP era referred to the set of policy strategies aimed at achieving increased bumiputera participation in the modern rural and urban sectors through (i) the increase of bumiputera employment in sectors traditionally dominated by other races in proportion to the national racial composition; and (ii) the increase of bumiputera share capital in the corporate sector to at least 30 per cent (based on the government's aim to structure Malaysia's economic wealth according to the ratio of 30:40:30, that is, 30 per cent for bumiputeras, 40 per cent for Malaysians in general, and 30 per cent for foreigners) (Chan and Horii 1986: 5) of the total by 1990 (Shamsul 1986: 98–99; Stoever 1985–86: 90–91).

Malaysia's political economy and informal dual legal order

Government intervention in multiracial Malaysia's economy is to a large extent politicized to project a nationalistic outlook so as to play up the ruling BN coalition's (which comprises, amongst other political parties, UMNO, MCA[11] and MIC)[12] popularity among the electorate through redistributive domestic economic policies, although such measures have on occasion been labelled as 'illiberal economic policy measures' which, together with other liberal economic policies meant to benefit foreign investors, have been 'driven, to a large extent, by coalitional priorities' (Ritchie 2004).

During the NEP era, attempts were made by the government to liberalize foreign investment in Malaysia. For example, the creation of ten 'free trade zones' (FTZs) in the early 1970s 'improved Malaysia's desirability as a host for low-cost assembly and re-export of electronics and other products' through 'provid[ing] advantages of tax free operation, elimination of import and expert duties, and exemptions from many NEP and [Industrial Coordination Act 1985] … requirements' (ibid.). However, it was also obvious that the Malaysian government, particularly in having '[a] combination of Mahathir's extreme pro-Malay position and his nationalist "Look East" policy' (ibid.), did not want to lose sight of the political imperative simultaneously to impose nationalist controls on domestic economic policies through interventionist measures that emphasized a redistribution of domestic wealth among the local population[13] – which obviously contained much to benefit the Malays.

On the other hand, the concomitant marginalization of the minority races by the NEP was delicately managed through political rhetoric by the ruling coalition. For instance, during the NEP era, it was observed that

> [a]s state intervention in the economy increased, the MCA and MIC began to argue that it was important for them to participate in business to accumulate wealth on behalf of the communities they claimed to represent … The argument by the MCA and the MIC proved effective in mobilizing support from the non-Malays, many of whom felt alienated by the NEP.
>
> (Gomez 2002)

The result was that the ruling coalition in Malaysia seemed to have politicized its economic policies with a keen mind on playing to the gallery so as to sustain its popular appeal to the electorate regardless of race and ethnicity.

The NEP transitioned in 1990 into the NDP (National Development Policy). Many observers have argued that despite a few changes and modifications, the NDP is a continuation of the NEP, both in substance and spirit. For example, while the overriding objectives of 'political stability and national unity' are still in place, the NDP retains 'the ongoing thrust of the NEP in eradicating poverty and restructuring society', as it continues to foster conditions conducive to the creation of a Malay commercial and industrial community (Leong 1992: 210). The government heavily politicized the NDP in the 1986 general election (Leong 1992: 212; Leong 1988). It was carried out in the mid-1980s through a 'seemingly more consultative process of policy-making' (ibid.),[14] unlike its predecessor, under which the designated instrument, the Economic Planning Unit (EPU), formulated policy with little or no consultation with interest groups and political parties in general (ibid.: 209).

The post-NEP privatization of state assets in Malaysia has also often been perceived to be associated with rent-seeking behaviour in Malaysia's political economy 'which have probably undermined the effectiveness of privatization, and allowed questionable executive decisions that have enabled greater control over resources to pass into the hands of a corporate sector dominated by politically-linked companies'.[15] The function of such extensive political patronage and interference in the privatization process arguably was to promote a government-selected elite class of wealthy and influential bumiputera businessmen which was 'crucial for continued political hegemony as rent-financed patron-client relations continue to be important in Malaysian politics' (Gomez and Jomo 1999: 99), thereby perpetuating an oligarchy in the Malaysian political order (Likosky 2004: 44–45).

Is it then accurate to say that such seemingly politically-driven economic policies in Malaysia were *non-democratic* or *authoritarian* policy manipulations for electoral gains?[16] On the surface of the government initiatives such as the NEP, NDP and other high-key economic corridor projects this might seem to be so if one were to adopt the view thus expressed:

> [N]on-democratic states where regimes face competitive elections should show predictable swings in their fiscal policy decisions that coincide with elections. Specifically, these regimes will, *ceteris paribus*, spend more in periods preceding an election. This increased spending may fund any number of electorally popular governmental initiatives, including increasing direct government transfers and implementing indirect transfers such as public works projects and bail-outs for failing industries that are key sources of electoral support. Such spending need not be 'bad' or 'wasteful' spending, but if spending consistently increases before elections – when controlling for other economic determinants of spending – then this is strong evidence the elections influence budgetary decision making.

> Controlling for other determinants of spending, we should observe higher government deficits in periods where the government faces elections.
>
> (Pepinsky 2007: 143)

However, it should be noted that such a view would not provide a complete picture of the political dynamics of Malaysia's economic policies since the view expressed above is essentially only concerned with fiscal policy decisions. In other words, policy decisions which are not classified as fiscal in character (e.g. purely affirmative-action driven policies aimed at artificially creating demand for Malay workers through ethnic employment quotas)[17] are not accounted for in this view.[18] Thus, although the politicization of Malaysia's economic policies over the years is clearly apparent, it is much more difficult to say with the same breath of confidence that such political behaviour was the only major factor driving Iskandar Malaysia.[19]

So far we have been looking at influences emanating from Malaysia's domestic political affairs and their role in shaping Malaysia's economic policies. Transnational commercial factors, on the other hand, also play a crucial role in developing an informal dual legal order[20] that provides the legal infrastructure necessary to advance Malaysia's economic policies.

Malaysia's dual legal order is unique because it is not organized purely through constitutional drafting or constitutional documentation (Likosky 2004: 85). It is informal in the sense that its duality is essentially adapted through contract, legislation and executive action (ibid.: 83, 85). These adaptations are ultimately the outcome of the assimilation of exogenous interests like transnational commercial interests into Malaysia's domestic socio- and politico-economic domain for the purpose of facilitating the integration of Malaysia into the global economy (Likosky 2002: 221–58). Paradigm examples in Malaysia include its post-independence move towards a strategy of export-led growth in the 1970s resulting in the opening of several export processing zones (EPZs) (sometimes also referred to as special economic zones [SEZs]) (ibid.: 232), the establishing of the state of Penang as a haven for offshore manufacturing of sophisticated high technology goods (Likosky 2004: 82–83), and the re-orientation of Malaysia's economy towards multi-media via the launching of the Multimedia Super Corridor (MSC) in the 1990s (Likosky 2002: 233). All these specially designated projects can generally be regarded as SEZ initiatives[21] whereby a substantial reformulation of Malaysia's domestic legal order for the sake of facilitating transnational commerce was carried out.

The reformulation of Malaysia's domestic legal order has been generally carried out in two ways: first, legal reform on a localized level to encourage foreign direct investment (i.e. the employment of investment incentives to attract foreign investors to invest in the host state) (Muchlinski 2007: ch. 6) and second, legal reform on a wider national level in alignment with certain SEZ objectives. A straightforward example of the former is the intra-corridor policies promulgated across the MSC in the form of a Bill of Guarantees granting privileged status to certain qualified companies (Likosky 2002: 236). An immediate example of the latter is the MSC, where reform aimed at boosting the influx of foreign IT-related businesses within the designated development corridor was publicized in the seventh Malaysia Plan.[22] Other less IT-related domestic legal reformulations which sought to foster a business-friendly environment for these foreign investors operating in the MSC were also put in place in the 1990s. For instance, in addition to the new cyberlaws enacted (such as the Digital Signature Act 1997, the Computer Crimes Act 1997, the Telemedicine Act 1997 and the Multimedia and Communications Act 1998), amendments to immigration laws, affirmative action laws, and a host of other measures have been undertaken in order to ensure a legislative environment suited to developing the IT sector in the country (Likosky 2002: 233). These measures, among others such as the establishment of the Special Copyright Task Force which was a part of the Enforcement Division of the Ministry of Domestic Trade and Consumer Affairs, were seen to be extra-corridor reforms undertaken to 'ensure that MSC-status companies would enjoy their Bill of Guarantee rights' (ibid.: 236–37). The bottom line here seems that as far as the Malaysian dual legal order is concerned, its SEZs are not entirely isolated from its local political domain as long as the need for Malaysia to liberalize its national economy remains.

However, in light of Malaysia's long-standing unique socio-economic bumiputera policy – which has recently been reaffirmed by the current prime minister Najib Razak when he launched the Ekuiti Nasional (Ekuinas) which aims to 'assist Bumiputera companies in competing in the domestic and global markets'[23] – it could thus be expected that the need for a strictly geographically de-limited dual legal order in Malaysia remains.[24]

In fact, as will be seen below, Iskandar Malaysia – one of the most recent SEZs established in southern Peninsular Malaysia – still preferred to adopt a restrained investment incentive policy by only confining the liberalization of the bumiputera quotas to within the geographical boundaries of the development region – thereby suggesting that the Malaysian government is still reluctant to align its extra-corridor legal domain with the intra-corridor commercial objectives in an entirely unreserved manner.

Iskandar Malaysia

Iskandar Malaysia was officially launched in 2006 under the South Johor Economic Region (SJER) project.[25] The Iskandar Regional Development Authority (IRDA) was established under the Iskandar Regional Development Authority Act 2007[26] with the objective of 'develop[ing] the Iskandar Development Region into a strong and sustainable metropolis of international standing' (s. 4). Accordingly, the IRDA is responsible, inter alia, for 'establish[ing] national policies, direction and strategies in relation to development within the Iskandar Development Region' (ss. 5, 6).

An interesting feature of Iskandar Malaysia is the Initial Incentive and Support Package (ISP) that significantly departed from the traditional bumiputera policy by making a concession to foreign investors seeking business opportunities in Iskandar Malaysia.[27] This concession entails, inter alia, tax incentives and entitlement for companies operating within Iskandar Malaysia to employ foreign employees freely within certain approved zones as long as such companies are granted IDR status.[28]

Basically, eligibility for the ISP is based on six key qualifying activities which have been identified by the IRDA: the creative industries, educational services, financial advisory and consulting services, healthcare services, logistics services and tourism.[29] The list of qualifying activities is, however, not exhaustive and may be reviewed and revised from time to time by the IRDA in line with the needs of investors, the region, and also the nation.

The most remarkable non-fiscal incentive granted to Iskandar Malaysia-status companies is the exemption from the Foreign Investment Committee (FIC) rules.[30] The legal status of the FIC rules has been explained as follows:

> The FIC is a committee and not a statutory body. The FIC Guidelines are not issued pursuant to any power granted by legislation, unlike the requirements under the National Land Code. Malaysian courts have held that the FIC Guidelines are simply administrative guidelines and do not have the force of law. Non-compliance however may have practical consequences particularly if the foreign investor needs to apply for any governmental licence, permit or approval such as employment work passes for expatriate personnel, or if the foreign investor wishes to participate in a government regulated sector as many governmental departments in Malaysia choose to conform to the views of the FIC.[31]

One immediate example of an exemption from the FIC rules is found in the *FIC Guideline on the Acquisition of Properties by Local and Foreign Investors.*[32] Section 9.3 of this guideline specifically provides that the guideline shall not apply to 'any acquisition of property by companies operating in the approved area in the Iskandar Regional Development and have been granted the status by the Iskandar Regional Development Authority', the effect of which directly affecting the bumiputera policy is that requirements under section 13 of the guideline (referring to equity, share capital and employment conditions for acquisition of properties by local and foreign interests) are waived.

Another example is the *FIC Guideline on the Acquisition of Interests, Mergers, and Take-overs by Local and Foreign Interests.*[33] Section 8.6 of this guideline expressly states that the provisions found in the guideline shall not apply to 'any acquisition of interest in a local company which operate in the approved area in the Iskandar Regional Development and have been granted the status by Iskandar Regional Development Authority (IRDA)' (ibid.). This similarly exempts approved companies from the equity, share capital and employment conditions imposed under sections 11–14 of the guideline.

Difficulties with the dualistic regime

Why the special status of Iskandar Malaysia?

Iskandar Malaysia is not the sole economic corridor established in Malaysia. In addition to the Multimedia Super Corridor,[34] there are two other economic corridors in Peninsular Malaysia, namely the Northern Corridor Economic Region (NCER)[35] and the East Coast Economic Region (ECER);[36] whereas in East Malaysia there are the Sabah Development Corridor (SDC)[37] and the Sarawak Corridor of Renewable Energy (SCORE), launched in 2008.[38]

In the NCER, there seem to be no non-fiscal incentives similar to those found in the ISP; the NCER only provided for certain financial and fiscal incentives as part of its strategy to 'provide an environment conducive to business'.[39] Similarly, the ECER only expressly provided for fiscal incentives within its region,[40] essentially leaving out any exemption from the bumiputera policy. Both SDC and SCORE in East Malaysia also did not seem to offer non-fiscal incentives similar to the ISP.[41] However, such a move to offer incentives under the ISP to lure foreign investments is nothing new to Malaysia, since it was reported that similar measures were undertaken in the 1980s and, more recently, under the Multimedia Super Corridor (MSC) status initiative:

> As far back as the 1980s, the government offered fiscal stimuli to the manufacturing sector that included full foreign ownership and unrestricted employment of foreign knowledge workers. More recently, the government also provided special privileges to companies awarded with Multimedia Super Corridor, or MSC, status.[42]

Why then the differential treatment in Iskandar Malaysia today? There is no immediate explanation, but it can be surmised that the Malaysian government is well aware that the success of the high-value[43] Iskandar Malaysia will ultimately depend on its ability to match with its far more urbanized and modernized immediate neighbour across the Johor straits – Singapore (Bhaskaran 2008: 66).

This, however, is not to say that Iskandar Malaysia is an outright aggressive project to challenge Singapore's status as a well-reputed financial hub which has more recently been focused on developing modern industries such as biotechnology, medical tourism and its flagship Integrated Resorts (IRs). Rather, economists prefer to view Iskandar Malaysia and Singapore as complementing each other in economic progress by way of synergizing the two states 'to generate greater economic benefits for both economies'.[44] It has also been reported that investors from Abu Dhabi and other parts of the Middle East have made it clear to the Malaysian government that their interest in Iskandar Malaysia would 'evaporate without the Singapore factor'.[45]

This indicates that '[i]nterest from Singapore is important for the success of [Iskandar Malaysia], which hopes to create a new economy by leveraging on proximity to the island'.[46] Unfortunately, such a view has not been warmly received by former prime minister Dr Mahathir Mohamad, who has been acrimoniously critical of Singapore and its government.[47]

However, it should be noted that while there has been no express exemption provided for the four other economic corridors in Malaysia, the FIC rules contain provisions that enable the local authorities of the respective economic regions to grant any exemption. For instance, section 8.7 of the *FIC Guideline on the Acquisition of Interests, Mergers, and Take-overs by Local and Foreign Interests* provides that the guideline shall not apply to 'any acquisition of interest in a local company which operates in the approved area in any regional development corridor by companies that have been granted the status by the local authority as determined by Government'.[48] Nevertheless, and as seen above, there is no clear indication of any such express exemption offered by the respective local authorities in the four other economic regions.

Uncertainty over the intended lifespan of the ISP

The objective of the ISP was expressly worded as follows:

> The development of [Iskandar Malaysia] requires a substantial amount of investment given the bulk of the development is targeted to be undertaken over the next 15 years. Developing a comprehensive ISP to attract private investors to invest these monies over the short-to-medium term is critical to kick start the development of [Iskandar Malaysia]. The ISP is structured to encourage early investment.[49]

It is noted that the ISP is likely to be a temporary measure aimed at kick-starting early economic development in Iskandar Malaysia by drawing foreign investment to the region. This is because of the usage of the word 'initial' together with 'incentive and support package' connoting a temporary nature of the ISP (ibid.).

However, there has been no clear indication of when exactly the ISP would be withdrawn, especially where predictions of when Iskandar Malaysia would actually develop to its maturity and self-sustainability remain unknown.

Is the ISP compatible with the twin-pronged strategy under the NEP and NDP?

The question of whether and when the ISP might be terminated is an important one especially in light of the longstanding objectives of the NEP (and subsequently, the NDP) in Malaysia.

To recapitulate briefly, the overarching objective of the NEP is to achieve national unity through a twin-pronged strategy aimed at eradicating poverty regardless of race, and by restructuring Malaysian society by closing the economic gap between the bumiputeras and the minorities. These objectives continue to be of ongoing pressing importance in the government's nation-building agenda.[50]

Here, the immediate difficulty with the ISP is its apparent incompatibility with the national aim of facilitating economic equality between the bumiputeras and non-bumiputeras in Malaysia, since the ISP now allows exemption from the employment and equity quotas reserved for the bumiputeras. Indeed, IRDA advisory council member Tun Musa Hitam already conceded that 'it was time to give up the New Economic Policy (NEP) for the success of [Iskandar Malaysia]'.[51] As such, the ISP would not come across as a welcome move to avid supporters (and especially the intended beneficiaries) of the NEP. As of 22 March 2007, former prime minister Abdullah Badawi had declared that Iskandar Malaysia would not have to require bumiputera equity participation in the six earmarked sectors.[52]

On the other hand, however, some commentators have applauded the Malaysian government's establishing of Iskandar Malaysia as a 'laboratory of "no-affirmative action" special economic zone' whose success 'may well be critical for a thorough review of the NEP, especially if Malay Malaysians do well there' (Rahman 2007). The existence of such sentiments is probably due to the strong criticisms that the NEP has drawn over the years since its implementation.[53] Another possible reason is that affirmative action in Malaysia has not worked well for the bumiputeras overall:

> Malay dissatisfaction has increased with growing awareness that better-off and politically connected Malays benefit disproportionately from the NEP. The majority resented the use of public funds to rescue a few wealthy Malay businessmen during the 1997–98 Asian financial crisis. It is a source of anger that Malay millionaires, for example, can take advantage of a 5 per cent housing discount for bumiputeras. In addition, the children of newly rich Malays seem to be the ones best placed to capitalise on ethnic preferences in the future, leaving their country cousins and poorer city relatives further behind.
>
> (Wain 2009)

Although the ISP would arguably provide the best opportunity for the bumiputeras to prove their ability to match, if not surpass, foreign and local non-bumiputera investors in terms of commercial and business competence, it is doubted whether this test could be passed in at least the next decade or so. The government has conceded that while the current economic policies continue to be committed to 'ensur[e] that the benefits of economic growth are shared equitably among all Malaysians',[54] the attainment of at least 30 per cent bumiputera equity ownership 'will only be achievable within a longer time frame' which essentially translates to the year 2020.[55]

Another difficulty with the ISP is that it seems to contradict Johor UMNO's 'main concern … that benefits arising from [Iskandar Malaysia] should not go to outsiders'.[56] In fact, one might immediately have thought that Johor UMNO's statement was wholly inconsistent with the general spirit of the ISP. Although it may be said that a balance could be struck between drawing foreign investors to kick-start the Iskandar Malaysia project and preserving the special position of the bumiputeras in Malaysia, it is less than clear how such a balance would be achieved in practice as long as the ISP initiative is in the way.

Conclusion

Iskandar Malaysia marks a significant departure from the NEP (and the NDP), essentially removing the bumiputera policy that has been serving to the advantage of the Malays and natives of Sabah and Sarawak for years. This is something that is not uniformly applied to the other economic corridors launched across Malaysia at around the same time.

However, such a departure from the nation's socio-economic bumiputera policy is geographically restricted, thereby suggesting that the Malaysian government is still reluctant to align its extra-corridor legal domain with the intra-corridor commercial objectives in an entirely unreserved manner. Thus put, it seems that a total homogenization of what was traditionally regarded as the dual legal order within Malaysia is still far from actual realization.

Notes

1 The author is grateful to Andrew Harding for his comments on an earlier draft, and Colin Seow for excellent research assistance.

2 The Federation of Malaya (in Malay, Persekutuan Tanah Melayu), a federation of eleven states in Peninsular Malaysia, existed from 31 January 1948 until 16 September 1963.

3 See Department of Statistics Malaysia, available online at www.statistics.gov.my/portal/index.php?lang=en (last accessed 20 February 2010); US Department of State on Malaysia, available online at www.state.gov/r/pa/ei/bgn/2777.htm (last accessed 20 February 2010).

4 Malay for the National Front. It was formed in 1973 as a successor to Perikatan (Malay for the Alliance) which had been Malaysia's ruling political party since independence.

5 It should also be noted that the words 'bumiputera' and 'native' do not correspond to any definable ethnic grouping in Malaysia, and can be used to refer to two broad categories of people, namely the Malays as defined in Article 160(2) of the Federal Constitution, and the natives of Malaysian Borneo (comprising the states of Sarawak and Sabah) as defined under Article 161A(6) of the Federal Constitution: see King 1995: 292.

6 See, e.g., Article 1 of the Third Part of the Constitution of the State of Johor.

7 Ninth Malaysia Plan. The Tenth Malaysia Plan – which will take effect in 2011 – is expected to be tabled at the Parliament in June 2010: '10th Malaysia plan will be

based on new economic model', *The Malaysia Insider*, 30 May 2009; '10th Malaysia Plan will be comprehensive, says Nor Mohamed', *Bernama*, 15 January 2010.

8 Although the Indians constituted a smaller portion of the population and were not as wealthy as the Chinese, they were still generally considered to be better-off than the Malays economically at that time: see Idriss 1990.

9 See also *Second Malaysia Plan* (1971–76) Kuala Lumpur: Government Printer, 1973.

10 See also *Mid-Term Review of Second Malaysia Plan*, Kuala Lumpur: Government Printer, 1973, 1.

11 Malaysian Chinese Association, representing the Chinese community.

12 Malaysian Indian Congress, representing the Indian community.

13 Such nationalist policies were propelled to the extent of 'increasingly ignor[ing] market forces': Ritchie 2004.

14 The consultative process was carried out by the National Economic Consultative Council (NECC).

15 See, e.g., Gomez and Jomo 1999: 98. The authors continued: 'This form of power centralisation and political involvement in the companies which have obtained privatised rents has meant that there is little protection of investments, sometimes even through the judicial process, from arbitrary executive decisions'.

16 See Pepinsky 2007: 142. The author continues: 'In cases where the expected costs of voter fraud or severe voter restrictions are high, incumbents choose to manipulate macroeconomic policy'.

17 As well as the encouragement of the rise of Malay supervisors and managers in Malaysia's overall labour force: Ritchie 2004.

18 See also Pepinsky 2007: 146 where after the author opined that 'Malaysia's political economy provides the foundation upon which the regime uses economic performance to enhance its rule. The regime openly affirms that economic performance is central to its political support, and throughout Malaysia's history it has acted accordingly', he specifically made reference to the regime having 'an incentive to manipulate *fiscal* policy when Malaysian citizens go to the polls' (emphasis added).

19 Previously known as South Johor Economic Zone as well as Iskandar Development Region: Pepinsky 2007.

20 On the concept of dual legal orders, see Likosky 2004: 83.

21 The essence of a SEZ (or EPZ) is that it 'represents a specialized form of investment incentive regime that has played a significant role in the evolution of globalised production by [multinational enterprises]': Muchlinski 2007: 226.

22 Section 14.142 of the Seventh Malaysia Plan states: 'A comprehensive review of IT-related legislation will be undertaken to promote more orderly development of IT and ensure that prevailing laws and regulations do not constrain the nation's efforts of becoming an information rich-society.'

23 'New approaches needed to help Bumis, says Najib', *New Straits Times* (Malaysia), 3 August 2009.

24 In April 2009, Prime Minister Najib Razak announced that the longstanding requirement that foreign investors in the services industry must fulfil the requirement of bumiputera equity ownership of 30 per cent of any joint venture, would be lifted immediately for twenty-seven sub-sectors, including health and social services, tourism, transport, business and computer-related services: Hazlin Hassan, 'Malaysia eases ownership rules', *Straits Times* (Singapore) 3 April 2009; Abid Zalkapli, 'Najib drops bumiputra quota for services sector', *Malaysian Insider*, 22 April 2009.

25 It is named after the Sultan of Johor, 'as a tribute to the role played by the sultanate in the development of modern Johor': 'Growth area to be named after Sultan', *New Straits Times*, 31 October 2006.

26 Available online at www.irda.com.my/pdf/act/IRDA_Act_2007_(EN).pdf. (last accessed 20 February 2010). The IRDA is co-chaired by the prime minister and the *menteri besa*r (chief minister) of the state of Johor: see s. 8 of the Act.
27 See media statement released by the IRDA on 22 March 2007, available online at www.khazanah.com.my/docs/ISP-IRDA%20Announcement_220307.pdf (last accessed 20 February 2010)
28 Ibid.
29 See press release at www.iskandar.com.my/index.php?option=com_content&task=view&id=190 (accessed 28 February 2010).
30 Ibid. Foreign investors must apply to Malaysia's Foreign Investment Committee (FIC) of the Economic Planning Unit, Prime Minister's Department, for approval in certain transactions as set out in its guidelines (FIC Guidelines): See online at www.irda.com.my/media-faqs.aspx?mid=10&smid=0&cid=9.
31 See www.iskandar.com.my/index.php?option=com_content&task=view&Itemid=8 (accessed 28 February 2010).
32 See www.wct.com.my/CMS/Contents/205/Full/wctfic.pdf (accessed 28 February 2010).
33 Available online at www.epu.gov.my/html/themes/epu/images/common/pdf/form_download/GP_SyerBI.pdf (last accessed 20 February 2010).
34 Called MSC Malaysia, it covers an area that stretches from Kuala Lumpur to the southern part of the state of Selangor, and carries the official mission of developing Malaysia's information and communications technology sectors. See online at www.mscmalaysia.my/home (last accessed 20 February 2010).
35 This encompasses the states of Kedah, north of Perak, Perlis and Pulau Pinang (Penang). The NCER initiative was launched in 2007 and is expected to span from 2007 to 2025 when the government is expected to release its Twelfth Malaysia Plan. The objectives of the NCER are as such:

> Firstly, the programme is part of the Government's commitment to helping the Region maximise its economic potential and closing the development and income gap between the different regions in Malaysia. Secondly, the Malaysian economy aims to move towards higher value-added and knowledge-based economic activities to drive further increases in per capita income.
> (See www.ncer.com.my/en/about/index.html (accessed 28 February 2010)

The development of the NCER is overseen by the Northern Corridor Implementation Authority established by the Northern Corridor Implementation Authority Act 2008: see www.ncer.com.my/ (accessed 20 February 2010).
36 This encompasses the states of Kelantan, Pahang and Terengganu as well as the district of Mersing in the state of Johor. The ECER was launched in 2007 and is expected to last for a period of twelve years: see www.ecerdc.com.my/ecerdc/about.htm (accessed 28 February 2010). This project is run by the ECER Development Council established under the East Coast Economic Region Development Council Act 2008: see www.ecerdc.com.my/ecerdc/dc.htm (accessed 28 February 2010).
37 See www.kln.gov.my/perwakilan/karachi/event/1265 (accessed 20 February 2010).
38 See www.sarawakscore.com.my/ (accessed 20 February 2010).
39 See www.massa.net.my/news/y7_q3_a8.htm (accessed 28 February 2010).
40 See www.ecerdc.com/2008/about7.htm (accessed 20 February 2010).
41 See, e.g., for SCORE, www.sarawakscore.com.my/modules/mbr/components/incentive/?mainpageid=incentive (accessed 20 February 2010).
42 'New parameters to attract investors', *New Straits Times*, 21 April 2007. But it should be noted that these measures were intra-corridor measures.
43 And reportedly Malaysia's 'largest undertaking yet, worth an estimated RM383 billion (US$109 billion)': ibid.

44 'S'pore can be catalyst for Iskandar success: DBS', *Business Times* (Malaysia), 14 April 2007.
45 'Singapore-in-Iskandar will test Najib-Dr M ties', *Malaysian Insider*, 14 April 2009.
46 'Iskandar: S'pore investors tread cautiously', *Straits Times* (Singapore), 29 August 2009.
47 'Beware the IDR falling into S'pore's hands', *Straits Times* (Singapore), 5 September 2007; 'Singapore-in-Iskandar will test Najib-Dr M ties', *Malaysian Insider*, 14 April 2009.
48 See also section 9.4 of the *FIC Guideline on the Acquisition of Properties by Local and Foreign Interests.*
49 See statement released by the IRDA on 22 March 2007, at www.khazanah.com.my/docs/ISP-IRDA%20Announcement_220307.pdf (last accessed 20 February 2010).
50 See, e.g., chapter 16, Ninth Malaysia Plan.
51 'Musa: Brief UMNO on why it has to give up NEP', *Star*, 23 March 2007.
52 Lim Kit Siang, 'Why Iskandar Development Region will fail', at http://blog.limkitsiang.com/2007/03/24/why-iskandar-development-region-will-fail/ (last accessed 20 February 2010).
53 See, e.g., the opposition Democratic Action Party's (DAP's) criticism of the NEP at www.dapmalaysia.org/english/2007/july07/lge/lge679.htm (last accessed 20 February 2010).
54 Chapter 16, Ninth Malaysia Plan, 323.
55 Chapter 16, Ninth Malaysia Plan, 347. However, there have been allegations that the 30 per cent target 'was achieved as early as 1997': Wain, 2009; or that the bumiputera equity ownership has exceeded the 30 per cent target: Surin, JA et al., 'Lim stands by reports, quits ASLI', *News Without Borders*, 11 October 2006.
56 'Iskandar to be on everyone's lip at UMNO meet', *New Straits Times*, 4 November 2006. Johor UMNO information chief Senator Dr Moh Puad Zarkashi was quoted as saying: 'We are talking about job and business opportunities. It would defeat the purpose if the local people do not become the direct beneficiaries of [the Iskandar Malaysia project]'.

Bibliography

Abdul Rahman, Abdul Aziz (1994) 'Nurturing of Bumiputera SMIs through PROTON's vendor scheme: A case study of Tracoma', in Fujio, H, ed., *The development of bumiputera enterprises and Sino-Malay economic cooperation in Malaysia.* Tokyo: Institute of Developing Economies.

Bhaskaran, M (2008) 'The Iskandar Development Region and Singapore', in Huang, Y and AM Bocchi, eds, *Reshaping economic geography in East Asia*. Washington, DC: World Bank Publications.

Chan, P and K Horii (1986) *Impact of the New Economic Policy on the Malaysian economy: With special reference to ownership and control.* Tokyo: Institute of Developing Economies.

Gomez, ET (2002) *Political business in East Asia.* New York: Routledge.

Gomez, ET and KS Jomo (1999) *Malaysia's political economy: politics, patronage and profits.* Cambridge: Cambridge University Press.

Idriss, Ahmad (1990) *Malaysia's New Economic Policy.* Petaling Jaya: Pelanduk Publications.

Jomo, KS (1990) *Beyond the New Economic Policy? Malaysia in the nineties* (The Sixth James C Jackson Memorial Lecture presented at Griffith University, Brisbane, 2 July 1990, Malaysia Society of the Asian Studies Association of Australia.

King, VT (1995) 'Indigenous people and land rights in Sarawak, Malaysia: To be or not to be a bumiputra', in Barnes, RH, A Gray and B Kingsbury, eds, *Indigenous peoples of Asia*. Ann Arbor, MI: The Association for Asian Studies.

Leong, HK (1988) 'The 1986 Malaysian elections: Analysis and results', *Asian Profile* 16(3): 239.

—— (1992) 'Dynamics of policy-making in Malaysia: The formulation of the New Economic Policy and the National Development Policy', *Asian Journal of Public Administration* 14(2): 204.

Likosky, M (2002) 'Cultural imperialism in the context of transnational commercial collaboration', in Likosky, M, ed., *Transnational legal processes: Globalization and power disparities*. London: Butterworths.

—— (2004) *The silicon empire: Law, culture and commerce*. Aldershot: Ashgate.

Muchlinski, P (2007) *Multinational enterprises and the law*, 2nd edn, Oxford: Oxford University Press.

Pepinsky, T (2007) 'Autocracy, elections, and fiscal policy: Evidence from Malaysia', *Studies in Comparative International Development* 42: 136.

Rahman, Azly (2007) 'Slaying an immortal tiger: Malaysia's New Economic Policy', *OpinionAsia*, 16 July.

Ritchie, B (2004) 'Politics and economic reform in Malaysia', William Davidson Institute Working Paper no. 655.

Shamsul, AB (1986) *From British to bumiputera rule: Local politics and rural development in Peninsular Malaysia*. Singapore: ISEAS.

Stoever, W (1985–86) 'Malaysia, the bumiputra policy, and foreign investors: An evaluation', *Studies in Comparative International Development* 20(4): 86–107.

Wain, B (2009) 'Not as simple as Mahathir paints it', *Straits Times*, Singapore, 24 July.

8 SEZs in India

An economic policy or a political intervention?

Shankar Gopalakrishnan

India was among the first Asian countries to institute 'export processing zones' (EPZs), with the creation of an EPZ at Kandla in the state of Gujarat in 1965. Yet such zones did not form a part of India's overall economic strategy until the passage in 2005 of the Special Economic Zones Act (SEZ Act) (Harding, this volume), which catapulted these zones to the centre of India's economic 'reforms'.

The SEZ Act was justified as a measure to give statutory status to these zones and provide them with a uniform, comprehensive policy framework. With the debate framed in this manner, much of the discussion on SEZs in India and elsewhere has focused on the question of whether or not these zones will fulfill such objectives and improve upon the earlier EPZ model. Secondarily, as a result of an explosion of protests across India against forced acquisition of peasants' lands by state governments for the purpose of SEZs, there has also been considerable discussion of how 'development' and 'industrialization' can take place in a predominantly agricultural society.

This paper argues, however, that both these approaches do not engage with the far deeper and more complex implications that SEZs have for India's polity and economy. SEZs are not merely another incentive policy for exports and foreign investment; they are rather a political intervention in India's governance institutions. This is apparent if we place the Indian zones in the context of India's own developing political economy and the international history of the concept of special zones. It is as a result of the real impact of SEZs and the far-reaching nature of this policy that the zones have, since early 2006, become such a flashpoint of conflict. The long term impact of these dynamics will be of interest not only in India but internationally as well.

Background: the Indian polity and economic 'reforms'

Between 1965 and 2000 a total of seven EPZs were set up in India. These zones were small in size, relatively low in investment and employment and subject to the same laws and procedures as the rest of the country (excepting some tax concessions and specialized infrastructure facilities). The zones drew relatively small amounts of foreign investment. In 1985 the zones were producing roughly 4.4 per cent of India's manufactured exports (Aggarwal 2004). Yet, both in terms of policy and in terms of their contribution to India's larger economy, the zones occupied a relatively marginal position.

To understand why the concept of special zones made the transition from this marginal position to the central one it has acquired today, it is important first to map the changes in the Indian polity that took place during this period. After a balance of payments crisis in 1991, India began to implement a structural adjustment programme, including the elements of regulatory rollback, fiscal conservatism, and trade and financial liberalization. These economic reforms have continued to the present day. Rather than the more ambiguous terms 'globalization' or 'liberalization' usually used to describe these changes, I will here use the term 'neo-liberalism', since it appears to more accurately describe the phenomena at work.

The details of the politics around these reforms are beyond the scope of this paper, but a very brief outline of some trends can provide the broad context for understanding SEZs. First, unlike in the case of, for instance, Britain under Thatcher, the Latin American nations under their military dictatorships or the USA under Reagan, neo-liberalism in India lacked (and continues to lack) a coherent institutional and political base. The support for neo-liberalism has, as in most countries, come from certain sections of the bureaucracy in alliance with large finance and industrial capitalists and the urban elite, but there has been no single political formation that has served to generate, organize and focus popular support for these policies.

From the point of view of supporters of reforms, this has been both a positive and a negative feature. The positive aspect has been that it has been possible to win over elements from most political parties, as well as selected powerful forces at various political levels, to specific reformist agendas at various points. This was described by Jenkins (1999) as 'reforms by stealth': a process of sweeping and deep policy changes achieved through behind-the-scenes negotiations and engagements, without involving either public debate or open involvement of democratic institutions. This has produced in turn an apparent 'consensus' whereby all major political parties in one way or another endorse at least some aspects of neo-liberal reforms in their policy statements.

The advantage of this becomes doubly apparent when one notes that there has been an intensifying resistance to neo-liberal reforms. As in most other developing countries, the impact of neo-liberal reforms has been an intensification of rural distress, a collapse of state welfare systems and a sharp decline in the security and rights of workers (both in the formal and in the unorganized sectors). While the neo-liberal reforms have produced a rapidly rising rate of GDP growth, they have had simultaneously negative results for most Indians – in particular farmers, agricultural and urban workers and other segments of the poor – and have caused utter devastation for a significant section.[1]

In such a context, the 'reforms by stealth' strategy has helped diffuse resistance and prevent it from consolidating, producing a paradoxical situation where mass discontent with neo-liberalism is widespread but there is no national-level, coordinated political force that can articulate this discontent. As election analyst Yogendra Yadav put it in his response to the last general elections, '[t]he case that this was a mandate against policies of economic reforms is an overstatement … having said this, it is equally necessary to realize that … if this election could [have been] a referendum on economic reforms, the policies of liberalization would have been rejected' (Yadav 2004).

Yet, even as this is a strength of the reformists, it is also a significant weakness. The lack of an organized political support base means that discontent can be diffused, diverted or ignored, but it cannot be confronted and overcome. Hence, where the neo-liberal agenda requires direct confrontation with an organized political force, reformists have frequently been forced to compromise on their goals. The result is that several 'big ticket' reforms, as the Indian media refers to them, have been stalled for many years. Some of these include:

- the dismantling or dilution of India's formal sector labour laws;
- the withdrawal of food subsidies and the dismantling of the public distribution system, which procures certain food items from farmers at a prescribed minimum price and supplies this food at subsidized prices through a national network of 'fair price' shops;
- the privatization of major public sector enterprises and of the nationalized banks (government owned banks taken over from the private sector in 1971);
- the withdrawal of subsidies to farmers, in particular on fertilizer and electricity supplies;
- liberalization of restrictions on the retail trade and allowing foreign investment in the retail sector.

These are only some examples, but in each case, the reformists have only been able to push through partial and incomplete measures. Examples of this include limited dilution of labour laws through court rulings and the application of poverty line-based targeting to the public distribution system (which many state governments have now begun to overrule). Neo-liberal commentators frequently note that 'second generation' reforms (as many of these areas are described) are 'stuck', with many lamenting the prominence of 'populist politics' in blocking such measures. Nor has this frustration been limited to Indian big business or Indian neo-liberal commentators – it has been echoed by international neo-liberal agencies such as the World Bank, the IMF and other such organizations.

In reaction to these tendencies, there has been a growing shift in the manner in which Indian companies and multinationals seek to address these barriers. Part of the growth in corporate profits and elite incomes in India has been driven by the reasons cited in the media and in most economic debates, including lower taxation, implicit or explicit subsidies, greater freedom of action, trade liberalization and lower import prices, and so on. But this is only part of the story. The other part of this sector's gains has come through a process best captured by David Harvey's (2003) concept of 'accumulation by dispossession'. This term refers to the use of state power, usury and other forcible means to seize resources and expropriate smaller producers and smaller capitals. Integral to capitalism at all times, this is accentuated under neo-liberalism, where both state assets and the assets of small commodity producers (such as peasants and artisans) become far easier to seize as a result of deflationary and 'rollback' policies. In the Indian case, its importance is clear from recent history. Hence the repeated attempts at easing private companies' access to forest, water and other common resources, the use of debt and credit as a method of extracting surpluses (with devastating impacts on agriculture), and, most obviously, the use of colonial-era laws to forcibly acquire private agricultural lands upon payment of paltry cash compensation. The last is meant to occur only where such acquisition is required by a 'public purpose', but in practice the courts and the administration have defined that phrase so broadly that acquisition for private projects is now the norm.

The changing Indian political situation has made such options increasingly attractive for corporations seeking super-profits. In the face of rising political barriers and limitations on policy changes, it is easier to attempt to seize resources through manipulation of the state machinery than to continue focusing on changing larger policies. A classic instance is the huge increase in mining activity, an extractive industry where companies receive both land and ore either for free or at very low royalty rates. The Orissa government claims to have signed Rs2 trillion (US$43 billion) worth of mining projects since the current government came into power (Merchant 2006). One of these new projects is India's largest proposed foreign investment, a gigantic steel project by Pohang Steel Corporation (POSCO) of South Korea – which incidentally has been granted SEZ status. Estimates say that the company will receive a minimum of Rs960 billion (US$2 billion) in windfall profits because of undervaluation of land, tax incentives and extremely low royalties on iron ore (Pati 2005). Similarly, the Jharkhand government has fifty-four memoranda of understanding for steel and power plants pending. Meanwhile, over 500,000 hectares of forest land have been diverted for various projects in the last five years alone, with much of this land being transferred to private companies (Chopra et al. 2006). India's real estate sector is witnessing a boom based on cheap handovers of government land and state acquisition of private lands for 'development' purposes. It is hence no surprise that seven of the top ten most profitable companies in India are either involved in real estate or in natural resources (*Business World* 2008).

Once again, there are limits to this strategy. Unlike the diffuse mass discontent produced by earlier neo-liberal policies, such efforts lead directly to violent conflict. The state of West Bengal for instance saw two mass uprisings against land acquisition, in one of which (Nandigram) more than fifty people were killed by the state machinery and the ruling party. In Orissa, POSCO's steel project is facing a three-year rebellion by the people of the area, who have cordoned off the proposed project site and refused to allow entry by any administrative officials until the project is withdrawn. The expansion of the armed Maoist organizations in large parts of central India has so alarmed the central (federal) and state governments that it has led to moves to fast-track changes in the Land Acquisition Act 1894 (after decades of apathy on the issue) as well as extremely brutal security responses, such as the *salwa judum* state-sponsored militia in the state of Chhattisgarh.

The overall result of these battles is that the neo-liberal process in India, and indeed the Indian polity in general, is in a highly fluid and contested situation which is increasingly polarized between corporate capital and mass anger. It is against this background that the SEZ policy should be viewed.

The formation of the Special Economic Zones Act 2005

From 1 April 2000, under India's new Export-Import Policy, the existing EPZs were renamed 'special economic zones' and other changes made to the EPZ policy, including allowing for private SEZs. Around fifty-three new zones were approved over the following five years, though most did not become operational prior to the passage of the SEZ Act.

Many of the features of the current SEZ Act were brought in through this policy. Private sector SEZs were allowed for the first time; prior to this, all zones were set up by the state governments. Incentives were greatly increased, and both SEZ units and developers were provided with duty-free imports of raw materials and capital goods.[2] Further powers were delegated to the top government official in the zone, known as the development commissioner, including the authority to serve as the labour commissioner (the nodal officer for administering labour laws) for the zones. The structure of overall governance was reduced to a three-tier system, with the SEZ cell in the Ministry of Commerce at the top, followed by a Board of Approvals at the Centre which would decide on units' applications to locate into SEZs, and finally the development commissioners of the zones themselves. Regulations on foreign investment were greatly eased.

Yet, the central government argued that there was a lack of coherence in SEZ administration, given that various ministries were required to take independent action in order to implement this policy. Hence in 2004 the central government revived a bill that had been drafted by the previous government. This eventually became the SEZ Act when it was passed by Parliament in 2005.

The new Act set in place an SEZ policy with the following characteristics. Three basic types of SEZs were provided for: 'multi-product' zones that could have multiple types of industry within them, 'single sector' zones that were focused on one or the other industrial sector, and 'free trade and warehousing zones' that were focused on storage and trade (ports, for instance). Each zone has a minimum area requirement – 1,000 hectares for multi-product zones, 100 for single-sector zones and 40 for free-trade and warehousing zones. These limits were reduced for less-developed states as an incentive. After the conflict over SEZs began, the central government also introduced a ceiling of 5,000 hectares for all zones.

The legislation allows any private company, state government, or the central government, to apply to the Board of Approvals at the central level for designation as the 'developer' of a SEZ. The Board may grant an 'in principle' approval if the land is not yet in the possession of the developer or a 'formal approval' once the land is in the developer's possession. The Board then is to approve the developer's plan for the SEZ before the zone is finally notified by the central government (Harding, this volume). Once a zone is notified, both the developer of the zone and units within it are provided a sweeping incentive package including exemption from all import duties and tax holidays (a ten-year holiday on income tax for the developer and a five-year full holiday, along with a five-year partial one, for units). Sales from an SEZ into the rest of the country (the 'domestic tariff area') would, however, be subject to customs duties. The zones are further divided into two parts, a 'processing area' that must consist of at least 50 per cent of the zone's total area, and a 'non-processing area'. The processing area is for authorized industrial units. Land in the non-processing area may, however, be used for 'business and social purposes such as educational institutions, hospitals, hotels, recreation and entertainment facilities, residential and business complexes'; the developer can also lease this land to any company authorized as a 'co-developer' for similar purposes.[3] All such developments will also be eligible for tax and other concessions if they are part of the 'authorized operations' within the zones.

The zone is to be headed by a single officer, appointed by the central government, known as the development commissioner. Regulatory requirements are also relaxed and the powers of regulatory bodies (such as those responsible for pollution and environmental clearance) are devolved to the development commissioner. The rules further compel the state governments to ease the process of receiving various clearances and to restrict strikes within the zones.

The international context

On the face of it, these features of the policy look similar to those of other EPZs and SEZs around the world. But the first indicator of the distinct political purpose of Indian SEZs can be seen if we place them against the international background (Muchlinski, this volume). Even if one takes the government's policy statements at face value, in view of recent international developments, it is unusual for the government to have justified a policy choice like SEZs on the basis of export-zone justifications. The export-zone model has come under increasing criticism even from its original supporters, for it fails to satisfy demands for generalized trade liberalization, is increasingly ineffective at attracting FDI in the face of competition between different developing countries, and often generates an 'enclave' economy with few linkages with the host economy. As a result of these changes, by the late 1990s the international financial institutions and the international development agencies – nearly all of whom, except to some degree the ILO, had earlier supported EPZs – now began to sound increasingly sceptical. Thus by 1998 the World Bank had declared that they were a 'second-best policy choice' and 'should not be established in liberal, low protection economies'. Meanwhile, steps in the WTO to bar export subsidies in general as 'anti-trade' mechanisms led eventually to the application of the Agreement on Subsidies and Countervailing Measures, which bars any form of specific export subsidy, to all developing countries (UNCTAD 2003).

Why then rely on such a model, when it is out of favour with the international agencies and institutions to which Indian neo-liberals normally look for direction? The reason is that the international shift has not been as simple as a rejection of special zones: even as the international climate has moved against EPZs, it has shifted in favour of other types of zone. Indeed, policy-makers in India and elsewhere have eulogized one particular model of zone – the Chinese SEZ – as truly effective, unlike the old EPZs, in particular on grounds of size and 'political will'.

If one looks closely at these shifts, it becomes apparent that there have been roughly three 'phases' of zone policies across the world (Gopalakrishnan 2008). These can roughly be summarized as follows:

- *Phase 1: zones as part of export-oriented developmentalist states.* In this phase, zones were set up in the Asian nations of South Korea and Taiwan as an integral part of a larger export-oriented development strategy. Rather than being areas of general liberalization, zones in these countries combined some forms of deregulation with very specific regulations in others (such as requirements for increased value addition and restrictions on repatriation of capital). This ensured that the zones fit into a larger strategy of increasing domestic value addition and exports together. This phase largely became obsolete when the rise of neo-liberal policies rendered such targeted developmentalist strategies impossible.
- *Phase II: zones as a crisis response.* In this phase, when zones became much more common, they were prescribed by international financial institutions as a remedy for several common international trade problems in developing countries – particularly foreign exchange shortages and trade deficits. The zones here, typified by the EPZs of Latin America, essentially sought to offer incentives to international capital in whatever way possible to draw export-oriented production to their areas. While zones proliferated, few achieved their goals; and it is these zones that

today attract such sharp criticism from international financial institutions and other agencies.

- *Phase III: zones as territories for accumulation*. But it is the third phase that has remained largely unnoticed in the Indian context. This phase is marked by the Chinese SEZs, which began with the traditional goal of earning foreign exchange but soon morphed into something much larger – a 'laboratory' for changes in economic and political institutions in a manner that would favour private investment and capital. The difference was the sheer size of the Chinese SEZs together with the staggeringly sweeping manner of policy transformations within them (including experiments with individual land rights, contract labour, competitive bidding, floating wages, withdrawal of banking restrictions, and so on). It is critical to understand the importance of this change. Chinese SEZs now ceased to be exporting centres; their primary importance became explicitly *political*. They were to be areas where new methods of capital accumulation could be applied, in the context of policies that increasingly treated rapid accumulation as the goal of state action. Ironically, the praise these zones have received comes at a time when there is serious rethinking on their meaning within China as well (Gopalakrishnan 2007).

Where on this continuum do Indian SEZs lie? As we saw above, the international financial institutions and international capital have largely lost interest in the second type of zone, though the Indian government still uses the conceptual framework of that phase to describe SEZs. For this reason many neo-liberal commentators within and outside India have been sharply critical of SEZs. Yet, this stems from a fundamental misunderstanding, for the purpose of Indian SEZs is not to create the second type of zone, but the third one, and in a more extreme fashion than has ever been attempted before.

The political nature of SEZs

This reality becomes clearer if we consider certain striking features of the Indian SEZ legislation and policy. Indeed, if one discards the EPZ conceptual framework and simply reads the SEZ Act as a legal instrument, one begins to find that the Act's stated goals and its actual content are entirely at variance with each other (Harding, this volume).

Zones created 'on demand'

The first and most salient point in this regard is the concept of *declaring an SEZ 'on demand'*. An SEZ is created not as a result of a planning exercise by the government, but as a result of an application by a government or a company. But SEZs, EPZs or other types of zone are quintessentially tools of industrial policy – created in order to generate exports, promote certain types of industry, and encourage development of backward areas. They may be *run* by private parties, but the concept of systematically *creating* them as a result of private initiative runs against the grain of the concept.

No doubt one response will be that allowing private initiative makes the policy more 'investor friendly' by offering more choice, and in any case the overall goals of the SEZ policy will be maintained by the central government when approving SEZ applications. Is this not, after all, the function of the Board of Approvals at the centre? However, the legal provisions are such that this is entirely untrue. Section 5 of the SEZ Act does provide that, at the time of notifying an SEZ, the central government should be 'guided' by considerations of:

- generation of additional economic activity;
- promotion of exports of goods and services;
- promotion of investment from domestic and foreign sources;
- creation of employment opportunities;
- development of infrastructure facilities; and
- maintenance of the sovereignty and integrity of India, the security of the state and friendly relations with foreign states.

Three issues should be noted. First, this consideration occurs not at the stage of approval – the logical stage for it to occur, for it is there that a specific authority (the Board of Approvals) considers SEZ proposals – but at the stage of final notification, when land acquisition is complete. Second, no authority is made responsible for ensuring this 'guidance' is followed. Third, the specified factors are extremely nebulous, and it would be difficult to find any industrial or service project that did not satisfy at least one. These three factors combined make this provision essentially meaningless.

Therefore, the *only* factor that is required to be taken into account at the time of approving an SEZ is whether the developer company (or government) is in possession of, or intends to acquire, the minimum area of land specified for that type of SEZ. It is this that accounts for the ease with which the Board of Approvals has issued dozens of approvals in every meeting – with a total of more than 500 in principle and formal approvals issued so far. In short, an SEZ in India has been defined in legal practice – official rhetoric notwithstanding – as essentially a space to be created when sufficiently big companies demand it. Its other objectives are at best secondary, if not irrelevant.

Encouragement of non-industrial and speculative activity

This leads us to a second strange feature of the legislation: the decision to throw open the zones to non-export and even non-industrial uses. As mentioned above, the zones are divided into processing areas and non-processing areas. Within processing areas, any unit can be set up with approval from the

Board of Approvals, and once again only one requirement is imposed: the units should have a 'positive net foreign exchange earning in the first five years' (SEZ Rules 2006: rule 53). In single-sector SEZs, these units must all belong to the sector in question; but in multi-product SEZs, they can belong to any sector.

In the non-processing area, the land can be used for 'business and social purposes'. Two reasons are frequently cited as to why such a non-processing area should be necessary in an SEZ: (i) to provide adequate housing and other amenities for the workers in the zone; and (ii) as an additional incentive to developers to help them make the zone 'profitable'. Neither of these seems entirely logical. The former can be provided outside the zone as well, and there is no need to allow them to enjoy tax exemptions. As for the latter, it amounts to stating that the developer is not expected to make a profit from industrial units in the zone.

Indeed, the latter logic compounds the sense that the key focus of SEZs is the creation of a *space* rather than any particular activity. From the central government's list of permitted activities in the non-processing areas of SEZs, we can gain a sense of what is expected from the use of this space. This list includes restaurants, housing and apartments, club houses, gymnasia, shopping arcades and retail space, multiplexes, schools, 'convention or business centres' and – oddly enough – swimming pools. Hotels are allowed in all SEZs except IT, biotech and gems SEZs.[4]

In short, real estate activity is regarded as integral to SEZ areas. This is no 'aberration', as it is sometimes described by defenders of the SEZ policy. Rather, as we saw above, the SEZ Act, rules and guidelines together present a consistent picture emphasizing allocating a space rather than encouraging any particular activity. This space is then explicitly allowed to be used for real estate purposes, indicating that real estate speculation is in no way seen as objectionable.

Extreme centralization of governance institutions

In sharp contrast to the nebulous regulation of economic activities in the zone, there is a remarkable clarity within the SEZ policy on the state structures that will control the zone. These matters have received relatively little attention in the policy debate.

The SEZ governance model relies on a single supreme authority: the zone's development commissioner. Provisions in the Act and the rules essentially transfer most state regulatory powers to this commissioner. This not only includes powers over environmental regulation, labour inspections, and so on, but also control over infrastructure and public services, which cannot be provided except with the commissioner's permission and by agreement with the developer (section 3(11) of the Act). The stated policy justification for these measures – reducing 'bureaucratic red tape' – essentially means the centralization of all regulatory powers.

Accompanying these regulatory relaxations are changes in judicial and policing functions. 'No investigation, search or seizure shall be carried out in a Special Economic Zone by any agency or officer' except with the permission of the development commissioner (section 22 of the Act). The only exception is in the case of 'notified offences', which the central government can notify under section 21 of the Act. Even in the case of such offences, the development commissioner must be intimated before any investigation (section 22 of the Act). The Act also provides that there will be special courts set up in SEZs for both civil and criminal matters, and these courts will be the only courts that can hear any civil dispute within an SEZ or any trial of a 'notified offence' (section 23 of the Act). Ordinary criminal trials of non-notified offences can take place in ordinary courts, but note that no investigation of such crimes is possible without the authorization of the development commissioner. Appeals from the special courts will lie directly to the High Court of the state (section 24 of the Act). These provisions together thus produce a system of a separate judiciary for the SEZ (Harding, this volume) where, once again, the development commissioner plays a key role.

Third, local governance institutions are essentially dissolved. The state SEZ policies of Andhra Pradesh, Gujarat, Jharkhand, Karnataka, Kerala, Madhya Pradesh, Orissa, Rajasthan, Tamil Nadu, Uttar Pradesh and West Bengal[5] all declare that SEZs will be notified as 'industrial townships' under Article 243Q of the Constitution. This exempts them from the provisions of Part IX of the Constitution, which provides for elected municipal governments. Instead, an industrial township authority is constituted with the same powers and duties as a municipal body, but without any elected members. In West Bengal, as per section 28(2) of the West Bengal Special Economic Zones Act, the governing body consists of three government representatives, one representative of the developer and two representatives of the units in the zone. In Maharashtra, in the case of SEZs the draft Maharashtra Special Economic Zones Act states that this body would have three nominees of the developer and two of the state government. In such a situation, the developer will be both the private party responsible for constructing the zone and effectively in control of the local government.

In sum, this means that power over all three arms of the state – executive, elected institutions and judiciary – is centralized in the hands of the development commissioner and/or the developer company. Complementing this is a section of the Act (section 49) that grants the central government the power to repeal or modify any law, insofar as it applies to SEZs, excepting labour laws. Together these clauses place SEZs outside the normal structures of the Indian state.

Finally, the SEZ Act insists that 'Every person, whether employed or residing or required to be present in a Special Economic Zone, shall be provided an identity card' (section 46). The rules originally went even further and, in an astonishing exercise of detail, stated that the

> processing area and Free Trade and Warehousing Zone shall be fully secured by boundary wall or wire mesh fencing having a height of at least two meters and forty centimeters above plinth level with top sixty centimeters being barbed wire fencing with mild steel angle with specified entry and exit points.
>
> (Rule 11(2))

This clause has now been modified, but the intent remains.[6] The rules also provide that only 'authorized persons' may enter the processing area (Rule 11(4)).

These are matters that would normally be dealt with by the local administrator concerned or the state government at most. It is a sign of how important the authorities see such matters that they were included in the central legislation – and indeed, in the case of ID cards, given statutory force. Clearly there is an overwhelming concern to ensure that SEZs throughout the country are walled off, and particularly that there be very tight control on entry and exit into the zones.

This completes the isolation of SEZs. Institutionally, legally and physically, the institutional structure of SEZs is to be totally cut off from practically all institutions outside of it. Inside the SEZ, all control lies with the instruments of capital – the development company itself and the development commissioner, whose mandate is simply the 'promotion' of the SEZ.

The SEZs as territories

As has been seen, the effective impact of the SEZ policy is the creation of a particular type of political-economic *territory* throughout India – these territories being marked by a close alliance between big capital (the developer) and the state, indeed effectively a merger of the two. Furthermore, the tight control over state activity (and therefore by implication over democracy) is in sharp contrast to the near absolute freedom granted to units and the developer, who are subjected to practically no regulation.

This model is distinguished by the total lack of connection between the zones' stated goals and the way the policy has actually been laid out. The question then is, why design such zones at all? Why create SEZs in such an irrational manner? Why take a Chinese model, remove even its few restrictions and limitations, and implement it in an extreme fashion?

It is here that we have to return to the political conjuncture described above. India's big capitalists, and their supporters among the state machinery and the urban elite, are today facing a choice. With their efforts to totally transform the Indian state in their favour having been stymied, they had attempted to use the existing state machinery in a 'robber baron' fashion; but this too has run into roadblocks. Yet, at the same time, the opposition to neo-liberal reforms is neither coherent nor politically organized enough to pose a real threat to their immediate power. The choice therefore is between compromising and attempting to build 'reforms with a human face' (incidentally a slogan with which the present government came to power, but now quietly buried) and repressing popular discontent further, which remains an option in the absence of a powerful opposition. From the latter point of view, the problem is not popular discontent as such, but the current institutional structure, which has developed too many points at which resistance can occur. Hence the focus once again shifts to intensified accumulation by dispossession on a smaller scale, but this time through an institutional structure that does not allow space for too much opposition. It is arguable that this is precisely what SEZs are; the unusual, but very real, parallels with the Chinese situation are striking.

Hence the peculiar features of SEZs, and the reason why the stated goals of export and investment promotion find so little reflection in the actual policy. An Indian SEZ is essentially a territory for super-accumulation by large capital. Within the policy, it is clear that opportunities for such accumulation abound. At the time of the creation of the SEZ, forced land acquisition and the handover of forest and common lands offer one major opportunity. As one example, in the Mundra SEZ in Gujarat, the Adani Corporation received more than 5,000 hectares of common land (without the consent of the communities that own the land) at approximately Rs1 per square metre, whereupon the same lands were resold at between Rs800–2000 (US$17–43) per square metre (Langa 2008). Allowing for real estate activities in the non-processing area is a clear invitation to further property speculation through such methods.

Once the zone is operational, the total control of the developer would create an effective monopoly over all infrastructure and public services. The use of the state machinery would allow for the expulsion of workers and the poor over time, allowing their areas to be expropriated as part of a steady process of further seizure of resources. Finally, the use of violence, fraud and intimidation against workers, rivals and smaller capitals will certainly take place. A further method of such accumulation is guaranteed by the Act itself: the sweeping tax incentives provided, which go beyond any rational justification. Most central taxes are withdrawn within an SEZ, and states are urged to waive their taxes as well. Kavita Rao (2007) has calculated that the result would be a net loss of Rs3.48 per rupee invested for multi-product SEZs and Rs0.45 for single-sector SEZs; even if the investment is entirely new (i.e. not transferred from other areas), and taking into account all possible accruals from personal income taxes, there is still a loss of Rs0.16 for single sector SEZs and Rs1.60 for multi-product SEZs. As such, these incentives amount to a massive net transfer of resources from other economic sectors to capital operating in SEZs.

This slant towards accumulation by dispossession might lead one to expect that the SEZ policy will be short-lived, as this kind of profiteering will have negative political consequences and lead to a moderation of the policy (which seems to be the implicit goal of the many pro-neo-liberal but anti-SEZ critics). But the consequences could be considerably more complex than this, and the results far-reaching for the economy as a whole.

The 'lock in' effect

It is well known that many neo-liberal economic policies are aimed precisely at rendering future rollbacks or changes impossible. This is often referred to as the 'lock in' effect, most well known in the case of financial sector liberalization and capital account convertibility. These latter policies ensure that future economic policies perceived to be against the interests of financial speculators will lead to capital flight. A particularly glaring example is the current fiscal crisis, in which private financial institutions have held the sword of Damocles of global financial chaos over the heads of those who oppose bailing them out from the consequences of speculative activity.

SEZs enhance the power of finance and big capital in similar but more indirect ways. First, as most critics point out, the volume of money transferred to SEZs via incentives will add to the fiscal crisis facing both the central and state governments. One should note that, as per the Parliamentary Standing Committee on Finance, in 2004–5 export promotion schemes were already resulting in a loss of Rs410 billion (US$9 billion) to the exchequer annually – equivalent to 72 per cent of customs revenues and 23 per cent of total indirect tax revenue of all kinds (33rd Report of the Parliamentary Standing Committee on Finance). SEZs will multiply this figure by several times. In turn the resulting fiscal impact would particularly handicap the state governments, reducing public investment and forcing them into further dependence on private investment for provision of public services and generation of employment. For the central government, the same would apply, also leading to greater borrowings and corresponding increases in debt.

Second, the SEZ scheme would distort investment and infrastructure patterns in the country. Certain companies – those able to access SEZs – and certain sectors of capital, such as real estate, construction and finance, would be at an advantage compared to other producers. This would have multiple impacts. On the level of individual companies, it would have a tendency to promote migration into SEZs by existing firms, as several critics have argued. On a sectoral level, investment – particularly speculative and volatile flows such as FDI – would flow towards SEZ-based capital and to real estate companies. Infrastructure would also tend to focus on the zones, particularly as the SEZ rules require that state governments have to provide as much water and electricity as the developer demands (Rule 5(5)(d)). The resulting distortion in investment and infrastructure patterns would have negative impacts on other sectors, decreasing access to capital and facilities for non-SEZ activities.

Third, pressure will build from other sectors of capital to ensure that SEZ-style concessions and legal frameworks are extended to larger and larger areas of the country, in order to 'compete' with SEZ firms. This would occur in part on the basis of direct market competition between SEZ and non-SEZ firms – the only restriction against which is the duty on sales in the domestic tariff area, which is already low and in any case unenforceable. In this context it is striking to find that an audit by the Comptroller and Auditor General (2008) of twenty-two SEZ units found that only 28 per cent of their 'export' earnings were from actual exports; the remainder were from 'deemed exports' into the DTA. It also found that more than Rs17.2 billion (US$370 million) of tax revenues were lost in just the case of the small sample of units surveyed by it, simply because there was no legal provision to recover these revenues. Meanwhile, recent news reports indicate that, in response to the 'problems' being faced by developers in the wake of the financial crisis, the government is considering allowing SEZ units to formally sell within the DTA without paying duties.

Fourth, such pressure to extend SEZ concessions will also be based on a 'demonstration effect' on other companies of the 'successes' of those within SEZs. It is already the case that large companies and multinationals are unwilling to invest in any state that does not offer them either SEZ status or equivalent concessions. The net result would be a 'race to the bottom' on a national scale. Smaller capitals meanwhile would decline, unable to survive this form of 'competition'.

Overall, these processes would mean a growing dependence on SEZ enclaves for overall economic performance – and for employment and investment. But this dependence would be inherently fragile, as a great deal of SEZ 'performance' would be based on unstable speculative activity and dependent on the peculiar pro-capital financial and state structures of SEZs. In this sense overall instability would increase as collapses occur frequently. In China, for instance, the increasingly heavy involvement of public banks in financing the real-estate boom in SEZs has led to major bankruptcies among public institutions (Gopalakrishnan 2007).

Moreover, this fragility would also essentially block moves to reduce SEZ concessions by future governments. Reduction in tax concessions, effective enforcement of labour, environmental or other laws, would lead to either withdrawal of capital (in the case of speculative and foreign investors) or to 'slowdowns' in activity. This would in turn impact the rest of the economy, both through the financial system and through direct losses of employment and wastage of resources. Thus the longer the SEZ strategy continues, the worse the lock in would be, and the more difficult to alter the policy in future.

Conclusion

As discussed earlier, SEZs have already triggered snowballing conflicts around acquisition of lands and handover of common lands. But this is only the beginning. As this policy begins to play itself out, with severe and complex consequences both within and outside the zones, the true implications of SEZs will become apparent. Even as this happens, they will increasingly entrench themselves at the centre of India's economy. The dynamics that this will produce are difficult to predict, but one result is almost certain. In an abiding irony, the SEZs will eventually become the engine of precisely what they sought to avoid – an explosion of popular anger and resistance that may well change India's polity.

In the Asian and international contexts, the Indian experience will be of particular interest for one reason above all: it constitutes the logical culmination of the zone concept. It is difficult to imagine a more extreme or more dangerous formulation of the concept of the SEZ than the Indian one. If the resulting conflicts force a rethink of the dynamics and consequences of SEZs in other nations, this might well be one of the few positive outcomes of this policy.

Notes

1 A detailed overview of the impact of the post-1991 reforms can be found in Chandrasekhar and Ghosh 2002.
2 See customs notifications 39/2002 Central Excise and 82/2002 Customs, both dated 13 August 2002, for developers, and 52/2000-CE and 137/2000-Cus, both dated 19 October 2000, for units.
3 Rule 11(10) of the Special Economic Zones Rules, 2006.
4 Notification SO 1846(E) of the Ministry of Commerce and Industry, Department of Commerce, dated 27 October 2006.
5 See http://sezindia.nic.in/state_policy_ent.asp (accessed 1 on March 2007). Note that this list of states includes only all the states whose policies are posted on the website, and it is hence a reasonable assumption that this is the case across the country.
6 In March 2007, this clause was replaced with a requirement that the processing area and an FTWZ shall be 'fully secured with measures approved by the Board of Approval'.

Bibliography

Aggarwal, Aradhna (2004) 'Export processing zones in India: Analysis of the export performance', Working Paper no. 148, Indian Council for Research on International Economic Relations. New Delhi: ICRIER, November.

Business World (2008) 'Top 100 most profitable companies', 27 October.

Chandrasekhar, CP and J Ghosh (2002) *The market that failed: A decade of neoliberal economic reforms in India*. New Delhi: Leftword.

Chopra, K, VB Eswaran and G Kadekodi (2006) *Report of the Expert Committee on Net Present Value, Supreme Court of India*, submitted in pursuance to court order dated 26 September 2005, in IA no. 826 in IA 566 of Writ Petition (Civil) 202/95.

Comptroller and Auditor-General of India (2008) *Report no. 6 on indirect taxes*, Central Government Performance Audit, available at: http://cag.gov.in/html/reports/PA2008.htm.

Gopalakrishnan, S (2007) 'Negative aspects of Chinese special economic zones', *Economic and Political Weekly* 42(17) (28 April): 1492–94. Mumbai: Sameeksha Trust.

—— (2008) 'Signs of an impending disaster', *Seminar* no. 582 (February): 25–31. New Delhi.

Harvey, D (2003) 'New imperialism: Accumulation by dispossession', *Socialist Register 2004*, 63–87.

Jenkins, R (1999) *Democratic politics and economic reform in India*, Cambridge: Cambridge University Press.

Langa, M (2007) 'Villagers veto sale of grazing land to Mundra's special economic zone', *Business Standard*, 27 May.

—— (2008) 'Villagers veto sale of grazing land to Mundra SEZ', 30/5/2008, available at www.environmentportal.in/node/247960

Merchant, K (2006) 'Investors fly in to tap Orissa's riches', *Financial Times*, 28 July.

Pati, J (2005) 'Signing away the state to POSCO', *People's Democracy*. New Delhi: Communist Party of India (Marxist), 7 August.

Rao, KR (2007) 'Impact of SEZs on the Indian economy: An initial evaluation', Paper presented at UGC–SAP Seminar on Special Economic Zones, Department of Geography, Delhi School of Economics, 16 March.

Special Economic Zones Rules (2006) Available at www.taxmanagementindia.com/Site-Map/SEZ/List_Rule.asp

UNCTAD (UN Conference on Trade and Development) (2003), *World Investment Report 2003*, New York and Geneva: United Nations.

Yadav, Y (2004) 'The elusive mandate of 2004', *Economic and Political Weekly* 39(51) (18–24 December): 5383–85, 5388–89, 5391–98 (article consists of 13 pages). Mumbai: Sameeksha Trust.

9 The Indian Special Economic Zones Act 2005

Implications for modelling the law and governance of SEZs

Andrew Harding

Introduction

Sharp debates in India since 2005 have deteriorated more recently into widespread protest against SEZs and even serious violence (Gopalakrishnan, this volume). Dohrmann (2008: 74–76) refers to an alarming instance in 2007 of a proposed 'chemical hub' SEZ involving Indonesian investment, at Nandigram, West Bengal, encompassing no less than 57 square kilometres and twenty-nine villages, which led to serious clashes involving thousands of police and protesters and fourteen deaths. This and other instances have resulted in the placing of a vague and temporary ceiling on SEZ sizes. The opposition to SEZs comes from both left-wing politicians and industrialists (*Economist* 2006: 78).

Controversy has focused on the legitimacy of SEZs as social and economic policy. Those who are opposed to SEZs would indeed have little interest in the law and governance of SEZs, because they would rather simply abolish them. At the same time defects in law and governance are reasons to oppose them being set up, have the SEZ structure changed, or subject SEZs to some form of global regulation. While entertaining some sympathy with this point of view, this chapter assumes nonetheless that SEZs are, in some form at least, here to stay, but consistently with the theme of this book it does not assume that they will or should take a particular form. It is, on the contrary, assumed here that the SEZ concept will prove to be capable of adapting to new circumstances and requirements, and possibly being used for a variety of purposes, provided our deep concerns about the consequences of SEZs can be put to good use in making dramatic improvements in refining SEZ law and governance. It seems inescapable that these new circumstances and purposes include the greater prevalence and dissemination of standards of legality and good governance, human rights and environmental and labour standards (all of which are discussed in this volume), and a greater willingness to challenge the injustices and abuses of privilege that can arise in the context of SEZs. Unhappily this chapter, analysing the example of India's Special Economic Zones Act 2005, finds that appropriate standards of law and governance are far from being met in this example; indeed accusations of almost every conceivable defect in law and governance have been levelled at the Indian SEZ structure (Dohrmann 2008; Gopalakrishnan, this volume).[1]

The chapter therefore considers the possibilities for law and governance in relation to SEZs, taking as its starting point the proposition that at present there is little in the way of accountability or transparency in respect of any aspect of SEZs: the decision to set up a zone in a particular place and in a particular form; the manner of operation of the zone; the regulation of the zone in the context of particular issues such as labour rights, human rights, environmental protection, corruption, and so on; and of course macro-accountability in terms of the costs and benefits of continuing a zone or more generally a national SEZ policy. The chapter takes India's Special Economic Zones Act 2005 ('the SEZ Act') as the latest example[2] of hard legal material on which to base some ideas about law and governance in SEZs. The chapter is concerned ultimately with imagining what an appropriate system of governance for SEZs would look like, and how the concepts of public law can be profitably brought to bear on the problems of SEZs. In this context we can look at legal structures or models that could be used, examining them against familiar constitutional and governance parameters and standards, using India as an example. For this purpose it will be necessary to set out in some detail in the next section of the chapter the governance structure envisaged by the SEZ Act, which will indicate several areas of concern. The chapter then considers the public law tensions around the discrimination that SEZs, by definition, involve. It concludes by looking at possible forms of national regulation based on public law principles.

India and China are of course the two epicentres of SEZ activity in contemporary Asia. In the case of China it is difficult to imagine rigorous application of public law principles at the present time. While China has had an Administrative Litigation Law and administrative divisions of the courts since 1990, the entrenchment of the rule of law in practice is barely under way in this area (Peerenboom 2004). The policy imperatives of SEZ growth and more generally the domination of the Communist Party make accountability and transparency problematical. Indeed, it came to light in China that more than one sixth of all SEZs (broadly defined) had actually been illegally established (Carter, this volume). If China cannot be regarded as likely to develop public law to the extent that accountability for SEZ-related acts and decisions will be speedily developed, the same is not true of India, where public law and in particular constitutional law and public interest litigation have been extensively developed. India is a mature democracy in which the rule of law is usually taken for granted as a guiding principle (Perry-Kessaris 2008). However, as we will see in the light of the SEZ Act, considering the rule of law difficulties to which the SEZ regime gives rise, one would have cause to doubt this assumption.

There is therefore some point in attempting to analyse the SEZ Act on a law-and-governance basis. Having said that, it is still the case that economic regulation and state investment are less likely to prove amenable to accountability and transparency than other areas of activity, a point which is explored further below. In addition there is obviously in the case of SEZs a difference between accountability and transparency. The state has an interest in 'talking up' SEZs, which are after all mainly designed to attract investment in a particularly sensitive market. Thus complete transparency might actually damage the progress of an SEZ and even cramp the ability of government to correct that which is wrong. At the same time the state itself presumably needs to know what the actual situation is so that it can maximize performance, hold responsible those who have made mistakes, ensure that basic standards are being met, and justify its policy on the basis of hard facts.

Many questions arise here. At the international level, we can consider what kinds of treaty or other instrument are used and what issues arise with regard to rights, obligations, applicable law and dispute resolution processes, and how these are dealt with. At the national level, we can consider who has power to set up an SEZ and what structures of governance can be implied or applied. How are divisions of power between federal, state and local governments brought to bear on SEZs, particularly for example in the context of land acquisition, investment, and the application of labour and environmental laws? What structures generally exist for regulating SEZs, particularly where an SEZ is set up as a private, local government or statutory development project, and are these adequate? To what extent is SEZ governance accountable to democratic and legal process? These are just some of the questions to which answers will be adumbrated in this chapter.

The Special Economic Zones Act 2005

SEZs are not new in India, the first 'export-processing zone' having been set up in 1965; but the SEZ Act, the outcome of a new investment policy announced by minister Murasoli Maran in 2000, was passed in order to encourage the creation of large numbers of new SEZs with the benefit of public-private partnership. Its long title is an Act 'to provide for the establishment, development and management of the Special Economic Zones for the promotion of exports and for matters connected therewith or incidental thereto'. It applies to the whole of India and makes extensive provision in the manner of a regulatory statute for the progress of setting up new SEZs but also for their effective governance. The Act has been justified in terms of economic growth: it has been claimed that 'GDP will rise by 2 per cent and that 30 *lakhs* [three million] jobs will be generated by SEZs … [which] will attract global manufacturing through foreign direct investment (FDI), enable transfer of modern technology and will also create incentives for infrastructure'.[3] Proceeding under the SEZ Act the authorities had approved in principle or inherited no less than 760 SEZs by February 2008. The structures involved are remarkably complex; however, they also involve some innovative but at the same time troubling notions of governance.

Constitutional issues

In federal states in particular the power of regulation of economic affairs is a notoriously elusive and debateable matter due to the preference of constitutional drafters for a combination of extreme vagueness and a lamentable tendency to reduce the economy to discrete and familiar, narrowly defined, sectors. The Constitution of India, which clearly bears the imprint of lawyers rather than economists, barely mentions economic regulation, and it does not mention SEZs at all, or anything adjacent or similar to them. Arguments as to the constitutionality of the SEZ Act have not been raised on grounds of interference with state powers, but it could be challenged on grounds of interference with fundamental rights such as the right to life and the right to equal protection. In practice legal challenges have been public interest cases related to compulsory acquisitions of land for SEZs on the basis that these are not for a 'public purpose'.[4]

The Act certainly contains some remarkable provisions. Section 49, for example, empowers the central government to direct that *any of the provisions of the Act or any other central Act or any rules, regulations, notifications or directions made under it* shall not apply to an SEZ or a class of SEZs, or shall apply to them only with such exceptions, modification and adaptation, as may be specified. The only thing excepted from this provision is the law relating to labour and trade unions. There is no obligation to report such direction to Parliament. In other words, notwithstanding the extensive provisions of the Act, the central government can suspend the Act or any other law or decision in any given SEZ or any given class of SEZs. It is hard to believe this provision could be found to be constitutionally valid. Not since the seventeenth century and the divine right of kings has it been normal for a government in a common law system to enjoy the power of simply suspending or overriding laws, unless emergency powers are being exercised. This breathtaking provision gives the central government very extensive direct or reserve powers over every aspect of SEZs and their functioning. This is a pattern which we see repeated in relation to other details of the SEZ Act.[5]

Procedure for approval of an SEZ

A proposal for setting up an SEZ 'for manufacture of goods or rendering services or for both or as a Free Trade and Warehousing Zone' may be made (jointly or severally) by any legal person, the state government, or the central government ('the Developer').[6] The developer identifies the area proposed and applies to the state government for the area. The developer can also apply directly to the Board of Approval (see below), and obtain the concurrence of the state government later if approval is given. Applications are to be approved by a statutory board, the Board of Approval ('the Board'). The central government, however, may after consulting the state government identify the area and *suo motu* set up an SEZ, by-passing the Board's approval procedure. The Board may approve a proposal, subject to such terms and conditions as it may deem fit, or modify or reject the proposal. The Board is required to give the developer reasons for rejecting a proposal and to report its decisions and reasons to the central government, which has the final say, at the end of the process, in approving the SEZ (or 'notifying' as the Act puts it).

Subject to any conditions imposed being accepted by the applicant, the central government then issues a 'letter of approval' to the developer. Anyone intending to provide infrastructure facilities, or undertake any 'authorized operation' (e.g. construction of a factory, mall, or infrastructure) in the SEZ must, after entering into an agreement with the developer, make a proposal to the Board for its approval, in which event the same procedure as for a letter of approval applies.[7] The developer is required to submit the exact particulars of the SEZ to the central government, which then satisfies itself that all requirements have been fulfilled and notifies the SEZ. The Board then authorizes the developer to undertake the authorized operations. The central government has power to designate areas within the SEZ as processing (manufacturing, services, warehousing) or non-processing areas.

In deciding whether to notify an SEZ the central government must have regard to: the generation of additional economic activity; the promotion of exports of goods and services; the promotion of investment from domestic and foreign sources; the creation of employment opportunities; the development of infrastructure facilities; and maintenance of the sovereignty and integrity of India, the security of the state and friendly relations with foreign states. In other words its discretion is virtually complete, and it does not apparently even have to consider the wider social, economic and environmental impacts of its decisions. The central government has responded to criticism and widespread protests by announcing an 'R&R' policy (relief and rehabilitation).[8]

Agencies and their roles

The Board comprises up to twenty civil servants from various relevant areas of government, and has the duty of promoting and ensuring orderly development of the SEZs. Specifically the Board has power, as indicated, to determine applications for approval of SEZs and authorized operations; it also has power to approve foreign collaborations, foreign direct investments, infrastructure facilities, and industrial undertakings in an SEZ. Interestingly enough, it is bound by such directions on questions of policy as the central government may give to it, and the decision of the central government whether a question is one of policy or not is final (once again the central government enjoys practically absolute power). There is no sense of democratic participation in governance via the Board.

An important reserve power of the Board is that of suspending the letter of approval for up to one year if it is of the opinion that the developer is unable to discharge the functions or perform the duties imposed on him; has persistently defaulted in complying with any direction given by the Board; or has violated the terms and conditions of the letter of approval; or if his financial position is such that he is unable fully and efficiently to discharge the duties imposed on him by the letter of approval, and circumstances exist which render it necessary for it in the public interest so to do. In this case the Board appoints an administrator to discharge the duties of the developer.[9] It must give three months' notice to the developer and allow him to show cause against the suspension.

The lines of accountability are rendered rather complex by the creation of three different SEZ agencies under the SEZ Act.

First, the central government has power to appoint a development commissioner ('DC') for one or more SEZs, who has overall charge of the SEZ and is sometimes described as the 'governor' of the SEZ, ensures its speedy development and the promotion of exports from it, coordinates with state and central governments and monitors the performance of the developer and the individual 'units' (e.g. factories) in the SEZ. The Board can also delegate its functions to one or more DCs.

Second, the central government must appoint an Approval Committee ('Committee') for the SEZ, comprising nine people (eight officials and one representative of the developer, chaired by the DC). Its main functions are to approve, modify or reject proposals for setting up units; approve the import or procurement of goods and provision of services in the SEZ; monitor activity within the SEZ and compliance with conditions attached to the letter of approval; and allow, on receipt of approval, foreign collaborations and foreign direct investments. Again there is no democratic participation for the benefit of those affected by the SEZ. A person aggrieved by an order of the Committee has a right of appeal to the Board. A letter of approval is also issued to an entrepreneur permitted to set up a unit on much the same terms as for the developer in relation to the SEZ itself.

Third, a Special Economic Zone Authority ('SEZA') of six people (four officials and two entrepreneurs appointed by the central government, also chaired by the DC – yet again there is no democratic participation) must be appointed for each SEZ, chaired by the DC. Its functions hardly differ from those of the DC, the main ones being to undertake such measures as it thinks fit for the development, operation and management of the SEZ; develop infrastructure; promote exports; and review the functioning and performance of the SEZ.

The central government has the power to issue directions to SEZAs and to DCs as well as to the Board. The SEZAs are required to report to the central government. The central government also has power to supersede the SEZA if it is of the opinion that the SEZA is unable to perform, or has persistently made default in the performance of the duty or has exceeded or abused its powers, or has wilfully or without sufficient cause, failed to comply with any direction issued by the central government. In practice it looks as though the structure is designed to make the DC all-powerful as long as the SEZ performs economically in the eyes of the central government.

The single window

One of the supposed advantages of having SEZs is that relevant approvals can be given on a 'single window' basis.[10] The Act is no exception. The relevant section (s. 19) is remarkable and worth quoting in full:

> Notwithstanding anything contained in any other law for the time being in force, the central government may, if required,
>
> (a) prescribe a single application form for obtaining any licence, permission or registration or approval by a Developer, or an entrepreneur under one or more central Acts;
>
> (b) authorize the Board, the Development Commissioner or Approval Committee, to exercise the powers of the central government on matters relating to the development of a Special Economic Zone or setting up and operation of Units;
>
> (c) prescribe a single form for furnishing returns or information by a Developer or an entrepreneur under one or more central Acts.

This means nothing less than that, in the attempt to consolidate all approval processes, the SEZ officials can be authorized to exercise *all public powers conferred by any applicable central legislation*. Potentially this provision if used widely could lead to the taking over by the SEZ officials, at a single stroke, of practically all existing forms of government and regulation applicable to SEZs.[11] The SEZ would in these terms become very much like a local government authority enjoying wide powers equivalent to powers at all levels of government and having its own laws (see below), but being unanswerable to the people it governs. It raises at the very least the possibility of various forms of regulation such as environmental protection, being legally outflanked by the single window principle. Given that the regulatory agencies being supplanted are the guardians of the relevant legislated principles, it seems remarkable that the various SEZ authorities, whose object is expressly to develop the SEZ, could override these principles in pursuit of an accelerated approval process. The dangers involved in this system of governance of placing economic development, or more strictly, profit, above all other considerations, seem all too apparent.

An SEZ legal system

The Act interestingly and controversially also takes a large stride towards the setting up of a separate legal system for SEZs.

First, the central government can authorize any official to be the enforcement agency for an SEZ in respect of any criminal offence and such official can exercise any of the enforcement powers under the relevant legislation, subject to the approval of the DC unless specifically authorized to act without such approval. Thus an SEZ may be able to (literally) police its own area.

Second, the state government may, with the concurrence of the chief justice of the High Court of that state, designate one or more courts, exclusively, to try all suits of a civil nature arising in the SEZ, and to try notified offences committed in the SEZ. Appeals from designated courts lie to the High Court itself. Arbitration is provided for in the absence of such designated courts.

It is not clear why these provisions were enacted. They are redolent of consular courts and special police in treaty ports, and raise the possibility of constitutional challenge. Presumably it is an attempt to circumvent the delays and other problems associated with the general legal system (Harding and Nicholson 2010). Although the judicial powers involved remain with the judiciary rather than some kind of administrative tribunal, it may be that the creation of special courts would lead to something like the development of a distinct approach or understanding of general law as applied in SEZs. To a large extent SEZs are indeed also 'special legal zones' (SLZs), and this legal distinctness essentially defines what we mean by 'special' in the term 'SEZ'. Carter (this volume) points out that China's SEZs are governed by a 'labyrinth' of special regulations, and SEZs in Guangdong have special laws on wages, migrant workers, and movement of goods; while Suzhou SEZ has transplanted virtually the entire system of town planning, construction, environment and social security from Singapore – 'software' which Carter describes as 'a euphemism for law'. The possibility of Indian SEZs becoming SLZs is clearly envisaged by the SEZ Act, but in a manner that potentially takes SEZ law far beyond what even China has done. From a constitutional law perspective this is an uncomfortable prospect. It implies not only special laws but special interpretations or applications of ordinary laws, a situation which is contrary to the rule of law.

Law, governance and SEZs

The overwhelming impression left by the provisions of the SEZ Act is that SEZs are considered sufficiently important in India that truly vast powers have been assumed by the government to enlist both private resources and state power in support of the creation of SEZs. The powers under the SEZ Act are quite out of the ordinary in their extent and implications, and although there is some reckoning of governance principles in terms of rights to be heard and rights of appeal from various decisions, these seem faint in comparison to the vast executive powers being exercised, and there is little guarantee of independence being exercised by the various boards and officials involved. Developers will no doubt consider that virtually any adverse decisions of any of these entities could skew their prospects and inhibit their profits; but they are represented on these bodies. Communities likely to be affected on the other hand clearly have more at stake and are not represented and have no rights of redress save through judicial review via public interest litigation. Although there are indeed some avenues of redress, the governance mechanisms seem to be geared entirely towards the successful implementation of the SEZs as an economic innovation rather than the enforcement of protective law in respect of human rights, agriculture, labour, or the environment.

The lines of accountability extend up to the central government, which is itself accountable only to Parliament for its actions under the Act. That Parliament may well be unable or unwilling to hold the executive to account is indicated by the fact that the Act was passed without any debate and within two days. It is no wonder that activists and others are in protest against the SEZ Act and the creation of literally hundreds of new SEZs under it. It will be interesting to see how the judiciary responds to this when faced with disputes over SEZs (or arising within SEZs). There are clearly plenty of junctures where judicial review is potentially available; but it will depend on judicial perception both of the Act and the judicial role in relation to economic policy whether judicial review can claw back some of the virtually unlimited powers conferred by the Act.

Finally, the elaborate structure created by the SEZ Act raises the possibility of a considerable confusion of jurisdiction which is quite at odds with the 'single window' thinking of the SEZ Act. Clearly the DCs are envisaged as having almost unlimited local power, and will control the Committee and the SEZA as well as sometimes exercising the functions of the Board.

The injustice of exceptions

In this section it is proposed, in the light of the above discussion, to take up a central feature of SEZs, the notion of special laws for SEZs, which seems to require some further consideration.

An obvious starting point is that in the rule-of-law ideology that lawyers tend to espouse, which speaks also to general social concerns, law is of general application and all cases should be treated similarly. This is a position which, however, resonates much more in Europe and North America than it does in Asia (Peerenboom 2004), which is more used (and India is certainly no exception) to forms of legal pluralism and unofficial law – special laws for special cases and the entrenchment of social status in spite of law to the contrary.

Although the making of exceptions is by no means a mode of reasoning which is foreign to the rule of law, exceptions are regarded with some suspicion and require clear justification and limited application. In the case of SEZs it might be plausibly maintained that the very notion of an SEZ is inherently of dubious constitutionality, because by definition SEZs involve the adoption of special laws and the making of exceptions, usually in favour of already privileged entities such as multinational enterprises, or against already unprivileged groups such as female workers. Muchlinski (this volume) even refers to SEZs as involving a 'dual legal order' and a 'distinct regime'; Carter (this volume) refers to the Suzhou SEZ as 'a particular model of law and development'. Typically SEZs involve provision of special customs and trade laws, lower standards of labour protection, and tax concessions.

It is therefore with good reason that some people regard SEZs as fundamentally unjust. Not all of these critics are rabid nationalists or incipient revolutionaries. Indeed we can identify with many of their concerns and try to see how the problem of the unjust exception can be overcome or reconciled with the policy of creating economic growth. At the same time it might be noted that a dual legal order can provide for *raising or protection* of legal standards just as well as it can provide for their lowering; Richardson (2004) for example finds that environmental standards are higher in Asian SEZs than in the domestic tariff areas.

Of course the concept of constitutional equality expressed in statements such as that all citizens or all persons are equal before the law easily recognizes that literal or strict equality is neither desirable nor possible: for example who would advocate that the rich and the poor should be subject to precisely equal taxes, or that both innocent and convicted accused persons should be sent to gaol? Accordingly we recognize the right of state organs to draw distinctions between all kinds of (juristic) persons provided they do so on a *rational* basis; in other words there must be a logical nexus between the group of persons identified and the reason for treating them differently, because without such insistence the distinction would almost certainly be arbitrary and oppressive.

Further, it is correct to say that in addition some distinctions that could be drawn, and also some reasons for drawing a distinction, are simply inherently repugnant and unconstitutional. For example, the objective of economic efficiency could not possibly justify the assassination of economically unproductive citizens;[12] and in some systems of law at least it is prohibited to draw a distinction which is based on ethnicity for *any purpose* whatever. Having said that, there are instances where ethnic distinction is regarded as wholly valid and desirable and very much an issue for SEZs; for example, with Malaysia's *bumiputera* policy, for which see below, and also Tey Tsun Hang (this volume) and in India with regard to scheduled castes and scheduled tribes. An obvious main concern in the context of SEZs is that distinction is often based on nationality, not, as is usual in other fields such as citizenship and immigration law, in order to discriminate *against* foreign nationals, but in order to discriminate in their *favour* and against home nationals. This is part of a best-of-both-worlds economic policy designed to encourage foreign direct investment within the SEZ while also providing protection for local industries outside it. Here those who take a strict constitutional-equality stance might find their position hard to articulate: if it is valid to discriminate in favour of home nationals for one purpose why is it invalid to discriminate against them for another purpose, if the result is rationally arrived at and argued to be in the broader national interest?

The overall objective of the SEZ is indeed ostensibly to secure the economic interest of the nation as a whole, which is practically by definition a proper objective of government. SEZs can deliver the notching up of skills, technology, management standards, and employment opportunities. At the same time, as explained above, this objective cannot in itself justify literally *any* form of distinction. It therefore makes good sense constitutionally speaking to dissolve the distinction between nationals and foreigners for SEZ purposes and provide for an SEZ approval process which recognizes only the desirability of approving entities which are capable of serving the economic or other relevant interests of society as a whole.

One can see here that this is precisely in a sense consistent with the trend; the Indian SEZ Act refers to foreign cooperation and foreign investment, but does not make any special provision for it as against domestic investment. In some SEZ contexts, for example in information technology zones (which form 60 per cent of Indian SEZs) and elsewhere, some legal systems, such as those of Malaysia, provide for approval only of companies having the characteristics of a 'pioneer' industry.[13] Here the word 'pioneer' is presumably coined in order to direct attention to an industrial concern's growth or technological potential rather than its nationality, and can be claimed on the basis of fulfilment of some relevant criteria laid down in the law, in soft-law guidelines, or policy documents. This is not only good law but good policy in that it encourages nationals to develop the attributes necessary for them to be treated equally with non-nationals.

The case of Malaysia (Tey Tsun Hang, this volume), points to the fact that there is also a certain contingency in the definition of constitutionality as applied to economic regulation. The Malaysian Constitution provides at Article 153 a potentially broad exception to the principle of equality under which it is valid for the government to introduce a quota system for trade licences, scholarships, admission to higher education and positions in the public service, based on ethnic criteria. In other words the government can discriminate in favour of *bumiputera* (sons of the soil), defined as Malays and natives of Sabah and Sarawak. The rationale for this purely ethnic distinction is that at independence the *bumiputera*, a majority of citizens, owned only 1 per cent of the economy. Article 153 therefore authorizes affirmative action programmes (within certain limitations based on vested interests or the 'legitimate interests' of non-*bumiputera* communities) in favour of an underprivileged majority group. This applies very much to the context of investment, in which (to simplify somewhat a rather complex set of regulations) the normal rule is (or at least was until it was recently repealed[14]) that new industrial activity of a given size (national or foreign) must reflect 30 per cent *bumiputera* equity participation[15] and has to comply with similar requirements regarding the employment of its workforce.

It is of course an issue (indeed a highly sensitive one) whether the objective of such a policy, formulated in colonial times but very much strengthened from 1970 following inter-ethnic rioting in May 1969, has in fact by now been fulfilled, or would not be better fulfilled in practice by using opportunity rather than ethnicity as a criterion justifying special treatment. While this general issue is not a concern in the present context, it is highly relevant to SEZs in the sense that it has become increasingly usual for the '*bumiputera* policy' (as we may call it for the sake of simplicity) to be *disapplied* in the case of Malaysian SEZs such as the Multimedia Super Corridor (Likosky 2005) and the Iskandar Development Region (Tey Tsung Hang, this volume) in order to encourage foreign investment in the broader national interest. Thus in Malaysia it is almost more plausible to argue that *equal* rather than unequal treatment is unconstitutional, except for the fact that Article 153, although recognizing an obligation on the government to protect the interests of the *bumiputera*, does so by vesting it with discretion, i.e. a power rather than a duty, to discriminate on an exceptional basis. Thus the government can legally, it would appear, not only rescind the *bumiputera* policy in SEZs but abolish it comprehensively.

This example, in furtherance of the argument set out above, is advanced to show that the area of political economy is one in which it is difficult for courts to enforce constitutional rights, and this might prove to be problematical if we expect courts to play a significant role in the law and governance of SEZs, both in India and elsewhere. Indeed in general terms it is true that courts often regard themselves as ill-equipped to make decisions which have potentially significant national economic or budgetary consequences. This can be seen from decisions regarding privatization/nationalization issues where courts either seem reluctant to intervene or else do so in dysfunctional ways (Butt and Lindsey 2008). The Indian judiciary too is no stranger to the notion that programmes or projects having great national economic significance should be treated with some care (Upadhyay 2000). The conclusion seems to be that although the courts might play a role in relation to the constitutional principle of equality, it is probably more promising to think in terms of a legislative regime that deals carefully with the delicate balancing of considerations that is involved in providing special laws for special cases. This is what the Indian SEZ Act signally fails to do.

Regulation

The SEZ as conceived in European social-democratic corporatism of the 1960s and 1970s (e.g. in Ireland and the UK), and in the Asian development state of the 1970s and 1980s (e.g. in Taiwan and Singapore), assumed that government had the principal responsibility to organize and manage SEZs, although the choice of central or local government was an issue. Consequently, the usual method of providing for SEZ regulation was to create an ad hoc statutory board with overall responsibility for creating, providing infrastructure for, regulating, and promoting all SEZs, and processing and facilitating applications from investors, as occurs in India. A variation of this is to have a separate authority for *each* SEZ, which could presumably only occur where there are relatively few of them and they have little in common. With the shift of emphasis in the 1990s towards market forces and privatization, as Muchlinski (this volume) notes, SEZs have been deeply affected, to the extent that it is now more usual than not that an SEZ will be under private rather than public ownership, or at least privately managed even if other functions are still vested in a statutory body. One can speculate as to the reasons for this, but they are probably partly a reflection of the political ideology of the time, partly the result of depleted government resources, and partly the result of an understandable desire to reduce bureaucracy and trump entrenched departmental interests. Typically these days, and especially in India, SEZs are the outcome of public-private partnership.

This creates a potentially problematical, even dangerous, situation. The more SEZs are privatized the more their success will be tested according to profit rather than adherence to stringent legal and human rights standards or even a broad definition of 'development' (Rittich 2005), all of which are likely to become degraded under this assumption. Regulation thus becomes a critical issue, and the best hope is that increased privatization would bring with it increased state regulation and supervision, and therefore more articulated mechanisms of transparency and accountability. In this connection one wonders if British-style 'development corporations' of the 1960s and 1970s, incorporating industrial zones and housing projects, schools, parks and so forth, might offer a better model than the current model of the SEZ; it may well be that the current model is indeed evolving in that general direction. Undoubtedly in practice, in Asia at least, the public/private distinction is more of a grey area than perhaps it should be from a legal perspective. Privatization does render fuzzy the lines of responsibility and accountability, both in parliament and outside it. Muchlinski (this volume), indicating a tall order for SEZ regulation, concludes as follows:

> The implications of the use of PPPs [public-private partnerships] need to be considered more fully. In particular the precise relation between the private and public elements needs to be clarified, the relationship between private profits and public service provision determined and the social and environmental aspects of the partnership regime need to be addressed. This is, after all, a form of business association used in specific industrial projects. How it needs to be adapted to the operation of SEZs is not a well understood issue.

Where then do the issues of accountability actually arise?

First one can mention the issue of criteria for investment approval. Typically, as in India, approval will depend on broad considerations of national interest, and the authority endowed with the power to approve the SEZ investment (i.e. to set up a SEZ, or to set up a factory in a SEZ) will have a broad discretion. Considerations to be taken into account would be, for example, extent of capital investment; pioneer status; technological expertise; export orientation; use of local natural resources; or labour-intensiveness. SEZ legislation itself usually provides little in the way of regulation as the discretion is usually very broad and the considerations and guidelines expressed very subjectively. There will often be an appeal process, but there is little hope that an appeal process would provide accountability, since the investor is asking for a special privilege rather than the observance of a right; the sympathy of the authorities is critical to the success of the investment; and the grounds of appeal will be very hard to formulate convincingly.

Judicial or quasi-judicial scrutiny therefore looks like an unpromising direction if we are interested in accountability, although it could play an important role in terms of enforcing rules of administrative procedure and rational decision-making. More likely is legislative scrutiny via ministerial responsibility, but of course this can be circumvented to a certain extent where the oversight function is placed with an independent statutory board. It is therefore of some interest how such boards can be constituted and structured and how they can be empowered to ensure that SEZs are managed in a responsible fashion.

It might be thought that regulation and accountability are merely a kind of luxurious transaction cost to the operation of the system, and it is the precise purpose of the SEZ to avoid them. However, proper regulation should ensure that SEZs are operated according to the desired principles and standards, making a genuine contribution to the national economy, but, in addition a contribution to development in the broader sense of upgrading technology and skills and improving standards in employment, environmental protection and corporate and social responsibility. SEZs should deliver more than the temporary and often illusory gains of the sweat-shop economy, or the subsidizing of cronyism. They should be points of productive partnership of government, the private sector and the local people and their representatives; templates and catalysts for development; examples of best rather than most exploitative practice; engines of growth; and sites of global economic integration. Regulation and accountability should be geared toward these larger objectives and should apply to every aspect of the SEZ experience, from the decision to create (often the most crucial one in terms of location and orientation) to the ensuring of continued adherence to the principles of good SEZ-governance. The purpose of this chapter has been to articulate in outline how this might be achieved.

Notes

1 For some fascinating and critical material on SEZs in India, which has greatly informed this chapter, see further the papers at www.india-seminar.com/2008/582.htm (SEZ Seminar, February 2008).

2 The Act came into effect in February 2006. State enactments have followed to supplement the main Act. Interestingly, Russia also adopted a Law on Special Economic Zones in the Russian Federation in 2005.

3 Commerce and industry minister Kamal Nath, cited at www.india-seminar.com/2008/582/582_factfile.htm (accessed 20 January 2010).
4 I.e. under the Land Acquisition Act 1894: Dohrmann 2008: 73. A current case of this kind in the Gujarat High Court also encompasses the possibility of a right of the local *panchayat* to be consulted about a proposed SEZ: http://timesofindia.indiatimes.com/city/rajkot/HC-wants-panchayat-to-have-a-say-in-SEZs/articleshow/5434411.cms (accessed 28 January 2010).
5 Section 51 can also be criticized on similar grounds: 'The provisions of this Act shall have effect notwithstanding anything inconsistent therewith contained in any other law for the time being in force or in any instrument having effect by virtue of any law other than this Act.'
6 For detailed discussion of the procedure, see Chaturvedi 2007; and Dohrmann 2008, who also lists, at 64–65, all the various privileges which are afforded SEZ investors. Note that it is also possible for there to be more than one developer provided the lands in question are contiguous.
7 The Act appears to envisage the developer as the owner of the land, but presumably in the ordinary case the land is acquired only after the letter of approval is given, since the outcome of an application cannot be assumed. It is the acquisition of agricultural land that has caused most of the protests against SEZs in India. The right to property in Article 31 of the Constitution, which was repealed in 1978, authorized compulsory land acquisition only for a public (and not a private) purpose. It is not therefore possible now to argue that a compulsory acquisition of land for SEZ purposes is unconstitutional. The acquisition of land for SEZs creates significant opportunities for land speculation, so that SEZs could become (as in the language of opposition to SEZs) REZs ('real estate zones').
8 See http://pmindia.nic.in/nac/concept%20papers/rehabilitationmay2005.pdf (accessed 20 January 2010).
9 It can also simply impose further conditions on the developer or agree to an application to the transfer of the letter of approval to another person.
10 For bureaucracy-related problems encountered by investors, see Sanyal 2007: 45.
11 SEZs are in fact notified as 'industrial townships' under Article 243Q of the Constitution. This exempts them from the provisions of Part IX of the Constitution, which provides for elected municipal governments.
12 This is what practically did occur under the Khmer Rouge in Cambodia in the late 1970s.
13 Promotion of Investments Act 1986 (Malaysia).
14 This was removed in 27 sectors in April 2009: http://biz.thestar.com.my/news/story.asp?file=/2009/4/24/business/3759119&sec=business (accessed 20 January 2010).
15 Contrary to most systems where local equity participation is prohibited or largely restricted in SEZs.

Bibliography

Butt, S and T Lindsey (2008) 'Economic reform when the constitution matters: Indonesia's Constitutional Court and Article 33', Bulletin of Indonesian Economic Studies 44(2): 239–62.

Chaturvedi, T (2007) *Guide to Special Economic Zones*, 2nd edn, Delhi: Commercial Law Publishers.

Dohrmann, JA (2008) 'Special economic zones in India: An introduction', *ASIEN* 106: 60–80.

Economist (2006) 'Cash cows: India's special economic zones', 381: 78.

Harding, AJ and P Nicholson, eds (2010) *New courts in Asia*, London: Routledge.

Likosky, M (2005) *The Silicon empire: Law, culture and commerce*, Aldershot: Ashgate.

Peerenboom, R, ed. (2004) Asian discourses of rule of law: Theories and implementation of rule of law in twelve Asian countries, France and the US, London and New York: RoutledgeCurzon.

Perry-Kessaris, A (2008) Global business, local law: The Indian legal system as a communal resource in foreign investment relations, Aldershot: Ashgate.

Richardson, B (2004) 'Is East Asia industrializing too quickly? Environmental regulation in its special economic zones', *UCLA Pacific Basin Law Journal* 22(1): 150–244.

Rittich, K (2005) 'The future of law and development: Second generation reforms and the incorporation of the social', *Michigan Journal of International Law* 26: 99; also published under the same title as ch. 6 of Trubek, D and A Santos, eds (2006) *The new law and economic development: A critical appraisal*, Cambridge: Cambridge University Press.

Sanyal, S (2007) 'Legal woes entangle Indian growth', *Far Eastern Economic Review*, Jan–Feb, 45.

Upadhyay, V (2000) 'Changing judicial power: Courts on infrastructure projects and environment', *Economic and Political Weekly* 35(43/44): 3789–92.

Resources

World Wide Web

National special economic zone websites

Cambodia

www.ppsez.com/ (Phnom Penh)

China

www.qdepz.com/en/jgqgk.htm (Qingdao)
www.weihai.gov.cn/weihai/en/Investment/DevelopmentZones/ET_ExpoProcess.asp (Weihai)
www.yantaimarket.com/en/city/export.htm (Yantai)
http://en.investteda.org/aboutteda/sections/exportzone/default.htm (Tianjin)

India

http://sezindia.nic.in/index.asp

Pakistan

www.epza.com.pk/

The Philippines

www.bcda.gov.ph/ (Bases Conversion and Development Authority)

Vietnam

www.linhtrungepz.com/english/loaddata.php?page=aboutus

International organizations and civil society groups

Global Policy Forum

www.globalpolicy.org/nations-a-states/state-sovereignty-and-the-global-economy/export-processing-zones.html

ILO

www.ilo.org/public/english/dialogue/sector/themes/epz.htm

UNCTAD

www.unctad.org/Templates/StartPage.asp?intItemID=2068

World Export Processing Zone Authority

www.wepza.org/

World Bank

http://www-wds.worldbank.org/external/default/main?pagePK=64193027&piPK=64187937&theSitePK=523679&menuPK=64187510&searchMenuPK=64187283&theSitePK=523679&entityID=000334955_20081007064814&searchMenuPK=64187283&theSitePK=523679

In print

Alter, P (1990) 'Export Processing Zones for Growth and Development: The Mauritian Example' IMF Working Paper.

Carter, C (2003) 'The Clonability of the Singapore Model of Law and Development: The Case of Suzhou, China' in Christoph Antons (ed.) *Law and Development in Asia*, London: Curzon/Routledge, chapter 10, 271–86.

Chan, T, Chen, E and Chin, S (1986) 'China's Special Economic Zones: Ideology, Policy and Practice' in YC Jao and CK Leung (eds) *China's Special Economic Zones: Policies, Problems and Prospects*, Oxford: Oxford University Press.

Chaturvedi, T (2007) *Guide to Special Economic Zones*, 2nd edn, Delhi: Commercial Law Publishers.

Creskoff, S and Walkenhorst, P (n.d.) 'Implications of WTO Disciplines for Special Economic Zones in Developing Countries' World Bank Policy Research Working Paper 4892.

Dohrmann, J (2008) 'Special Economic Zones in India: An Introduction' *ASIEN* 106: 60–80.

Engman, M, Onodera, O and Pinali, E (n.d.) 'Export Processing Zones: Past and Future Role in Trade and Development' OECD Trade Policy Working Paper no. 53.

ESCAP/UNCTC (1985) *An Evaluation of Export Processing Zones in Selected Asian Countries* United Nations: ESCAP/UNCTC Publication Series B, no.8.

Gerbracht, B (2006–7) 'Export Processing Zones and Free Trade Agreements: Lessons from the North American Agreement on Labor Cooperation' *Transnational Legal and Contemporary Problems* 16: 1029.

Gopalakrisnan, R (2007) 'Freedom of Association and Collective Bargaining in Export Processing Zones: Role of the ILO Supervisory Mechanisms' Working Paper no. 1, Geneva: ILO.

Guo, W, and Feng, Y (2007) *Special Economic Zones and Competitiveness: A Case Study of Shenzhen, the People's Republic of China*, Islamabad: Asian Development Bank.

Hein, P (1989) 'Structural Transformation in an Island Country: The Mauritius Export Processing Zone (1971 to 1988)' *UNCTAD Review* 1: 41.

International Confederation of Free Trade Unions (1983) 'Trade Unions and the Transnationals', Information Bulletin, Special Issue no: 3. 'Export Processing Zones', Brussels: ICFTU.

International Labour Office (ILO) (2003) *Employment and Social Policy in Respect of Export Processing Zones (EPZs)*, Governing Body GB.286/ ESP/3, 286th Session, Geneva, March.

—— (2008) *Report of the InFocus Initiative on Export Processing Zones (EPZs): Latest Trends and Policy Developments in EPZs*, Governing Body GB.301/ESP/5 301st Session, Geneva, March.

Jauch, H (2002) 'Export Processing Zones and the Quest for Sustainable Development: A Southern African Perspective' *Environment andUrbanization* 14: 101.

Kumar, R (1989) *India's Export Processing Zones*, Delhi: Oxford University Press.

Lai, H (2006) 'SEZs and Foreign Investment in China: Experiences and Lessons for North Korean Development' *Asian Perspectives* 30(3): 69–97.

Litwack, J and Qian, Y (1998) 'Balanced or Unbalanced Development: Special Economic Zones as Catalysts for Transition' *Journal of Comparative Economics* 26: 117.

Madani, D (1999) 'A Review of the Role and Impact of Export Processing Zones' Washington, DC: World Bank Policy Research Working Paper no. 2238.

Richardson, B (2004) 'Is East Asia Industrializing Too Quickly? Environmental Regulation in Its Special Economic Zones', *UCLA Pacific Basin Law Journal* 22(1): 150–244.

Sit, V (1985) 'The Special Economic Zones of China: A New Type of Export Processing Zone?' *The Developing Economies* 23(1) (March): 68.

Sklair, L (1988) 'The Costs of Foreign Investment: The Case of the Egyptian Free Zones', in Elie Kedourie and Sylvia G Haim (eds) *Essays on the Economic History of the Middle East*, London: Frank Cass.

—— (1991) 'Problems of Socialist Development: The Significance of Shenzhen Special Economic Zone for China's Open Door Development Strategy' *International Journal of Urban and Regional Research* 15(2), Special Issue: 'Urbanisation in the Hong Kong-South China Region', 197.

—— (1993) *Assembling for Development: The Maquila Industry in Mexico and the United States* (first published Unwin Hyman 1989, updated US publication by the Center for US-Mexican Studies, San Diego: University of California).

Torres, R (2007) 'Free Zones and the World Trade Organization Agreement on Subsidies and Countervailing Measures' *Global Trade and Customs Journal* 2(5): 217.

Warr, P (1989) 'Export Processing Zones' *World Bank Research Observer* 4(1): 65–88.

World Bank/FIAS (2008) *Special Economic Zones: Performance, lessons learned, and implications for zone development*, Washington, DC: World Bank Group.

Index